WHAT AFRICAN AMERICAN PARENTS WANT EDUCATORS TO KNOW

WHAT AFRICAN AMERICAN PARENTS WANT EDUCATORS TO KNOW

Gail L. Thompson

Rowman & Littlefield Education
Lanham • New York • Toronto • Plymouth, UK

Published in the United States of America
by Rowman & Littlefield Education
A Division of Rowman & Littlefield Publishers, Inc.
A wholly owned subsidary of The Rowman & Littlefield Publishing Group, Inc.
4501 Forbes Boulevard, Suite 200, Lanham, Maryland 20706
www.rowmaneducation.com

Estover Road
Plymouth PL6 7PY
United Kingdom

British Library Cataloguing in Publication Information Available

The hardback edition of this book was previously cataloged by the Library of
Congress as follows:

Thompson, Gail L., 1957–
    What African American parents want educators to know / Gail L. Thompson.
      p. cm.
    Includes bibliographical references and index.
      1. African Americans—Education. 2. African American parents—Attitudes. 3.
Educational surveys—United States. I. Title.
LC2731.T46 2003
371.829'96073—dc21   2002029888

Manufactured in the United States of America.

Contents

Tables

Acknowledgments

As always, I am thankful to God for an opportunity to share information that will hopefully improve the schooling experiences of African American students. This book would not have been possible without the assistance of numerous individuals. First, I am grateful to the African American parents, grandparents, and foster parents who took time out of their busy schedules to participate in this study and for their candor in discussing their own and their children's schooling experiences. I am also grateful to the two school principals who gave me access to their schools and to community officials who gave me access to their organizations. Editors and publishers of Black newspapers, such as the *Precinct Reporter, The American,* and *Westside Story* ran press releases urging African American parents to participate in the study. Wallace Allen permitted me to mention the study on his weekly radio program. My husband, Rufus, and children Nafissa, NaChe', and Stephen, were supportive. Dr. David E. Drew, a wonderful friend, mentor, colleague, and dean, gave me constructive feedback about this study, course release time for two years, and assistance in countless ways. I am also grateful to Ethel Rogers, Miriam Avila, Karen Lazarus, and Desiree Esparza for their assistance. In spite of being bedridden, Elanda Birchfield always has a smile and a kind word when I visit her in the hospital. My mother Velma Coleman and sisters, Tracy Smith (who assisted with survey distribution) and Michelle Harris, have also been supportive. I'm also sending a special "shout out" to my faithful friends Cynthia Hebron, Wanda Foster, Sharon Holmes-Johnson, Deborah Tavasti, and Pamela Samuels who have been supportive for nearly three decades and to my colleagues Dr. Mary Poplin and Dr. Lourdes Arguelles for lots of encouragement, good laughs, and good advice; my Great Aunt Ebbie Crear; aunts Dorothy Taylor, Wilma Hester, and Lillian Mitchell; and cousins Beverly Brookins, Carl Crear, Debbie Jo Crear, and Baby Brother (John Boyd) for words of encouragement. Last, but certainly not least, I would like to thank Jane Garry, a wonderful editor at Greenwood Publishing Group, Inc. for having faith in two of my writing projects and for being extremely supportive, and I am also grateful for the support of Marie Ellen Lacarda, my new editor at Greenwood.

Introduction

In September 2001, I had a conversation with one of my former graduate students. When I asked how his first year of teaching high school was going, even though he was still fine-tuning his discipline policy, he spoke excitedly about what had been a mostly positive experience thus far. His biggest disappointment, however, had been with parents. "Out of 147 parents," he exclaimed, "only 10 came to Back to School Night!" I understood his frustration for two reasons. First, when I taught in urban public schools for fourteen years, I, too, was often frustrated by the small number of parents who attended school events, such as Back to School Night and Open House. Second, I have heard many teachers—both veteran and new teachers—voice the same sentiment. In most cases, the teachers have concluded that parents who fail to attend school events do so because they simply do not care about their children's education. Indeed, some teachers spend an excessive amount of time during the school day engaged in "parent bashing."

In schools that are predominated by children of color, parent bashing and the belief that parents don't care are extremely common (Delpit, 1995; Flores, Tefft-Cousin, & Diaz, 1991; Poplin & Weeres, 1992; Thompson, 2002). Often, teachers in urban and high-poverty schools even use this belief as an excuse to shortchange children academically. When I was a high school teacher, for example, I actually heard a few teachers justify their low academic standards by implying that children of color and/or lower-socioeconomic-status children deserve less by way of academic challenge and quality instruction than middle- and upper-class children.

An extreme form of parent bashing takes the guise that certain parents/guardians—particularly African American parents/guardians—pass sociocultural deficiencies on to their children that the school system has to correct. However, it has become increasingly clear that parents/guardians play an important role in their children's education (Comer & Poussaint, 1992; Lynn, 1997a; Mapp, 1997; U.S. Department of Education, 2001a). Parents/guardians are their children's first teachers and the messages that they convey to them leave an indelible imprint on their psyche and outlook on life (Thompson, 2002). Schools that form strong partnerships with parents/guardians find that the relationship can become mutually beneficial (Bempechat, 1998; Routman, 1996; U.S. Department of Education, 2001a; Vail, 2001b). However, because of the persistent achievement gap between African American students and White students, there is a need for African American parents/guardians and educators to form stronger partnerships. Moreover, if educators are truly sincere about improving the academic achievement of African American students, they can no longer hold a negative view of African American parents/guardians or ignore their input as they have usually done (Scott & Marcus, 2001). Those who hold a negative view of African American parents/guardians, and African American culture and styles of discourse, must invariably view African American children in the same manner (LeMoine, 2001). This view will impact teacher expectations, and instructional practices, and it will determine the types and quality of curricula that are offered to African American students (Thompson, 2002).

WHY THIS BOOK IS NEEDED

In *African American Teens Discuss Their Schooling Experiences* (Thompson, 2002), I attempted to present educators with feedback from nearly 300 high school seniors. My goals were to show educators that there is a great need to improve the quality of instruction that many African American K–12 students—particularly those in urban schools—receive, and to stress the importance of positive relations between educators and African American students. The chapter pertaining to what the students said about their parents'/guardians' involvement in their elementary, middle, and high school education (which shall be revisited in Chapter 4 of this book) convinced me that, just as there is a need for educators to hear the voices of African American students, there is an equally strong need for them to hear the voices of African American parents/guardians.

This need is more pressing because of new legislation, "The No Child Left Behind Act" (U.S. Department of Education, 2001b), that was recently passed by Congress. In light of the dismal results of previous education reforms (U.S. Department of Education, 1998), this legislation holds educators responsible for educating all children through a multifaceted action plan that includes empowering parents. According to Rod Paige, U.S. Secretary of Education, "There is no more powerful engine for change than a parent who has information and who has options" (Paige, 2001). "The No Child Left Behind Act" is unique in that it promises to empower parents as never before. Parents/guardians of children in underperforming schools will have the option of transferring their children to better schools. If all schools were good schools, there would be no need for this option to exist. However, since lower-socioeconomic-status children and children of color in urban schools often get the worst teachers (Quality Counts, 2000; Thompson, 2002; Wilson, 1996), they are also more likely than other children to attend substandard schools. The outcome of the parental options component of "The No Child Left Behind Act" remains to be seen. In the meantime, however, educators, researchers, and policymakers must begin to improve underperforming schools. Inviting parents/guardians to participate is a crucial first step. The discussion of what should be done to improve the schooling experiences of African American children must include African American parents/guardians, a group that has historically been ignored and misunderstood by educators (Thompson, 2002). Therefore, the purpose of the current study is to provide educators with feedback from African American parents/guardians with the overall goals of (1) improving the quality of instruction that African American students receive, and (2) increasing parent/guardian participation in schools, so that the end result will be an improvement in the academic achievement of African American students.

METHODOLOGY

Quantitative and qualitative data were collected from African American parents/guardians. The study was designed to give African American parents/guardians of school-age children an opportunity to describe many aspects of their children's schooling experiences. A press release describing the study was published in three southern California regional newspapers that target African Americans, and a local radio talk show host permitted me to describe the study during an airing of his program; I invited African American parents/guardians who were interested to contact me. I also attended or sent a representative to four predominantly African American community-based events, including two graduations at predominantly African American schools in the targeted region. As a result, a purposive, nonrandom sample of 129 African American parents/guardians participated in the quantitative phase of the study and 23 were interviewed for the qualitative phase. The low response rate may be attributed to at least two factors: (1) Time constraints and the vicissitudes of life prevented many African American parents/guardians from participating; and (2) because of the negative ways in which researchers have traditionally used data about African Americans (Delpit, 1995), many parents/guardians may have been wary of participating in the study. For example, one of the mothers who participated in the current study said that her sister was afraid to participate because she feared that the results would be used to shut down her children's school. Although there were many problems at the school, she didn't want to contribute to its total demise.

THE QUESTIONNAIRE

An original questionnaire was distributed to the self-selected group of African American parents/guardians who were interested in participating in the study. The questionnaire consisted of thirty-nine Likert-type, dichotomous, and open-ended questions. In addition to demographic information, the survey instrument included questions pertaining to elementary, middle, and high school, racism at school, how parents/guardians perceived adults at school, suspension and expulsion, attitudes about college, literacy issues, academic problems, and specific ways in which African American parents/guardians assisted their children academically. The questionnaire was field-tested and approved for face validity by an Institutional Review Board. A test of inter-item reliability on the dependent variables yielded an alpha coefficient of .87, indicating high internal consistency. Additionally, a comparison between the questionnaire and interview responses of the parents/guardians who participated in both phases of the study resulted in a high level of test-retest reliability.

DATA ANALYSES

A standard statistical software program (SPSS) for the social sciences was utilized to analyze the questionnaire data. Univariate and bivariate statistics were examined and will be reported. Intertextual analysis was used to interpret interview data.

A PROFILE OF THE PARENTS/GUARDIANS WHO PARTICIPATED IN THE QUESTIONNAIRE PHASE

African American parents/guardians of school-age children in eleven southern California school districts participated in the study. However, 74 percent of the parents/guardians had children in one school district. Most of the schools in this district, which have high percentages of African American and Hispanic children, have been designated by the State Department of Education as "underperforming." In this school district, African American students comprise 12 percent of the total student population, but they are disproportionately represented among the students who are not faring well academically. For example, they have lower average standardized test scores than their peers of other racial/ethnic groups in the district and higher suspension and expulsion rates. When the new state-mandated High School Exit exam was given in 2001, the majority of African American students who took the test failed the math portion, and nearly half failed the English/Language Arts section (California Department of Education, 2001).

Approximately 80 percent of the parents/guardians who participated in the current study were women. Parents (78 percent), rather than guardians, accounted for the largest group of participants. The average parent/guardian had two school-age children, but 33 percent had three or more. Sixty-seven percent had at least one child in elementary school, 43 percent had at least one child in middle school, and 36 percent had at least one child in high school.

A PROFILE OF THE INTERVIEWEES

Twenty-three parents and guardians—such as grandparents, other relatives, and foster parents—agreed to participate in the interview phase of the study. As in the questionnaire phase, females predominated in the interview group with twenty females and three males. The youngest interviewee was twenty-eight years old and the oldest was sixty-seven. The average interviewee was forty years old. The interviewees were employed in a wide range of occupations. Interviewees included two business owners, a high school teacher, an elementary school librarian, two school recreational aides, a social worker, a software analyst, an administrative assistant, a church secretary, several stay-at-home mothers, a florist, a waitress, a receptionist, a cook, a mother on Welfare, a part-time graduate student, a full-time undergraduate student, and a full-time community college student. Five interviewees had each earned a bachelor's degree; six had completed some course work at four-year universities; seven had completed some junior college, community college, or trade school work; and three had failed to earn a high school diploma. Five interviewees had one school-age child; the average interviewee had three.

Although seven school districts were represented by the interviewees, fifteen of the twenty-three interviewees had children in the school district in which the majority of questionnaire respondents had children. All interviews were recorded on audiocassette. The shortest interview lasted twenty-five minutes and the longest interview lasted two hours; however, the average interview lasted forty minutes. There were forty-eight interview questions, most of which matched questionnaire items. Unlike the individuals who participated solely in the questionnaire phase of the study, interviewees were given the opportunity to describe their own upbringing, schooling experiences, occupations, and additional issues pertaining to college.

THE BOOK'S ORGANIZATION

This book is divided into three major sections: African American Parents/Guardians Discuss Their Children and Themselves; African American Parents/Guardians Discuss the Education System; and African American Parents/Guardians Discuss Other Issues. Most chapters contain questionnaire results, as well as direct quotes and detailed narratives from the interviews. The narratives were included in order to give educators a look at the diversity in background experiences, attitudes, and perceptions that exist among African Americans.

Chapter 1 describes how the parents'/guardians' children felt about school. Chapter 2 focuses on the academic problems that were of greatest concern to the parents/guardians. Chapter 3 explores numerous issues pertaining to literacy. Chapter 4 presents the results of the ratings that the parents/guardians gave to the quality of their involvement in their children's education and describes specific ways in which they assisted their children academically. In Chapter 5, the parents/guardians discuss discipline, suspension, and expulsion. In Chapter 6, they share their beliefs about teachers. In Chapter 7, they discuss the benefits of their children's course work and homework. In Chapter 8, they share their beliefs about school administrators. In Chapter 9, the parents/guardians suggest ways in which the public school system could be improved. In Chapter 10, they describe their children's experiences with racism at school and their perception of the racial climate in the school district. In Chapter 11, they discuss school safety. Chapter 12 describes the effects of peer pressure and the lure of street life on African American youths. Chapter 13 presents the parents'/guardians' attitudes about college, messages that they shared with their children about college, and how the education system can better prepare African American students for college. This section ends with a summary of major findings and recommendations for educators.

Part I

African American Parents/Guardians
Discuss Their Children and Themselves

How Their Children Felt about School

Much of the scholarly literature pertaining to African American students is negative, primarily because of the persistent achievement gap between African American students and Whites. Consequently, numerous researchers have sought to identify factors that might close the gap (Grissmer, Flanagan, & Williamson, 1998; Hedges & Nowell, 1998; Jencks, 1998; Phillips, Brooks-Gunn, Duncan, Klebanov, & Crane, 1998; Phillips, Crouse, & Ralph, 1998; Thompson, 2002; Wilson, 1998). Additional studies have examined how teachers, teacher qualifications, and the quality of teaching that students receive affect achievement (Drew, 1996; Ferguson, 1998a; Haycock, 1998; National Center for Education Statistics, 1996; Thompson, 2002). Other studies have examined the links between student attitudes and achievement. For example, Fordham and Ogbu (1986) concluded that some African American students become underachievers because they associate success in school with "acting White." However, Cook and Ludwig (1998) examined longitudinal data from Black and White tenth graders in order to ascertain how they felt about school. Cook and Ludwig found few differences between Black and White students' attitudes about achievement. Therefore, they concluded that peer attitudes about achievement were not responsible for the Black-White achievement gap. Conversely, Ferguson (1998a) identified many limitations in Cook and Ludwig's study, particularly because the data set that they utilized was inadequate for the hypotheses that they were testing. Therefore, Ferguson suggested that additional research is necessary.

In another study, White-Johnson (2001) conducted interviews with students, parents, and teachers to ascertain the reasons why five suburban African American male high school students had dropped out of school and ended up in an alternative education program. Differential treatment by teachers and administrators was one of the main factors that students cited. The students' parents pinpointed many factors, including cultural ignorance, a lack of understanding of their children by adults at school, an ineffective curriculum, underqualified teachers, negative labeling, poor instructional practices, and teachers who did not care about their children. On the other hand, when White-Johnson interviewed teachers, several believed that the school was not responsible for the students' academic problems. Instead, they believed that the students had chosen to fail, and that they did not care about their own education. Although teachers admitted that the school used a tracking system that promoted inequities, unlike the African American parents, they were pleased with the curriculum and with their instructional practices.

The differences between the perceptions of teachers and those of African American students and parents that White-Johnson (2001) described are indicative of the gulfs between these groups. These gulfs can only be bridged when honest communication that is based on mutual respect occurs. As noted in the Introduction, one of the primary purposes of this book is to give educators an opportunity to listen to the voices of African American parents/guardians. The study was designed so that the parents/guardians could provide educators with a comprehensive look at their children's schooling experiences through the parents'/guardians' eyes. This panoramic view begins with a discussion of how the parents/guardians thought that their children felt about school, related variables, and two detailed narratives from the interview phase of the study.

FACTORS RELATED TO CHILDREN'S ATTITUDE ABOUT SCHOOL

The majority (93 percent) of the African American parents/guardians who completed the questionnaire said that their children liked school. Children's attitude about school was linked to nine other questionnaire items. The two strongest correlations involved variables that were inversely related to their attitude about school: parent type and racism frequency. In other words, parents were more likely than guardians, such as foster parents or other relatives, to say that their school-age children liked school. Moreover the parents/guardians of children who experienced racism frequently at school were less likely than others to have children who liked school.

Seven variables were positively correlated to children's attitude about school. All but one—taking children to the public library—were related to parents'/guardians' perceptions and ratings of educators and the work that teachers assigned. These correlations indicate that African American parents/guardians who believed that most teachers care about students, and who gave high ratings to their children's high school teachers, high school course work, and high school homework, were more likely than others to believe that their children liked school. The same was true of parents/guardians who gave high ratings to their children's middle school course work and middle school homework. The weakest of the nine correlations was between taking children to the public library and liking school. In other words, parents/guardians who assisted their children academically by taking them to the public library were also likely to have children who enjoyed school (see Table 1.1). More details about children's attitudes about school will surface in ensuing chapters. The two narratives that follow are based on interviews with African American mothers whose children disliked school. Pseudonyms were used instead of actual names of participants.

THEY HATE TO GO TO SCHOOL!

Among the twenty-three parents/guardians who were interviewed, Peggy, a divorced mother of seven children, was one of the least satisfied with the quality of schooling that her children had received. Her youngest child was in preschool, so "he could get a head start," she stated. Five of her children were enrolled in the same school district in which the children of the majority of parents/guardians who participated in the study were enrolled. Out of frustration, however, Peggy had sent her eldest child, a tenth grader, to a high school in another district. Explaining why she had transferred her daughter, Peggy stated, "because they help her more when she asks for math help. In this district [the first district], they say, 'You guys don't want to learn.' This is what they were telling her."

Peggy believed that the transfer had been beneficial for her daughter, who had been moved up to the college preparatory academic track. However, she

Table 1.1
Variables That Were Correlated to Children's Attitude about School in the Order of the Strength of Each Correlation

Variable	Strength of the Correlation	Significance
Racism frequency	-.41	$p < .001$
Parent type	-.40	$p < .001$
Parents'/guardians' beliefs about whether or not most teachers care about students	.33	$p < .001$
Parents'/guardians' beliefs about the benefits of high school course work	.32	$p < .02$
Parents'/guardians' beliefs about the benefits of middle school course work	.30	$p < .02$
How parents/guardians rated high school teachers	.29	$p < .01$
Parents'/guardians' beliefs about the benefits of high school homework	.29	$p < .04$
Parents'/guardians' beliefs about the benefits of middle school homework	.25	$p < .04$
Taking children to the public library	.18	$p < .04$

$N = 120$

was so dissatisfied with the quality of schooling that her other children were receiving that she was contemplating transferring her middle school–age child to the second school district as well. "My kids hate school!" she exclaimed. "They hate to get up in the morning. They hate to go to school!" Peggy's frustration with the school district and her children's antipathy toward school originated from a series of negative experiences with teachers. Three themes surfaced repeatedly throughout the interview: (1) Peggy believed that most teachers do not care about African American children; (2) she believed that most teachers are unwilling to give African American children extra help when needed; and (3) she believed that teachers' negative attitudes, complacence, and unwillingness to give African American children additional assistance result in academic problems and discipline problems at school.

The main academic problems that Peggy's children had were with pronunciation and math, problems that she herself had experienced. Concerning the pronunciation problem, she said, "I can understand that one, because I had speech [therapy] too when I was in elementary school. So, I don't know if it's because we had parents that came from Texas and Alabama and we spoke like they did." Like her children, Peggy had also struggled with math. She explained:

Most of the parents, like me, when we went to high school, if we raised our hands and asked for extra help in math, we did not get that extra help, because we were Black kids. You know, from the ninth grade all the way to eleventh grade, I really wanted to drop out of school, because it was so hard. It was hard because we couldn't get the extra help. If one teacher cared, it could have pushed me to go to college. It wasn't only the White teachers; it was Black teachers too. If you didn't do what they wanted you to do, they didn't like you either. If Black teachers would stop acting like Uncle Toms, it would help a lot too. Black teachers could step in and say, "You know this is not right." We have got to help our kids. If we don't help our kids, who's going to help our kids? Nobody!

Regarding her tenth grader who transferred to another district, Peggy said:

My daughter was at the point where she wanted to quit school. That was because she wasn't getting the help she needed, just like me and math. I could have excelled at anything but math. Nobody wanted to help in math. That wasn't my fault. I couldn't teach myself geometry, trigonometry, or algebra. I could not teach myself this. I knew multiplication and division. Teachers have degrees in things that they should help kids with. A lot of Black kids do not succeed because of math. Do you know, I did not learn math until I went to a community college? Yet, I graduated from high school with a 3.3 grade point average!

I feel like we do not have a degree to teach our kids the math and social studies, the degrees that the teachers went to school for. Now, if we had degrees and if we went to school for it, then we should know how to apply it to the kids. But since we don't, all we can do is the best that we can as parents and be there for our kids.

My daughter in seventh grade is having problems with math, too. I went in and asked her teacher to give her extra help. He said, "Okay," but she never got it. I think I'll move her to the other district or to another school where I see people care about her. I don't want her to go into the ninth grade without knowing how to do math.

Peggy was also convinced that teacher apathy and an unwillingness to provide extra help to African American children create discipline problems. She described one teacher who not only fell asleep in class, but who actually allowed Peggy's daughter, a fourth grader, to teach the class. As a result, the entire class became disruptive. According to Peggy:

The whole class was being affected by this. If kids are sitting up cursing in school, who's learning? Nobody. Well, they're learning how to cuss, but they're not learning how to do math and what they need to know. A lot of things can be avoided by teachers stepping in and simply saying, "I'm not gonna have it." Then, you call the parents and let them do their job. Our job is to help our kids. Our job is to get our kids to school on time, so they can learn. But the teacher was sitting up there sleeping in class because they feel, "Well, this is a Black school, so they can cuss each other out."

The teacher told me "These are the best Black kids I've ever had." I've never heard anything like that in my life. He did not like these Black kids and he didn't care if they learned or not. This was his job. He got a check at the end of the month whether or not these kids learned, and these kids were not learning!

My kids are the opposite of me. I used to love school. My kids hate it. I can see that some of their teachers were really mean. It's not right to assume, but if I can see it, the kids can see it too.

HE FEELS SINGLED OUT A LOT

Venisha, a married mother of two school-age children, was one of two business owners who participated in the interview phase of the study. Her memories of her own K–12 schooling experiences in Chicago and California were overwhelming positive. She stated:

I was probably a better student than my kids are. I was focused, the kind of kid that wanted to get my work done. I loved school. I had a happy home life; I had good teachers and they tried to help me. They were really willing to help, willing to stay after school. So, I could tell that they were really into helping me learn. They were kind, concerned, and more passionate about helping than the teachers are today. I also had the pressure of my parents on my back. I always wanted to do good in school and I tried to keep my focus.

Like Peggy, she was disappointed that her own children's schooling experiences had been less positive than her own. She described her daughter, an eighth grader, as "just starting to have academic problems." Her main academic problem was with reading comprehension and "talking loud to teachers." According to Venisha:

Her behavior is great, but she's starting to talk back to teachers, not disrespectfully, but just to explain herself. She gets a little loud. I think a teacher thinks when you get a little loud, you're being a bit defiant. She's a loud person. My husband is a loud person, and when they get to explain themselves, they get loud. Their voices go up. Then, the teachers think she's being disrespectful. She's gotten a Referral [a discipline form that requires a student to go to the school office] for that once. Actually, she's just starting to have problems.

Because her daughter was tall for her age and overweight, she was experiencing some social problems as well. She was teased by her peers frequently. However, Venisha believed that a problem with a teacher, as opposed to teasing by peers, was the main reason that her daughter disliked school. Venisha explained:

There was an incident where she felt that a teacher had harassed her. He had touched her bottom, while reaching out to grab her. He was upset or frustrated with her. He went to grab her arm, and since her arm was out of reach, he grabbed the back of her pants. She was frustrated, and she was switched out of the teacher's class. But ever since then, her grades started going downhill. She was in seventh grade. Before that, she wasn't a bad student, but I think she has a comprehension problem. That's what the teachers say.

As a result of her reading comprehension problem, Venisha's daughter was placed in a special reading program. However, Venisha was dissatisfied with the program and with some of her daughter's teachers. She stated:

I've gone to her school and spent a whole day there, as if I'm a student. I have to, because I don't know what's going on. I'm wondering why her grades are like this. I've gone several times, particularly to her reading class. The way it's set up, you have to go to the library and check out a book. Once they check out the book, they read it, and take a test on a computer in order to get a certain number of points. Once she passes the test, she gets those points. Well, she hasn't been getting any points. Either she doesn't comprehend the test or doesn't understand the book. When I ask the teachers how to better assist her, there are no make-up tests for it. The only thing I can do is help her with the book by reading it to her and going through the chapters. She's gone to tutoring after school and they're still not helping.
We've tried everything. We have the letter of retention [a formal letter indicating that a student will probably not be promoted to the next grade level]. They've sent her many retention letters. She had mandatory summer school for sixth and seventh grade. I think the teachers need to try harder. I sat in one class where the teacher was ignoring all of the other kids who were raising their hands and only calling on one White girl. I was really mad and I wanted to talk to him about it, but my daughter told me that he was leaving the school. I was glad because I was really mad with him.

Whereas Venisha's daughter had recently begun to have behavioral problems at school, her son's problems had been ongoing, particularly starting in second grade. Unlike his sister, who struggled with reading comprehension, Venisha's son was an outstanding student academically, but he was exhibiting behavioral problems. She explained:

He gets really good grades. Some of the work is right at his level, but some of it is too easy. He's good at reading and his standardized test scores are above grade level. He really likes doing homework and schoolwork. But, because of his behavior, he gets suspended. He can't go to school, so that brings his grades down. He was suspended twice in second grade, once in third, and once in fourth, pretty much for defiance or for talking back. Once, it was for fighting, but he's not a regular fighter.

Venisha attributed her son's dislike of school and his behavioral problems to multiple sources: her son himself, school proctors (quasi–security guards), and teachers. She stated:

I can't totally blame the school or school district for everything, because I know what kind of kid he is. He craves attention, but I think he feels singled out a lot. I think a lot of it has to do with being defiant. He's just that way. He's a rough kid. He gets singled out a lot, even if he didn't do anything, just because of his reputation for doing things that have happened. They just kept throwing everything at him, and when he would stand up for himself, they didn't believe him.

At home, we let him explain himself. I think he feels that at school he gets singled out a lot and he knows that we'll listen to him, but no one else will. He thinks the teachers don't believe him when he's telling the truth. He knows we listen to him. Sometimes, he will be guilty and I'll believe him. He knows that I'll believe him, and he'll realize what he did or said was wrong. He'll come to me and say, "Mama, it was a lie." But when he does tell the truth at school, they never believe him. I don't care what it is.

Venisha shared a specific example of the pattern of early labeling of her son that she noticed when he was in third grade:

He was at a playground and the rules of the playground are that there is no food, no rough horseplay, basic things like that. He had some candy in his hand that didn't belong to him. He was holding it for someone else. He was probably snacking on it. I know my son; he was probably eating it, and he was not supposed to have candy at this time, because we thought he had a hyper problem from too much sugar. So, the teacher had suggested that we cut back on the juice and cereal in the morning.

He was at recess and the proctor blew the whistle for "Time Out" and everyone was supposed to freeze. My son was in one of those play tunnels and he was moving around. The proctor went over to him and said, "You are supposed to freeze when I blow the whistle." When she noticed the candy, he told her that he was holding it for someone else. The proctor didn't believe him. He kept trying to explain himself, but she kept saying that he was defiant. He calmed himself down, because he does get a little angry and they know that. He tried to calm himself down, and he tried to explain himself, but they still didn't believe him. So, he got angrier. He said, "I don't even want to go to school anymore. I hate this place! Nobody wants to believe me anymore, even when I'm telling the truth."

During that same year, her son's third grade teacher told Venisha that he suspected that her son suffered from Attention Deficit Disorder (ADD) and that she should have him checked by a doctor. "The teacher thought maybe he needed Ritalin," Venisha said. The teacher also recommended that she eliminate sweets from her son's diet. Venisha took the teacher's advice but saw no positive results. She explained:

He's still the same, with or without sugar. I even put him on some herbal products to cut back on sugar. We totally cut back on his sugar and he was still the same. He is just a talker. I think he's probably bored to death, because he'll do his work and once he's done, he's off. He'll go help without being asked to help, and the teachers don't want him to help. They think he's disrupting the class. When they find out that he's finished his work, they tell him to go back and read over his work. I feel he's been blackballed pretty much and feel that he doesn't even want to go back to school anymore. He wants to go somewhere else.

When Venisha discussed the possibility of ADD with her family doctor, the doctor "thought he didn't have any problems," she said. However, she was so frustrated by her son's problems, that she was planning to have him retested for ADD, and contemplating allowing him to be put on Ritalin, something that her husband opposed. In the meantime, she tried to assist her children academically by helping them with homework, having her daughter read to her, reading back to her daughter, teaching her son strategies to control his behavior, and holding him accountable for violating school rules. She also decided to move her son to another school, within the same district, so that he could get a new start. Although she felt that he was doing much better at the new school, mostly because the principal seemed to understand him better than school personnel at his previous school, she still had mixed feelings. Venisha explained:

The principal he has now swears that he is such a good kid. If he doesn't have something to do, he's going to find something to do. The principal knows that he's a good kid. I signed him up for a special class. It's not a behavior class, but when he gets frustrated or angry on the playground, he can go to this class and calm himself down. If he's angry with someone, they talk about it and try to solve it. I think it was a mistake to put him in that program because every time he has a problem, he goes there. I think it pretty much singles him out to make him seem like he is a problem kid.

Most of the work that he gets is challenging work and he likes to do his work. He's enthused about his work, but sometimes he wants to go out and play first. He really loves doing schoolwork and homework. He just gets unfocused. At his new school, he has better teachers than at his old school. Even though he has a few problems with some of them, I think he has better teachers and this time, the teachers are really into him.

SUMMARY

This chapter examined factors that were related to how the African American parents/guardians thought that their children felt about school. The overwhelming majority of parents/guardians said that their children liked school. The questionnaire results indicated that nine variables were correlated to how parents/guardians thought that their children felt about school. The two narratives provided more details.

Of the nine variables that were correlated to how parents/guardians thought children felt about school, experiencing racism frequently at school was the strongest link. The parents/guardians of children who experienced racism frequently at school were less likely than others to believe that their children liked school. This finding was underscored by Peggy's narrative. She described examples of institutional racism that manifested themselves through low teacher expectations and an unwillingness by teachers to provide extra help. She attributed these problems to the fact that teachers were working at a predominantly African American school. Regarding one teacher, Peggy stated, "He did not like those Black kids and he didn't care if they learned or not." Venisha felt that her son's earlier behavioral problems had started a cycle of negative labeling. Like Peggy, when Venisha transferred her child to a different school, she found that he had better schooling experiences. This finding underscores the need for all aspects of institutional and individualized racism to continue to be addressed in schools (Thompson, 2002). This topic will be discussed in detail in Chapter 10.

A second finding from the questionnaire data was that "parent type" was also linked to how parents/guardians thought their children felt about school. Parents were more likely than guardians to state that their children liked school. One reason might be that guardians may have spent less time with the children. For example, a foster parent might have only had custody of a school-age child for a short amount of time. Another possibility is that children who were living with guardians, as opposed to parents, might have been placed with guardians as a result of adverse circumstances, such as abuse, neglect, the death of a parent, or the like. Consequently, these adverse circumstances might have also affected children's attitudes about school. Having to change schools and adjust to new environments might be additional factors that resulted in a negative attitude about school. This finding suggests that schools may need to provide counseling, mentoring, and other services to help children who are not living with their biological parents have more positive schooling experiences.

A third finding was that parents'/guardians' beliefs about whether or not most teachers care about students was also correlated to children's attitudes about school. The parents/guardians who believed that teachers do care about students were more likely than the parents/guardians who did not believe this to have children who liked school. During her interview, Peggy repeatedly stated that her children's teachers did not care about African American children. She also said that her children "hate to go to school." This finding suggests that teachers' attitudes about African American students do have an impact on the students (Delpit, 1995; Foster & Peele, 1999; Ladson-Billings, 1994; White-Johnson, 2001). In *African American Teens Discuss Their Schooling Experiences*, Thompson (2002) concluded that African American students want to have better relationships with their teachers. Many of the students in her study were disappointed with teachers who were only at school "to collect a paycheck." If the achievement gap is to ever be closed, recruiting caring and well-qualified teachers for predominantly African American schools is imperative.

The fourth finding also emphasized the impact of teacher quality on African American students' attitudes about school. The parents/guardians who believed that their children had outstanding high school teachers and whose children had benefited from their middle school and high school course work and homework, were also more likely to state that their children liked school.

A fifth finding was that the parents/guardians who took their children to the public library on a regular basis were also more likely than those who did not to have children who liked school. One explanation for this finding is that children who used the public library frequently might have been better readers than those who did not. For decades, researchers have stressed the positive correlation between strong reading skills and academic success (Chall, 1967; Flesh, 1986; Harris & Sipay, 1990; Honig, 2000). A logical conclusion is that children who used the public library frequently may have had a more positive attitude about school because they may have also experienced greater academic success than other children. During Venisha's interview, she described her daughter's ongoing reading comprehension problem. Venisha felt that her daughter's teachers were using ineffective practices, but she was also unaware of additional ways to assist her daughter. Although she described numerous ways in which she attempted to assist her daughter and son academically, she did not mention that she took them to the public library. A suggestion by teachers that she consider using the public library might have been beneficial to Venisha's daughter. Many public libraries provide free tutoring and reading incentive programs. The link between taking children to the public library and children's attitude about school suggests that if educators can convince African American parents/guardians to take their children to the public library, the results might have a positive effect on African American children's attitude about school. Chapter 3 will examine additional issues pertaining to literacy.

A sixth finding was that both of the parents whose narratives were presented in this chapter were disappointed that their children's schooling experiences had been less positive than their own. Despite the fact that Peggy complained about the lack of extra help from her math teachers, she still remarked, "I used to love school." The same was true of Venisha, who said, "I loved school. . . . I had good teachers and they tried to help me." Four themes that surfaced in the narratives were that these parents had become convinced that, although their own schooling experiences had been better, in their children's cases, (1) most teachers did not care about African American children; (2) most were unwilling to give extra help; (3) the attitudes, assumptions, and practices of some teachers and other school personnel often lead to discipline problems; and (4) some African American parents feel frustrated by their inability to assist their children more. These issues and more details about children's attitudes about school will resurface in ensuing chapters and must be addressed if the achievement gap between African American students and others is ever to be eradicated.

2

Academic Problems

For decades, researchers have reported that, on average, African American children tend to have more negative schooling experiences than other children. They are disproportionately represented among children who are placed in Special Education classes (Ford, 1995; Graue & DiPerna, 2000; Hacker, 1992; Murrell, 1999; Oakes, 1999); suspended and expelled from school (Murrell, 1999); retained (Graue & DiPerna, 2000; Rodney, Crafter, Rodney, & Mupier, 1999); and who are not faring well academically (Jencks, 1998). The achievement gap is most apparent in the standardized test scores of African American students. Throughout the years, the National Assessment of Educational Progress (NAEP) has continuously documented the gap between the math, reading, science, and history scores of African American students and their peers of other racial/ethnic groups (National Center for Education Statistics, 2000). Furthermore, on average, African American students tend to have lower SAT and ACT scores than other students.

Graue and DiPerna (2000) found that lower-socioeconomic-status boys from ethnic minority groups are disproportionately chosen for early retention. They also noted that teachers' beliefs impact retention decisions, in that teachers who view children as "deficient" are likely to recommend retention. Therefore, they maintained that teachers' and administrators' perspectives about retention often stem from racist, sexist, and classist beliefs.

Rodney, Crafter, Rodney, and Mupier (1999) examined variables contributing to grade retention among 243 African American teenage boys. They found that the number of suspensions from school, the use of violence against others, and a lack of discipline in the home were positively associated with grade retention. Because numerous studies have found that, for the most part, grade retention is ineffective, the authors urged researchers to seek alternatives.

In another study, Roderick and Camburn (1999) examined patterns associated with course failure among high school students in Chicago. They found that a high percentage of students in urban schools failed high school courses, particularly during ninth grade, and males were more likely than females to fail courses. Absenteeism, failure to complete assignments, and test failure were the three main reasons why students failed high school courses. Often, course failure created a pattern of negative events, including more course failure, low achievement, and high dropout rates. The authors recommended early intervention and skill development assistance to help students in transitioning from middle school or junior high school to high school.

In *African American Teens Discuss Their Schooling Experiences* (Thompson, 2002), the students discussed retention, course failure, and academic problems. Ten percent of the students were retained at least once during elementary school. Whereas 15 percent failed one or more middle school course, nearly 60 percent failed at least one high school course. During both middle school and high school, students were more likely to struggle with math and to fail math courses than any other academic subject. A key finding was that students who were retained or placed in the Special Education program during elementary school were less likely to have positive elementary and secondary schooling experiences than students who were in the Gifted and Talented Education Program (G.A.T.E.).

Like the high school students who participated in Thompson's earlier study, the parents/guardians who participated in the current study were given opportunities to discuss their children's school-related problems. Questionnaire respondents were asked to identify their children's problems, and interviewees were asked to elaborate. Thirteen of the academic problems that were listed on the questionnaire concerned some of the parents/guardians who participated in the study (see Table 2.1). The six most frequently cited problems will be discussed in this chapter, along with grade retention and course failure. A related narrative has also been included.

GRADE RETENTION AND COURSE FAILURE

Twenty-two percent of the questionnaire respondents had children who were retained during elementary school or who failed at least one middle or high school course. Of this group, the majority (82 percent) had children who failed an elementary grade as opposed to a middle school or high school course. Eight variables were correlated to grade retention/course failure. Six were positively related and two were inversely related.

Elementary track, the strongest variable, was negatively correlated to grade retention/course failure. Therefore, parents/guardians who had children in elementary G.A.T.E. classes were less likely to have children who repeated an elementary grade or who failed a course during secondary school. Middle school course work was also inversely related to grade retention/course failure. Parents/guardians who rated their children's middle school course work as *beneficial* were less likely to have children who were retained or who failed courses.

Table 2.1
Academic Problems That Concerned Parents/Guardians

Problem	Percent
Math	38
Writing	29
Reading rate	25
Comprehension	25
Disliking reading	22
Grammar	21
Spelling	17
Poor Grades	16
Homework	16
Pronunciation	12
Science	11
Social Studies	9
History	8

$N = 129$

Several academic problems were correlated to grade retention/course failure. The parents/guardians of children who struggled with reading comprehension, grammar, and/or homework were also more likely to have children who were retained during elementary school and/or who failed at least one secondary school course. Additionally, parents/guardians who had children who were suspended from school and those who read to their children on a regular basis were also likely to have children who were retained or who failed a course. Moreover, the number of school-age children in a household was correlated to grade retention/course failure, in that larger families were more likely than smaller ones to have children who were retained or who failed at least one course (see Table 2.2). During the interview phase of the study, a mother whose daughter was retained during second grade voiced her opinion about retention. She stated:

These kids that they keep calling "problem child" will eventually end up being a problem if nobody cares. I had one daughter in the second grade. They told me, "Well, if you don't hold her back, she's gonna be a problem child." So, I kept my daughter back. They said what she was supposed to learn in the second grade, she still didn't know— multiplication and reading. She should have mastered them in the second grade. She spent two years in second grade. Now, she's in fifth grade and she still hasn't mastered

Table 2.2
Variables That Were Correlated to Grade Retention/Course Failure in the
Order of the Strength of Each Correlation

Variable	Strength of the Correlation	Significance
Elementary school track	-.30	p < .001
Parents'/guardians' beliefs about the benefits of middle school course work	-.29	p < .02
Reading regularly to children	.25	p < .004
Suspension from school	.22	p < .02
Number of school-age children	.22	p < .02
Reading comprehension problem	.21	p < .02
Homework problem	.21	p < .02
Grammar problem	.19	p < .04

$N = 28$

it because the teachers didn't care. So now I help her read. I feel that the teachers should give a little extra care to the children they call "problem child" and see how far that gets you, instead of always blaming the parents. It's not always on the parents.

ACADEMIC PROBLEMS

Math

Math was the most frequently cited academic problem: Nearly 40 percent of the questionnaire respondents cited it. One parent, who had a son in middle school and two daughters in high school, said, "They're doing math that my husband and I never did when we were in school." A mother of a seventh grade honors student said that although her daughter had a 3.9 grade point average, "She struggles with math. I get my boyfriend to help her." Math problems were also correlated to other questionnaire items.

Two variables were negatively associated with math problems: First, the rating that parents/guardians gave to the quality of the elementary course work that their children received was inversely related to math problems. In other words, parents/guardians who believed that their children's elementary course work was beneficial were unlikely to have children who had problems with math. The rating that parents/guardians assigned to how well they had assisted their children academically was also inversely related to math problems. Parents/guardians who gave themselves an *excellent* or *good* rating were unlikely to say that their children had problems with math.

Nine other variables were positively correlated to math problems. Parents'/ guardians' gender was associated, in that female respondents were more likely than males to state that their children had a problem with math. Homework problems were also correlated to math problems, as were poor grades. Problems with three academic subjects—history, science, and social studies—were also linked to math problems. Moreover, problems with pronunciation, grammar, and discipline were also correlated to math problems. In other words, the parents/guardians of children with these problems were more likely than other parents/guardians to have children who struggled with math (see Table 2.3).

Writing

Writing was the second most frequently cited academic problem that parents/guardians identified. Nearly 30 percent of the questionnaire respondents were concerned about their children's writing. As with math problems, writing problems were correlated to other questionnaire items. Twelve variables were positively related to writing problems and two were inversely related.

Middle school track and high school track were the only variables that were negatively correlated to writing problems. In other words, parents/guardians who had children in the highest level middle or high school academic tracks were unlikely to have children who had writing problems. Two writing-related

Table 2.3
Variables That Were Correlated to Math Problems in the Order of the Strength of Each Correlation

Variable	Strength of the Correlation	Significance
History problem	.31	p < .001
Pronunciation problem	.31	p < .001
Grammar problem	.30	p < .001
Parents'/guardians' gender	.29	p < .001
Homework problem	.28	p < .001
Poor grades	.24	p < .01
Discipline problem	.24	p < .01
Social studies problem	.24	p < .01
Science problem	.24	p < .01
How parents/guardians rated elementary course work	-.21	p < .02
Parents'/guardians' self-rating	-.18	p < .04

$N = 49$

variables were positively associated with writing problems. The parents/guardians of children with spelling and/or grammar problems were more likely than others to indicate that their children were poor writers. Three reading-related problems—comprehension, pronunciation, and reading rate—were also positively correlated to writing problems. Parents/guardians of children with writing problems also tended to have children who had problems with history, social studies, and science. Moreover, poor grades and discipline problems were correlated to poor writing. However, two unexpected variables were correlated to writing problems. Parents/guardians who said that they bought books for their children on a regular basis and parents/guardians who rated the public school system as *excellent* or *good* were also more likely to say that their children had writing problems (see Table 2.4).

Reading Rate

Twenty-five percent of the parents/guardians indicated that their children's reading rate was problematic. This problem was correlated to sixteen other

Table 2.4
Variables That Were Correlated to Writing Problems in the Order of the Strength of Each Correlation

Variable	Strength of the Correlation	Significance
Spelling problem	.40	p < .001
History problem	.39	p < .001
Social studies problem	.39	p < .001
Grammar problem	.39	p < .001
Middle school track	-.28	p < .01
High school track	-.27	p < .04
Pronunciation problem	.25	p < .004
Science problem	.22	p < .01
Discipline problem	.21	p < .02
Poor grades	.20	p < .02
Buying books	.19	p < .03
Reading comprehension problem	.19	p < .03
Reading rate problem	.19	p < .03
Parents'/guardians' public school system rating	.19	p < .03

$N = 37$

questionnaire items. Three were inversely related to reading rate and thirteen were positively related.

Elementary, middle school, and high school tracks were all inversely correlated to reading rate, meaning that parents/guardians who had children in the highest-level tracks were unlikely to have children who were slow readers. Of the variables that were positively associated with reading rate, poor grades had the strongest correlation to reading rate. In other words, the parents/guardians of slow readers were also likely to have children who had poor grades. Parents/guardians of slow readers also tended to have children who struggled with comprehension, spelling, writing, pronunciation, grammar, and homework. These parents/guardians also were more likely to have children who had problems with social studies, science, and history. Although these parents/guardians tended to give high ratings to the public school system, they had children who disliked school and who were considered to be discipline problems (see Table 2.5).

Reading Comprehension

As with reading rate, 25 percent of the parents/guardians who completed the questionnaire said that their children had problems with reading comprehension. Comprehension problems were correlated to twenty-four variables. Fifteen variables were positively related and nine were inversely related to reading comprehension problems.

Like reading rate and writing problems, having children with reading comprehension problems was inversely related to having children in the highest academic tracks. Parents/guardians who had children in G.AT.E. during elementary school and/or during middle school were unlikely to have children who had problems with comprehension. Second, parents/guardians who gave high ratings to their children's elementary course work, the public school system, and/or to their children's high school teachers were unlikely to have children who struggled with reading comprehension. The same was true of parents/guardians who rated their own involvement in their children's education as *excellent* or *good*, who encouraged their children to read on a regular basis, who talked to their children about college, and whose children owned books.

Conversely, parents/guardians of children who struggled with reading comprehension were most likely to also have children who had difficulty with grammar, spelling, writing, pronunciation, and reading rate. Their children tended to dislike school and reading and they were more likely to have been suspended, retained, or to have failed a course, have problems with homework, and earn poor grades. Furthermore, their children were also more likely to have difficulty with social studies, science, and history. Moreover, parents/guardians of children who struggled with reading comprehension were more likely to have reported to school officials that their children had experienced racism at school (see Table 2.6).

Table 2.5
Variables That Were Correlated to Reading Rate Problems in the Order of
the Strength of Each Correlation

Variable	Strength of the Correlation	Significance
Poor grades	.40	p < .001
High school track	-.37	p < .004
Spelling problem	.36	p < .001
Middle school track	-.31	p < .01
Homework problem	.30	p < .001
Reading comprehension problem	.29	p < .001
Parents'/guardians' public school system rating	.27	p < .003
Science problem	.26	p < .003
Elementary school track	-.26	p < .004
Social studies problem	.25	p < .004
History problem	.24	p < .01
Grammar problem	.23	p < .01
Discipline problem	.22	p < .01
Disliking school	.22	p < .01
Writing problem	.19	p < .03
Pronunciation problem	.18	p < .04

$N = 32$

Disliking Reading

Twenty-two percent of the parents/guardians who completed the questionnaire said that their children did not like to read. Thirteen questionnaire items
were correlated to disliking reading. Eight were positively correlated and five
were inversely related to disliking reading.

The strongest variable that was negatively correlated to disliking reading
was parents'/guardians' perception of whether or not most school administrators and counselors care about students. Therefore, parents/guardians who believed that most administrators and counselors care about students were
unlikely to have children who disliked reading. The second strongest inverse
relationship was between having children who disliked reading and how
parents/guardians rated their children's high school teachers. Parents/guardi-
ans who rated teachers as excellent or good were unlikely to have children who
disliked reading. The same was true of how parents/guardians rated their children's elementary teachers. Children's elementary and middle school track

Table 2.6
Variables That Were Correlated to Reading Comprehension Problems in the
Order of the Strength of Each Correlation

Variable	Strength of the Correlation	Significance
Reporting racism to school officials	.43	p < .01
History problem	.37	p < .001
Social studies problem	.37	p < .001
Spelling problem	.36	p < .001
High school teachers' rating	-.32	p < .004
Poor grades	.30	p < .001
Reading rate problem	.29	p < .001
Middle school track	-.29	p < .01
Disliking reading	.26	p < .003
Science problem	.26	p < .003
Suspension from school	.26	p < .003
Homework problem	.25	p < .004
Parents'/guardians' self-rating	-.24	p < .01
Grammar problem	.23	p < .01
Elementary school track	-.23	p < .01
Disliking school	.22	p < .01
Owning books	-.22	p < .02
Retention/course failure	.21	p < .02
Parents'/guardians' public school system rating	-.21	p < .02
Elementary course work rating	-.21	p < .02
Encouraging children to read	-.21	p < .02
Writing problem	.19	p < .03
Talking to children about college	-.19	p < .04
Pronunciation problem	.18	p < .04

$N = 32$

were also inversely related to disliking reading. Hence, parents/guardians who
had children in G.AT.E. were unlikely to state that their children disliked
reading.

The strongest positive correlation was between suspension level and a dislike
of reading. Parents/guardians who had children who were suspended from
school multiple times or who were suspended during middle school or high
school were more likely than others to have children who disliked reading.
Reading comprehension problems were also correlated to a dislike of reading,
as were poor grades and homework problems. Having children with problems

in three subjects—history, science, and social studies—was also associated with having children who disliked to read. Finally, as with several of the other academic problems that have been discussed thus far, having children who disliked school was also correlated to having children who disliked to read (see Table 2.7).

Grammar

Twenty-one percent of the parents/guardians who completed the questionnaire said that their children struggled with grammar. Sixteen variables were correlated to problems with grammar. Three were inversely related and thirteen were positively related.

All three of the variables that were inversely related to problems with grammar pertained to students' academic track. Parents/guardians whose children were in the highest-level tracks during elementary, middle, and high school were unlikely to have children who had problems with grammar.

Problems with four academic subjects were positively correlated to problems with grammar. Parents/guardians of children who struggled with social studies, history, math, and/or science were more likely to also have children who

Table 2.7
Variables That Were Correlated to Disliking Reading in the Order of the Strength of Each Correlation

Variable	Strength of the Correlation	Significance
Suspension level	.50	p < .01
Social studies problem	.35	p < .001
Disliking school	.33	p < .001
Science problem	.30	p < .001
Homework problem	.29	p < .001
Poor grades	.29	p < .001
Beliefs about whether or not administrators care	-.29	p < .01
High school teachers' rating	-.28	p < .01
History problem	.27	p < .002
Reading comprehension problem	.26	p < .003
Middle school track	-.26	p < .02
Parents'/guardians' rating of elementary teachers	-.23	p < .01
Elementary track	-.19	p < .03

$N = 28$

struggled with grammar. The same was true of parents/guardians whose children were considered to be discipline problems at school, who were retained/failed courses, and/or who had poor grades. Having children who experienced difficulty with spelling, reading comprehension, reading rate, pronunciation, writing, and homework was also linked to having children who had problems with grammar (see Table 2.8). The narrative that follows provides more information about the academic problems that concerned one parent.

MATH WAS NOT MY SUBJECT. I DON'T KNOW IF IT JUST RUBBED OFF ON MY KIDS

At the time of her interview, forty-five-year-old Beatrice, a laundress and cook, was rearing three teenagers. While her daughter, a tenth grader, was doing well in school, her sons, a ninth grade Special Education student and a tenth grade former G.A.T.E. student, were struggling with homework and math. Moreover, the tenth grade former G.A.T.E. student was a full year behind

Table 2.8
Variables That Were Correlated to Grammar Problems in the Order of the Strength of Each Correlation

Variable	Strength of the Correlation	Significance
Writing problem	.39	p < .001
Middle school track	-.39	p < .001
Social studies problem	.36	p < .001
History problem	.35	p < .001
Poor grades	.31	p < .001
Math problem	.30	p < .001
High school track	-.30	p < .02
Spelling problem	.27	p < .002
Elementary track	-.26	p < .003
Pronunciation problem	.23	p < .01
Reading rate problem	.23	p < .01
Reading comprehension problem	.23	p < .01
Discipline problem	.22	p < .01
Homework problem	.20	p < .02
Grade retention/course failure	.19	p < .04
Science problem	.19	p < .03

$N = 27$

in course credits. Beatrice feared that her sons' academic problems would cause them to eventually drop out of school, as she had done during her senior year of high school. She also feared that they had inherited their math problem from her. However, she also believed that her sons' academic problems stemmed, in part, from the school system, particularly the way in which teachers permitted students to behave in class, as well as peer pressure. Concerning her own K–12 schooling experiences, she stated:

I had a lot of friends and I had good teachers in elementary school and junior high school, but when I got to high school it was just different. I don't know if it was because it was harder or boring. I don't know what the problem was. It was little things. It was hard for me to begin a task and then just stay on it, and finish it. I've always had that problem for a long time and I think that was my problem in high school.

I wasn't getting bad grades, but I was behind in credits. I've always had a problem with math. Back then, we had basic math classes. If you couldn't do algebra or you couldn't do the hard math, they would put you in a basic math class, and I would usually pass it with an "A." But math was just not my subject. I don't know if it rubbed off on my kids.

When my son was in G.A.T.E., he was good in math. He used to come home with algebra problems and I couldn't really help him, because I didn't know how to do it. After he got out of G.A.T.E., it seemed like he couldn't do it anymore. I don't know what happened. I don't know if the problems got harder, or he just got lazy. I think he just got lazy. He was good in all of his subjects, and I don't know what happened to him.

Despite the fact that Beatrice did not have definitive proof of the causes of her older (the former G.A.T.E. student) son's academic decline, she had strong suspicions and noticed a steady downward spiral, starting when he began to attend a middle school in a different city. Beatrice explained:

He has always been the smartest of all of them. They always had him in G.A.T.E. Then, he started thinking that the G.A.T.E. program was too hard for him. So, he had to be taken out of it. Two years ago, he was taken out of G.A.T.E. and he's been failing ever since. He'll pass about two or three classes and then fail the rest. He's not taking school seriously.

I think it was the middle school that made him do bad. He wasn't doing bad at his other middle school. The second middle school seemed like a ghetto school. That's the term the kids use about that school. When I went up there, it did seem like it was a ghetto school. I would go into my other son's Special Ed class. I couldn't believe how those kids were acting. They had their feet on the table. They would be eating candy. There would be sunflower seeds and candy wrappers on the floor. They would be saying, "What's up Dog?" to the teacher. I was like, "What is this?" and the teacher would just be putting up with it. It was terrible. It reminded me of one of those schools that they show on TV, where the kids are bad and they have to bring in the principal to have a battle with them. It was a terrible school. I went to several classes that were like that. I said, "They need to do something about this." I never really complained but I think it was that school that made my kids bad. My daughter didn't have a problem but my sons went downhill.

Whereas Beatrice noticed that her older son began to decline academically when he changed middle schools and left the G.A.T.E. program, she noticed problems much earlier with her younger son. Although his behavior worsened when he went to the "ghetto school," Beatrice had concerns about him as early as kindergarten. She stated:

I noticed when he was in kindergarten and third grade, he was slower than other kids learning his name and learning his letters. He wouldn't catch on. When I had him tested, they diagnosed him as ADD. He's not hyper. He just has Attention Deficit Disorder. He just has a problem where he couldn't pay attention too good and that would interfere with his learning. They put him on medication so that it could control his impulses. He's been in Special Ed since he was in third grade. He would get suspended once every two weeks. It was for doing little things like throwing pencils in the classroom. He never got into any fights. The medication kind of helped him a little bit. Then, it wouldn't even help him. He never did like taking medication, so a lot of times I was keeping him off of it. I felt that he wasn't learning or doing as well as he was supposed to, so then I would put him back on the medication. Finally, I stopped, because I felt that it wasn't helping him. I didn't see any improvement. Now, he's been off for about a year and he's doing good without it.

"Doing good" without medication meant that Beatrice had to make fewer trips to school for her son's behavioral problems. When she did, however, she caught a bus to the school, and sat next to her son in his Special Education class. "He didn't like that," she said. "I told him, 'If you don't want me to come down here and sit with you, then you need to behave yourself.' That was when he was in seventh grade."

After that, Beatrice continued to assist her children academically in many ways. In addition to continuing to visit their classrooms, she attended school functions, helped them with homework, listened to them read, read to them, bought books for them, ironed their school clothes, cooked them hot breakfasts on school days, and tried to teach them to be responsible for their actions. "I try to encourage them and teach them the importance of getting an education," she said. "I talk to them all the time. We talk about everything. I try to show them examples of why they should get their education."

SUMMARY

This chapter identified variables that were correlated to grade retention/course failure, and it described the academic problems that concerned some of the African American parents/guardians who completed the questionnaire. The narrative provided additional information about these and other topics. Although the percentages of parents/guardians who were concerned about some of the problems were low, the related results underscore the need for more feedback from larger samples of African American parents/guardians.

One-fifth of the parents/guardians said that they had at least one child who was retained during elementary school and/or who failed at least one middle school or high school course. The majority of parents/guardians who stated that their children had experienced grade retention/course failure, said that it occurred during elementary school. Children's elementary school track was the strongest variable that was linked to grade retention/course failure. Parents/guardians of children who were in the Special Education program during elementary school were more likely than those whose children were in G.A.T.E. classes during elementary school to have children who were retained and/or who failed courses. These findings are similar to those of Thompson (2002). The majority of the African American high school seniors in that study who were retained during elementary school were also placed in the Special Education program. Moreover, Special Education students and retainees were more likely than other students to report negative schooling experiences. During her interview, Beatrice described some of the problems that her son, a Special Education student, experienced. He was a slow learner and he had behavioral problems that resulted in multiple suspensions from school. Beatrice had been told that he had ADD, but she believed that the medication that had been prescribed was ineffective. The finding in the current study, like that of Thompson (2002), reiterates the need to improve Special Education programs and to seek alternatives to retention (Rodney, Crafter, Rodney, & Mupier, 1999).

A second finding was that parents/guardians who were most satisfied with their children's middle school course work were unlikely to have children who had been retained in elementary school or who failed middle and/or high school courses. In Chapter 1, the rating that parents/guardians gave to middle school course work was also linked to their beliefs about their children's attitudes about school. Parents/guardians who believed that their children received beneficial middle school course work were also likely to believe their children liked school.

Several factors were positively related to grade retention/course failure. Parents/guardians of children who had been suspended from school were more likely than those whose children had not been suspended to have children who repeated an elementary grade or who failed one or more secondary school courses. Davis and Jordan (1995) found that the negative stigma associated with suspension can result in low self-esteem and other long-term consequences. Rodney, Crafter, Rodney, and Mupier (1999) found a positive correlation between grade retention and suspension. They concluded that grade retention is associated with numerous problems, including violence against others. Therefore, they advised educators to consider alternatives to retention, such as in-class and after school remediation. This suggestion is particularly salient since, in Chapters 1 and 2 of this book, the need for African American children to receive extra help from teachers surfaced repeatedly. This point was also stressed by the African American teens who participated in Thompson's (2002) study. Chapter 5 will examine the issue of suspension in greater detail.

Homework problems and three literacy-related issues were also positively correlated to grade retention/course failure. Parents/guardians of children who had a reading comprehension problem were more likely than those who did not to have children who were retained or who failed courses. Because reading is the foundation on which academic success rests (Chall, 1967; Flesh, 1986), the correlation between grade retention/course failure and problems with reading comprehension is logical. Reading (textbooks, worksheets, math problems, instructions, test questions, etc.) is required in every school subject. A child who cannot understand what he/she reads is destined for academic failure. In Chapter 1, Venisha described how her daughter's reading comprehension problem affected her schooling experiences and Venisha's own beliefs about the education system. Grammar was another literacy-related topic that was positively correlated to grade retention/course failure. Hence, parents/guardians of children who had problems with grammar were also more likely than others to have children who were retained or who failed courses.

The number of school-age children in the household was also positively correlated to grade retention/course failure. The parents/guardians with the most school-age children in the home were more likely to have children who were retained or who failed courses. An obvious explanation is that when there are many young children in the home, parents/guardians have less time to devote to each child on an individual basis. The academic needs of a child who is struggling academically may be overlooked until it is too late. This finding suggests that there is a need for schools to provide in-school and after-school assistance to children who are struggling academically, particularly those from large families. Another option is for schools to train older children in large families to tutor their younger siblings.

In addition to grade retention/course failure, the parents/guardians also discussed their children's academic problems. Six problems concerned 20 percent or more of the parents/guardians who completed the questionnaire. Math was the most common academic problem. Of the eleven variables that were correlated to math problems, two were inversely related. The parents/guardians who were most satisfied with their children's elementary school course work and with the quality of academic assistance that they themselves had given to their children were less likely to have children who struggled with math.

Conversely, the parents/guardians of children who struggled with history, pronunciation, grammar, homework, social studies, and/or science; who had poor grades; and/or who had behavioral problems at school were more likely to have children who struggled with math. Moreover, mothers, rather than fathers, were more likely to state that their children struggled with math. This may be attributed to the fact that, traditionally, males have been presumed to have a greater aptitude for math than females. Girls often receive negative messages about their math aptitude early in their schooling and these messages can have long-term adverse consequences (Drew, 1996).

The fact that nearly 40 percent of the questionnaire respondents said that their children struggled with math and that math surfaced as a huge concern for Peggy in Chapter 1 and Beatrice in Chapter 2, indicates that problems with math instruction and curricula must be addressed in order for the achievement gap to be eradicated (Drew, 1996; Moses & Cobb, 2001; Polite, 1999). NAEP scores underscore this need (National Center for Education Statistics, 2001). Moreover, many African American students in Thompson's (2002) study had failed math courses or identified math as their most difficult middle school and high school subject. Drew (1996), who described the long-term negative effects of poor math and science instruction and the impact of underqualified math teachers on students, urged educators and policymakers to improve the quality of elementary and secondary school teachers who teach math.

The feedback from the African American parents/guardians in the current study lends a sense of urgency to the work of Drew and other researchers. Starting in elementary school, African American children need outstanding math teachers who make the subject matter interesting and comprehensible and who are willing to provide extra help during class and at other times as well (Thompson, 2002). Furthermore, if schools are going to successfully form partnerships with African American parents/guardians, they must be willing to equip the parents/guardians with the math skills (and other skills) that they might be lacking. A recurring message in the study thus far has been that some African American parents/guardians who truly want to assist their children academically become frustrated by their inability to assist them with specific problems. For example, Beatrice stated that "when my son was in G.A.T.E. . . . he used to come with algebra problems and I couldn't really help him, because I didn't know how to do it." Therefore, it appears that math problems can become generational problems. Parents/guardians with weak math skills are not only unable to assist their children with challenging math problems, but they may also pass negative attitudes about their own and their children's math aptitude on to their children. For example, Beatrice remarked, "I've always had a problem with math. . . . Math was just not my subject. I don't know if it rubbed off on my kids." In Chapter 1, Peggy stated, "I could have excelled at anything, but math." In fact, there was a statistically significant relationship between children's math problems and how parents/guardians rated the quality of academic assistance that they provided to their children. Those who were most satisfied with the quality of their assistance were less likely to have children who struggled with math. Another message is that parents/guardians feel frustrated that teachers, whom they assume have been trained to assist their children in specific subjects, such as math, are failing to do so. These issues are ongoing problems that must be addressed.

Nearly 30 percent of the parents/guardians were concerned about their children's writing problems, the second most frequently cited academic problem.

Parents/guardians of G.A.T.E. students were unlikely to have children who were poor writers. As noted by Thompson (2002), African American students who are placed in the G.A.T.E. program during elementary school tend to have more positive schooling experiences, including a better caliber of instruction, than other students. The finding that middle school and high school track were correlated to writing problems suggests that students in Special Education and basic courses need more writing practice and a better quality of writing instruction. Problems with spelling, grammar, pronunciation, reading rate, and reading comprehension were also associated with writing problems, illustrating how much reading and writing are interrelated. Finally, the fact that the parents/guardians of students who had writing problems also tended to have children who struggled with history, social studies, and science—three subjects that usually require essays and reports—indicates that weaknesses in one area can have wide-ranging effects, including poor grades and behavioral problems.

3

Literacy Issues

In the United States, the ongoing debate over reading methods has resulted in many claims and counterarguments (Chall, 1967; Coles, 1999; Flesh, 1986; Goodman, 1996; Honig, 2000; McQuillan, 1998; Routman, 1996). Some researchers have vehemently argued that most American students read poorly. Others have maintained that these claims are spurious. Routman (1996) said that while most American students decode well, many have difficulty applying what they read to other contexts. Gardner (1991) found that the average American child learns how to repeat information that has been taught, but is unable, as Routman (1996) noted, to use it for other purposes. In other words, these students cannot move beyond the basic level of comprehension—the literal level—and use higher-order thinking skills.

One effect of the "reading wars" is that many teachers are genuinely confused about how to teach reading (Thompson, 2000). This problem undoubtedly has a deleterious effect on the literacy achievement of African American children, who, along with poor children and urban children, are more likely to have underprepared and underqualified teachers (Quality Counts, 2000). Although in African American culture, as in most cultures, literacy has always been highly esteemed (Anderson, 1988; Fleming, 1976; Harris, 1992), today African American fourth, eighth, and twelfth graders, on average, tend to have lower reading scores than their peers of other racial/ethnic groups (U.S. Department of Education, 2000b). In its most recent version of *The Nation's Report Card: Fourth Grade Reading Highlights,* the National Center for Education Statistics (2000) reported that African American fourth graders continue to lag behind White, Asian, Hispanic, and Native American fourth graders in reading achievement. Whereas there was a 29-point gap between White and Hispanic fourth graders, the gap between White and African American fourth graders was 33 points (p. 7).

One widespread belief about literacy development is that a print-rich home environment is an important determinant of future literacy skills. The positive correlation between home practices and strong literacy skills has been well documented (Scott & Marcus, 2001). Children from homes in which there are lots of books, where reading is modeled by adults, and who have been read to on a regular basis start school with advantages that other students lack. As a result, they are already reading when they start school or they are ready to begin reading soon after. These children are more likely to end up in the highest reading groups and are given the message early on that they are smart. On the other hand, when children start school with "limited" literacy skills, or when they are less advanced than other children, their home life is often cited as the culprit.

Scott and Marcus (2001) reviewed research that blamed the reading problems of African American children on dialect, discourse patterns, and home literacy practices. They urged educators to forge mutually beneficial "bidirectional" versus "unidirectional" home-school connections. These connections should use the "cultural capital" of African American students and parents to improve African American children's literacy development.

LeMoine (2001) described strategies that educators can use to improve the literacy skills of African American children who speak Ebonics. LeMoine referred to these children as "Standard English Language Learners" (SELLs) and said that the majority of African American kindergartners and first graders fit into this category. In order to instruct these children effectively, according to LeMoine, teachers must utilize six instructional practices: (1) They must increase their knowledge and understanding of SELLs; (2) they must learn to incorporate their knowledge of SELLs and their knowledge of language acquisition strategies into their instructional practices; (3) teachers must use effective second language acquisition strategies that will improve syntactic, phonological, and vocabulary skills; (4) they must use both whole language and phonics to improve literacy skills; (5) they must incorporate SELLs' history and culture into the curriculum; and (6) in designing lessons, teachers must take SELLs' learning styles into consideration.

The National Assessment of Educational Progress (U.S. Department of Education, 2000b) described some of the literacy practices of teachers and the effects of these practices on children. In another study, *The Nation's Report Card: Fourth Grade Reading Highlights,* the National Center for Education Statistics (2000) described correlations between reading achievement and home and school factors. The researchers found that the number of pages that fourth graders read daily during school and at home was associated with reading achievement. Fourth graders who read eleven or more pages daily had higher scores than those who read fewer pages. Time spent on homework was also correlated to reading achievement. Fourth graders who did not do their homework had lower reading scores than those who did their homework, and than those who reported that they did not have any homework. Fourth graders who read for fun on a daily basis also had higher scores than those who read for fun less frequently. Moreover, fourth graders who said that they discussed their "studies" at home on a daily basis had higher scores than those who did not.

In *African American Teens Discuss Their Schooling Experiences* (Thompson, 2002), the high school seniors who participated in the interview phase of the study discussed numerous issues pertaining to literacy. The majority of interviewees said that they liked to read when they were in elementary school, read during their spare time, owned children's books, used the school library, and used the public library. The majority of interviewees also said that, during elementary school, at least one family member modeled reading on a regular basis and that at least one family member read to them on a regular basis.

In Chapter 2 of the current study, several literacy-related problems that concerned the parents/guardians who completed the questionnaire were identified. Nearly 30 percent of the parents/guardians said that their children had a problem with writing. One-fourth of the parents/guardians said that their children had a problem with reading rate and one-fourth said that their children had a problem with reading comprehension. Furthermore, one-fifth of the parents/guardians said that their children disliked reading. Many variables were correlated to these problems.

The current chapter presents information about literacy practices in African American homes and includes two narratives. The goal of the chapter is to provide educators with more information about African American family literacy practices. Informing educators about specific ways in which the African American parents/guardians in this study assisted their children with literacy and descriptions of literacy practices in the home can help educators form stronger partnerships with African American parents in the hope of improving the reading and writing skills of African American children.

FAMILY LITERACY PRACTICES

Listening to Children Read

Eighty-two percent of the parents/guardians who completed the questionnaire said that their children read to them on a regular basis. The average parent/guardian said that his/her child read to the parent/guardian three days per week. However, 11 percent said that their children read once per week and 4 percent said they read at least six days per week. During the interview phase of the study, a mother of a seventh grade girl and a ninth grade girl spoke extensively about literacy practices in her home, stating:

The younger one has always been a reader from the beginning, but I have to encourage her to do outside reading on her own. At school, they have that Accelerated Reader program, so she has to read anyway, whether she likes it or not. But when they're off track [periodic breaks from year-round school] or out for the summer, I always make sure that she reads.

I have them read to me and I read to them. Even before my older daughter knew how to read, I read books to her. She would memorize the books and she would be reading. She really didn't know how to read yet, but when she was three or four years old, she would do that and she eventually started to read. Now, she and I will pick up a book—not as often as we used to—but we pick up a book and we read together. I do it more with the younger one than the older one. She reads to me a couple of times per week. The older one only does it when she's out of school for the summer. Otherwise, she just reads on her own.

Thirteen variables were positively correlated to reading to parents/guardians. The strongest correlation was between reading to parents/guardians and parents/guardians reciprocating by reading to their children. In other words, parents/guardians who read to their children also tended to be the parents/guardians who listened to their children read. Reading to parents/guardians was also correlated to several ways in which parents/guardians assisted their children academically, such as contacting teachers on a regular basis, encouraging children to read on a regular basis, helping with homework, taking children to the public library, buying books, encouraging children to check over their class work and homework, and limiting the amount of time that children spent watching television. Reading to parents/guardians was also linked to owning books. Therefore, the parents/guardians of children who owned their own books were also more likely to state that their children read to them on a regular basis. Parents/guardians who had elementary school-age children were also more likely than those with children who were in middle or high school to have children who read to them. The rating that parents/guardians assigned to the public school system, parents'/guardians' beliefs about whether or not most teachers care about students, and children reading to other members of the household were also linked to reading to parents/guardians (see Table 3.1).

Reading to Others at Home

Seventy-four percent of the parents/guardians who completed the questionnaire said that their children read to other members of the household. Some children read to more than one member of the household. The majority of children (58 percent) who read to other members of the household read to their siblings. Twenty-eight percent read to another parent, besides the parent who completed the questionnaire. Eighteen percent read to a grandparent, and 10 percent read to another relative who lived in the home.

Reading to others was correlated to five variables. The strongest correlation was an inverse relationship between having children who read to others and the level at which parents/guardians stated that their children had experienced racism at school. In other words, parents/guardians of children who experienced racism in elementary school were unlikely to state that their children read to other members of the household. Parents/guardians who had children

Table 3.1
Variables That Were Correlated to Listening to Children Read in the Order
of the Strength of Each Correlation

Variable	Strength of the Correlation	Significance
Reading to children	.76	p < .001
Encouraging children to read regularly	.36	p < .001
Encouraging children to check their work	.29	p < .001
Children reading to other members of the household	.27	p < .003
Helping with homework regularly	.26	p < .003
Having elementary school-age children	.26	p < .003
Children owning books	.25	p < .01
Taking children to the public library	.21	p < .02
Public school system rating	.21	p < .02
Buying books for children	.19	p < .03
Beliefs about whether or not teachers care	.19	p < .05
Limiting TV viewing	.18	p < .05
Contacting teachers regularly	.17	p < .05

$N = 106$

in elementary school instead of in middle school or high school were also more likely to have children who read to other members of the household. Parents/guardians who listened to their children read, who read to their children, and who encouraged their children to read regularly were more likely to have children who read to others in the home (see Table 3.2).

Parents/Guardians Reading to Their Children

Seventy percent of the questionnaire respondents said that they read to their children. The average parent/guardian read to his/her children three days per week. Ten percent read only once a week, but 19 percent read four or more days per week.

Reading to children was correlated to nine other questionnaire items. The strongest correlation was between listening to children read and parents/guardians reading to children. Additional ways in which parents/guardians assisted their children academically, such as by limiting television viewing, taking children to the public library, and encouraging children to read on a regular basis and to check their work, were also positively correlated to reading to children. Having children in elementary school, rather than in middle school or high school, having children who read to other members of the household, and how parents/guardians rated their children's high school teachers and the public school system were also linked to reading to children (see Table 3.3).

Owning Books

Ninety-two percent of the parents/guardians who completed the questionnaire said that their children owned books. Owning books was correlated to

Table 3.2
Variables That Were Correlated to Reading to Others in the Household in the Order of the Strength of Each Correlation

Variable	Strength of the Correlation	Significance
Level at which children experienced racism at school	-.46	$p < .01$
Encouraging children to read regularly	.33	$p < .001$
Listening to children read	.27	$p < .003$
Parents/guardians reading to children	.25	$p < .01$
Having elementary school-age children	.21	$p < .02$

$N = 96$

Table 3.3
Variables That Were Correlated to Parents/Guardians Reading to Children in the Order of the Strength of Each Correlation

Variable	Strength of the Correlation	Significance
Listening to children read	.76	$p < .001$
Encouraging children to read regularly	.36	$p < .001$
Parents'/guardians' public school system rating	.26	$p < .004$
Children reading to other members of the household	.25	$p < .01$
Parents'/guardians' high school teachers' rating	.24	$p < .04$
Taking children to the public library	.23	$p < .01$
Encouraging children to check their work	.23	$p < .01$
Limiting TV viewing	.22	$p < .01$
Having elementary school-age children	.20	$p < .03$

$N = 90$

seven other questionnaire items. The variable representing problems with reading comprehension was inversely related to owning books. Therefore, parents/guardians of children who owned their own books were unlikely to have children who struggled with reading comprehension. Owning books was positively correlated to parents/guardians listening to children read and how parents/guardians rated the public school system. Parents/guardians who said that their children owned their own books were also more likely than other parents/guardians to say that they bought books, encouraged their children to read and to use the school libraries, and believed that their children were college bound (see Table 3.4).

Buying Books for Their Children

Seventy percent of the parents/guardians said that they purchased books for their children on a regular basis, which was correlated to twenty variables. Most were positively correlated, but two were inversely related.

As noted previously, there were positive correlations between buying books for children, owning books, listening to children read, encouraging children to use the school libraries, and parents/guardians reading to their children. There were also positive correlations between buying books and assisting children academically by contacting teachers on a regular basis, limiting television viewing, encouraging children to read on a regular basis, taking children to the public library, assisting with homework, helping them study for tests, talking to children regularly about school, and encouraging children to check their schoolwork. Parents'/guardians' public school system rating and how they rated their children's elementary teachers were also correlated to buying books

Table 3.4
Variables That Were Correlated to Children Owning Books in the Order of the Strength of Each Correlation

Variable	Strength of the Correlation	Significance
Buying books	.29	$p < .001$
Listening to children read	.25	$p < .01$
Believing that children planned to attend college	.24	$p < .01$
Encouraging regular reading	.22	$p < .01$
Reading comprehension problem	-.22	$p < .02$
Public school system rating	.19	$p < .04$
Encouraging children to use the school libraries	.18	$p < .04$

$N = 119$

for children. Two variables also pertained to college. Parents/guardians who talked to their children on an ongoing basis about attending college and/or who believed that their children planned to attend college were also more likely to buy books for their children. Moreover, parents/guardians who said that their children's education was very important to them were more likely than others to buy books for their children. The most perplexing positive correlation existed between buying books for children and writing problems. This could indicate that some parents/guardians bought books for their children to assist them with writing problems. The source of the racism that children experienced at school was negatively linked to buying books for children. It appears that the parents/guardians of children who experienced racism from multiple sources at school, such as from students and adults on campus, or from more than one group of adults on campus, were less likely than others to buy books for their children. Having children who earned poor grades was also inversely correlated to buying books for children. Therefore, parents/guardians who purchased books for their children on a regular basis were unlikely to have children who had poor grades (see Table 3.5).

Encouraging Children to Use the Classroom or School Library

Forty-nine percent of the parents/guardians said they encouraged their children to check out books from the classroom or school library on a regular basis. In addition to owning books (as noted previously), this questionnaire item was positively correlated to sixteen others. The three categories of associations were (1) additional ways (which have previously been cited) in which parents/guardians assisted their children academically, (2) parents'/guardians' perception of school-related factors, and (3) academic problems.

The parents/guardians who encouraged their children to check out books at school tended to have children who had difficulty with their history and/or social studies classes. Parents/guardians of children who had been suspended from middle school and high school, or from all three levels of school, were also likely to encourage their children to use school libraries. Parents'/guardians' beliefs about the benefits of their children's middle school homework was also linked to encouraging children to use the school or classroom library. Moreover, parents'/guardians' perception of the racial climate in their children's school district was related to this variable. In other words, those who believed that racism was common in the school district were also likely to encourage their children to use these libraries. Racism at school will be revisited at length in Chapter 10.

Finally, assisting children academically by encouraging them to check their work; buying books for them; talking to them about college; contacting teachers regularly; encouraging children to read; helping with homework; taking them

Table 3.5
Variables That Were Correlated to Buying Books for Children in the Order
of the Strength of Each Correlation

Variable	Strength of the Correlation	Significance
Encouraging children to check their work	.51	p < .001
Helping children study for tests	.49	p < .001
Encouraging children to read regularly	.48	p < .001
Helping with homework	.43	p < .001
Racism source(s)	-.35	p < .04
Talking to children about school	.33	p < .001
Talking to children about college	.33	p < .001
Limiting TV viewing	.33	p < .001
Contacting teachers regularly	.32	p < .001
Children owning books	.29	p < .001
Encouraging children to use school libraries	.27	p < .002
Taking children to the public library	.27	p < .002
Believing that children planned to attend college	.26	p < .004
Public school system rating	.26	p < .003
Elementary teachers' rating	.20	p < .03
Value parents/guardians placed on children's education	.20	p < .03
Writing problems	.19	p < .03
Listening to children read	.19	p < .03
Parents/guardians reading to children	.18	p < .05
Poor grades	-.18	p < .04

$N = 90$

to the public library; limiting television viewing; helping children study for
tests; and talking with them about school on a regular basis were also positively
correlated to this variable (see Table 3.6).

Taking Children to the Public Library

Thirty-eight percent of the parents/guardians said that they took their children to the public library on a regular basis. Most had elementary school–age
children. However, twelve other variables were positively related. One variable,

Table 3.6
Variables That Were Correlated to Encouraging Children to Use the School
or Classroom Library in the Order of the Strength of Each Correlation

Variable	Strength of the Correlation	Significance
Encouraging children to read	.47	p < .001
Suspension level	.38	p < .04
Limiting TV viewing	.33	p < .001
Taking children to the public library	.32	p < .001
Helping with homework	.30	p < .001
Helping children study for tests	.28	p < .001
Encouraging children to check their work	.28	p < .001
Buying books for children	.27	p < .002
Parents'/guardians' perception of the school district's racial climate	.27	p < .01
Talking with children about college	.27	p < .002
Benefits of middle school homework	.26	p < .03
Talking with children about school	.25	p <. 004
Social studies problem	.22	p < .01
Contacting teachers	.22	p < .01
Children owning books	.18	p < .04
History problem	.18	p < .04

$N = 63$

the source of racism that children experienced, was inversely linked to taking children to the public library. This suggests that the parents/guardians of children who experienced racism from adults or from adults and children at school were unlikely to take their children to the public library on a regular basis.

Once again, numerous other strategies that parents/guardians utilized to assist their children academically were also positively correlated to taking children to the public library. These strategies included buying books for children, encouraging them to check their work, encouraging them to utilize school libraries, contacting teachers, encouraging children to read, parents/guardians reading to children, listening to children read, helping them study for tests, helping with homework, and limiting television viewing. However, the variable representing the number of days per week that parents/guardians read to their children was also linked to taking children to the public library, indicating that those who read to them frequently were more likely to take them to the public library (see Table 3.7). The two narratives that follow are based on interviews with parents/guardians of struggling readers.

I'M STILL WONDERING WHAT'S GOING TO HAPPEN TO MY SON

When she graduated from college with a business degree, Jocelyn, a divorced mother of two girls and two boys, had no idea that she would one day return to school to pursue a teaching credential, not to mention a master's degree in reading. Although she had initially taken courses to become a teacher, when she moved to California from Oklahoma, she changed her career plans. However, many years later, her love for her son, a seventh grader who was struggling with math and reading, motivated her to change careers. Her goal was to find the solution to his reading disability and to help other parents and children in similar predicaments. Whereas his math and reading–related problems were her primary concerns, Jocelyn's son had other problems that surfaced

Table 3.7
Variables That Were Correlated to Taking Children to the Public Library in the Order of the Strength of Each Correlation

Variable	Strength of the Correlation	Significance
Racism source	-.36	p < .04
Limiting TV viewing	.34	p < .001
Encouraging children to check their work	.33	p < .001
Contacting teachers	.33	p < .001
Encouraging children to read	.33	p < .001
Encouraging children to use school libraries	.32	p < .001
Buying books for children	.27	p < .002
Helping children study for tests	.26	p < .004
Number of days per week parents/guardians read to children	.25	p < .03
Reading to children	.23	p < .01
Helping with homework	.22	p < .01
Listening to children read	.21	p < .02
Having elementary school-age children	.20	p < .03
Children's attitude about school	.18	p < .04

$N = 49$

early in his schooling. These problems became more noticeable when he was in fifth grade. Jocelyn believed that these problems stemmed from his low birth weight, and the fact that she pampered him, because he was small for his age. She explained:

He's the oldest of my two sons. He's smaller than his brother, so you would think that he's the younger one. He has always had problems in elementary. He had a pronunciation problem, mostly with "G" words. He had to go to a speech therapist. Teachers showed concern for him back in kindergarten. He wasn't completing assignments on time, especially homework. They were concerned about the level at which he was completing sentences and his skills. He was always into everybody else's business in the classroom. Anything could easily distract him. He wasn't a discipline problem at home, but I saw the same school behaviors—as innocent as they are—at home. Before he started school, I put him in preschool, because I already suspected that he would have problems because of his size. During kindergarten, they had concerns about ADD because he's very active. They asked me to go have him tested.

Instead of having her son tested for ADD, when he became a first grader, Jocelyn enrolled him in a private school. When the school closed after one year, she placed him back in public school. The main difference that she noticed was that her son was teased about his size more in public school. The teasing not only intensified in ensuing grades, but resulted in her son lashing out at other children. According to Jocelyn, "He's been suspended several times and it is mostly related to teasing. Once, a little boy pushed him and my son hit him back. So there was an altercation. In that school district, they'll kick you out for anything."

When her son was a sixth grader, Jocelyn decided to have him tested for ADD. She told the doctor she believed that he needed medication because of what educators had told her. Although the doctor said that her son did not have any symptoms of ADD, he agreed to place the boy on Ritalin anyway. After giving her son the medication for one day, Jocelyn stopped giving it to him, fearing that it would have a long-term adverse effect on him. During that one day, she had telephoned the school five times to ascertain how her son was being affected by the drug. "I just didn't feel comfortable with it," she stated, "because I didn't know what effects it would have on my child."

When her son was in seventh grade, Jocelyn permitted him to be placed in the Resource Specialist Program (RSP), which would allow him to receive additional academic assistance. According to Jocelyn, "He felt like he was going too fast and was not catching on to what was happening in the classroom. In RSP, they have summer camp and after-school programs to work with him in reading and math." By the end of the year, however, Jocelyn was questioning whether or not she had made the right decision. She explained:

He doesn't know his multiplication still. And when I had specific concerns about the things my son could not do, I expect for some of that to happen if he's in a special program. He doesn't know his multiplication, but they're into that "Introduction to

Algebra," and pre-algebra. That's what they work with him on. So, my thing is, how can he do the algebra if he can't even do the multiplication or division? He's missing some basic math concepts. I even thought about homeschooling him. I may have to put him in another tutoring program. He has a sister that's very good in math, but because of that sibling thing I can't get them to work together. I think I'm going to try to put him into regular classrooms and pay tutors to help him, because I'm not satisfied with the system. He is in middle school and I have concerns because I do not want him to go into Special Ed in high school. I've visited some Special Ed classrooms and I don't feel like they're learning anything. I think it's just a holding tank. They're getting them through the system and not expecting much from the kids. In RSP, it's definitely watered down. It's almost like a form of remediation but they're not giving him work that will prepare him for the next level, because it's all watered down. So, how do we get him caught up and keep him there? That's my concern. That's what I'm trying to work on right now.

At home, Jocelyn used multiple strategies to assist her son and her other children academically. During the summer, she enrolled him in a reading and math program. When she decided to return to school to earn a teaching credential and a master's degree in reading, one of the underlying motives was to gather additional information that would enable her to better assist her son, particularly with reading. Moreover, in addition to hiring tutors to work with him, she also enrolled him in an after-school literacy program. In the meantime, she was still worried. "I'm still wondering about my son [and] what's going to happen," she said.

SHE READS VERY WELL, BUT SHE DOESN'T UNDERSTAND A LOT OF THE TIME

During her interview, Mrs. Washington, a fifty-seven-year-old church secretary, described her granddaughter's schooling experiences. When the girl was a year old, Mrs. Washington had become her guardian because the girl's parents were addicted to illegal drugs. Throughout the interview, Mrs. Washington's resoluteness about doing whatever she could to assist her granddaughter academically was evident. "I try to do everything I can for her, because I want her to be successful in life," Mrs. Washington stated.

Starting in elementary school, her granddaughter had struggled academically. Now, as a sixth grader, she continued to struggle with math and reading. Like Jocelyn in the previous narrative, Mrs. Washington was frustrated with the school system's response to her granddaughter's academic problems. Therefore, like Jocelyn, she became proactive.

In describing her granddaughter's early schooling experiences, Mrs. Washington stated, "She had a problem in learning. I think when you have a problem like this, the teacher has to spend a little more time with you. At first, I thought it was because her parents did drugs. At school, they tested her for Attention

Deficit Disorder. I never got the results. The doctor asked for the results, but we never could get them from the school."

Unlike Jocelyn's son, Mrs. Washington's granddaughter was never medicated for ADD. During her early school years, the granddaughter had exhibited signs of nervousness and appeared to have a short attention span. However, she was never a discipline problem, according to Mrs. Washington. Like Jocelyn, Mrs. Washington became frustrated by the school's inability to assist her granddaughter. "I don't think that they had my granddaughter's best interest in mind," she explained. "I wasn't too happy with that school. There were too many people in the classes and they weren't helping her."

Mrs. Washington was mainly concerned about her granddaughter's reading skills. Consequently, she decided to enroll her in a nationally known private reading clinic. Although she gave the clinic credit for helping her granddaughter overcome her shyness, Mrs. Washington was disappointed at how she and her granddaughter had been treated there. She remarked:

I think the guy who took over the clinic was a redneck who drank too much. I would sit in the waiting room, watching what they would do. One night, I watched this female tutor work with my granddaughter and a White child. She may have given my granddaughter fifteen minutes of her time, but she gave most of her time to the White child. So, I told the tutor about it. I said, "I'm not paying you for this session. If I had to sit out here and watch and bogard [to act assertively to get what one deserves] to see that my child is getting the right attention, then I don't need to be here. I'm not going to pay you for something I'm not getting."

As her granddaughter continued to struggle with reading, Mrs. Washington searched for other solutions. When her church started a weekend and after-school tutorial program, Mrs. Washington enrolled her granddaughter in the program. She soon noticed positive results. According to Mrs. Washington, "I think they did more for her at the church than the clinic or school did. This is what she needed. Her grades have improved. She reads very well, but she does not understand a lot of the times." In the meantime, Mrs. Washington was determined to continue doing "everything I can." Her ultimate goal was to send her granddaughter to college, "so she can make something out of herself."

SUMMARY

This chapter described the ways in which African American parents/guardians who participated in the study attempted to improve their children's literacy skills. Although some of the results were based on small subsets of the total sample of participants and many of the correlations were small, the details that surfaced can be useful to educators. Moreover, they underscore the need for more research with larger samples about literacy practices in African American homes.

In addition to listening to their children read on a regular basis, the majority of the parents/guardians said that they read to their children, bought books for them, and that their children read to other members of the household on a regular basis. However, less than half the parents/guardians stated that they encouraged their children to use the classroom and/or school library and less than 40 percent said that they took their children to the public library on a regular basis. Family literacy practices were linked to numerous variables, such as additional ways in which parents/guardians assisted their children academically, parents'/guardians' perception of teacher attitudes about students, their satisfaction with the public school system, having elementary school–age children in the home, academic problems, and issues pertaining to racism (which shall be discussed in detail in Chapter 10).

These findings are similar to those of Thompson (2002). In that study, the majority of the African American teens who participated in the interview phase of the study said that many of the aforementioned literacy practices were common in their homes during their elementary-school years. However, much smaller percentages of students reported that they had used the school or public libraries on a regular basis. The students attributed this to numerous factors, including that the books in the school libraries were boring and out-of-date. Some students also stated that they had enough books at home and did not need to use other libraries, unless it was for school reports that had been assigned.

The two narratives in this chapter provided specific examples of additional ways in which a mother and a grandmother sought to assist their children with their academic problems. The mother, Jocelyn, actually changed careers in an effort to help her son. She had placed him in private school, was considering homeschooling him, and was paying tutors to provide extra assistance. Mrs. Washington placed her granddaughter in a private, nationally known reading clinic, only to become disillusioned as a result of what she perceived to be racist treatment. Thereafter, she enrolled her granddaughter in a church-run, after-school and weekend tutorial program. In addition to their persistence in searching for solutions to their children's reading problems, these women's stories are similar in two other ways: First, both—like Venisha, in Chapter 1, and Beatrice, in Chapter 2—had been given the impression that their children suffered from ADD; second, both women—like Beatrice, Venisha, and Peggy (in Chapter 1)—had become extremely frustrated because of the school system's inability to help their children with their problems. These issues will be revisited in ensuing chapters.

4

How African American Parents/Guardians Assisted
Their Children Academically

Today, as noted in the Introduction, it is well known that parent involvement is positively correlated to academic achievement (Comer & Poussaint, 1992; Floyd, 1995; Lynn, 1997a; Mapp, 1997). In *Family Involvement in Children's Education: An Idea Book*, the U.S. Department of Education (2001a), reported that family involvement is related to higher test scores, better grades, better school attendance, a greater homework completion rate, better student attitudes and behaviors, higher graduation rates, and increased college attendance rates.

In examining the National Education Longitudinal Study (NELS) data, Cook and Ludwig (1998) found that African American parents were as involved in their children's education as White parents from similar socioeconomic backgrounds. In *African American Teens Discuss Their Schooling Experiences* (Thompson, 2002), the high school seniors discussed their parents'/guardians' involvement in their elementary, middle, and high school education. Seventy-four percent of the students rated their parents'/guardians' involvement in their elementary school education as *excellent* or *good;* 62 percent rated their parents'/guardians' involvement in their middle school education as *excellent* or *good;* and 59 percent rated their parents'/guardians' involvement in their high school education as *excellent* or *good* (pp. 154–155).

In a seminal study, *Family Life and School Achievement: Why Poor Black Children Succeed or Fail,* Clark (1983) contrasted family practices in the homes of five high-achieving African American high school seniors and five low-achieving African American high school seniors in low-income Chicago communities. He found that, regardless of the number of parents per household, numerous characteristics surfaced repeatedly in the homes of high achievers. One important characteristic of the parents of high achievers was they did not believe that the school was solely responsible for educating their children. Instead, they believed that parents should be responsible for making positive contributions to their children's education. Parents of high achievers also started preparing their children for academic success during the preschool years by helping them hone their speaking skills and by teaching them to read, spell, and problem-solve. A third characteristic of the parents of high achievers was that they had high expectations for their children regarding school attendance, punctuality, and class participation. Moreover, they created a homework routine that started with strict monitoring of their children's homework practices, and assistance with projects and reports. As the children grew older, the parents expected them to accept more responsibility for ensuring that homework was completed. Another characteristic was that the parents of high achievers taught their children that teachers' primary purpose was to assist students academically.

Conversely, the parents of the low achievers whom Clark studied had been enervated by the vicissitudes of life. These parents were preoccupied with immediate survival needs. Although their children's education was important to them, they failed to provide their children with the sustained academic support that the parents of high achievers provided. Furthermore, they placed the responsibility for their children's schooling on the children, instead of on themselves as parents or on the school system. Moreover, the parents of low achievers were grossly ignorant about many aspects of their children's education, including grades, test scores, and problems at school. These parents were unlikely to visit the school for any reason, unless they were advised to do so as a result of their children's misbehavior.

Although it is well known that parent involvement is important, it is also well known (as noted in the Introduction of this book) that many educators are displeased with the amount of parent participation in schools. For example, in its "Schools and Staffing Surveys" for 1990–91 and 1993–94, the *Digest of Education Statistics* (U.S. Department of Education, 1999) reported that lack of parent involvement was a great concern of many public school teachers. Often, this lack of participation leads teachers to assume that parents/guardians do not care about their children's education (Phillips, Crouse, & Ralph, 1998; Thompson, 2002). However, educators, themselves, contribute to this lack of participation by giving some parents/guardians the impression that they are not welcome at school (Comer & Poussaint, 1992; Mapp, 1997; Vail, 2001b). Additionally, many parents/guardians feel uncomfortable around school personnel (Comer & Poussaint, 1992; Delpit, 1995; Mapp, 1997). In contrast, urban and lower-socioeconomic-status schools and school districts that have been successful in increasing parent participation have done so by connecting with parents/guardians in ways that make them feel welcome and valued at school (Mapp, 1997; Vail, 2001b). Lynn (1997b) said that professional development that would train teachers to work with families is one way to begin the process of increasing parent involvement. Another option is for teacher education programs to train teachers to work with parents through field experiences.

Thus far throughout the current study, examples of how African American parents/guardians assisted their children academically have surfaced. This chapter seeks to increase educators' knowledge of additional ways in which the

African American parents/guardians in the study assisted their children academically. It also presents the results of the ratings that the parents/guardians gave to themselves regarding how well they assisted their children academically. Two related narratives are included.

AFRICAN AMERICAN PARENTS'/GUARDIANS' SELF-RATINGS OF HOW WELL THEY ASSISTED THEIR CHILDREN ACADEMICALLY

The majority of the parents/guardians who completed the questionnaire rated their academic assistance to their children as *excellent* or *good* (see Table 4.1), but 17 percent rated their assistance as less than good. In explaining why she gave herself a *good* rating, a mother of four explained:

Because I stay involved with them. I look at their reports. They carry Binder Reminders and I ask to see what they're up to. I speak with their teachers on occasion, when I have the opportunity to go to the school. I talk to my kids about the importance of education and where it's going to take them. You have all these parents bragging about "A + " students. I tell my kids to do their best. Their best may not be an "A." It may be a "C," but I want them to work on doing their best, and then we'll talk about getting better.

A mother who rated her involvement in her children's education as *good,* said she did so because "I'm very involved in their life. I don't just send them out there. I'm involved to make sure that they're doing the right thing, to respect adults, to listen, and learn. I tell them to work on their goals now, instead of waiting until they get to high school." A mother of a son in elementary school who rated her assistance as *good,* said that she did so because:

Whenever he needs help, I am there, whether we are at my business or at home. I'm there for him. I always encourage him to do his homework, as soon as he gets out of school. I say, "Get it done. Let's do it right." His dad does too. I wish that I was better

Table 4.1
How Parents/Guardians Rated Their Academic Assistance to Their Children

Rating	Percent
Needs to improve	5
Fair	12
Good	44
Excellent	36
No answer	3

$N = 129$

at it and was better acquainted with the work that they're doing. I don't want to help them do it all the way. I want them to figure it out, because I'm not going to be there with them in class when they're having a test. I help them enough, so that they can help themselves.

Parents'/guardians' self-rating was correlated to nineteen variables. Three of the ten variables that were inversely related to their self-rating pertained to racism at school. Parents/guardians who believed that their children had experienced racism at school, particularly those whose children had experienced racism frequently and those whose children had experienced it during more than one level of their schooling, were unlikely to rate their academic assistance as *excellent* or *good*. Suspension from school and discipline problems were also inversely related to parents'/guardians' self-rating. Therefore, those who gave high ratings to their assistance were less likely to have children who had been suspended from school or who were discipline problems. Three academic problems—math, history, and reading comprehension difficulties—were also negatively correlated to parents'/guardians' self-rating. Those who gave themselves high ratings were less likely to have children who struggled in these areas. Furthermore, parents/guardians who reported high involvement were unlikely to have children who disliked school. Moreover, parents/guardians who gave themselves a high rating were unlikely to serve as classroom volunteers.

Nine variables were positively correlated to parents'/guardians' self-rating. The strongest correlation was between this variable and how parents/guardians rated their children's high school teachers. Parents'/guardians' public school system rating, elementary teachers' rating, and their beliefs about the value of their children's elementary course work and homework were also linked to their self-rating. Additionally, there were positive correlations between their self-rating and their beliefs about whether or not most school administrators, counselors, and teachers care about students. Finally, parents/guardians who said that they placed a high value on their children's education and parents/guardians who had children in G.A.T.E. during middle school were also more likely to give themselves an *excellent* or *good* self-rating (see Table 4.2).

HOW PARENTS/GUARDIANS ASSISTED THEIR CHILDREN ACADEMICALLY

In Chapter 3, numerous ways in which African American parents/guardians assisted their children with reading were described. The majority of parents/guardians listened to their children read, they read to their children, and their children read to other members of the household. Seventy percent of the parents/guardians purchased books for their children. Nearly half of the parents/guardians encouraged their children to use the school libraries and 38 percent took their children to the public library on a regular basis. This section

Table 4.2

Variables That Were Correlated to Parents'/Guardians' Self-Rating in the Order of the Strength of Each Correlation

Variable	Strength of the Correlation	Significance
Experiencing racism at multiple levels	-.43	p < .001
High school teachers' rating	.41	p < .001
Experiencing racism frequently	-.34	p < .03
Public school system rating	.31	p < .001
Elementary teachers' rating	.31	p < .001
Disliking school	-.30	p < .001
Benefits of elementary homework	.29	p < .002
Discipline problem	-.29	p < .001
Parents'/guardians' beliefs about whether or not teachers care	.28	p < .004
The value placed on children's education	.25	p < .01
Reading comprehension problem	-.24	p < .01
Experiencing racism at school	-.24	p < .02
Benefits of elementary course work	.23	p < .02
Middle school track	.23	p < .04
Parents'/guardians' beliefs about whether or not administrators care	.22	p < .03
History problem	-.21	p < .02
Serving as a classroom volunteer	-.20	p < .03
Suspension from school	-.18	p < .04
Math problem	-.18	p < .04

$N = 129$

will provide more information about ways (which have been mentioned briefly in previous chapters) that African American parents/guardians assisted their children and it will describe several additional strategies that they utilized (see Table 4.3).

Helping with Homework on a Regular Basis

Seventy-four percent of the parents/guardians said that they helped their children with homework on a regular basis. Fourteen questionnaire items were correlated to this variable. Thirteen were positively related and only one—the

Table 4.3
How African American Parents/Guardians Assisted Their Children
Academically

Strategy	Percent
Listening to children read	82
Talking to children about school	82
Contacting teachers on a regular basis	76
Encouraging children to attend college	74
Helping with homework	74
Encouraging children to check their class work and homework	73
Buying books for children	70
Reading to children	70
Encouraging children to read	59
Limiting TV viewing	58
Helping children study for tests	57
Encouraging children to use school libraries	49
Taking children to the public library	38
Volunteering to help in classrooms	20
Other assistance	14

$N = 129$

source of racism that children experienced at school—was inversely related. Therefore, parents/guardians who helped their children with homework were unlikely to say that their children experienced racism from adults at school or from multiple sources.

Among the variables that were positively correlated to helping with homework, the variables that had the strongest correlations were encouraging children to check their schoolwork, helping children study for tests, limiting television viewing, contacting teachers, and buying books. Parents/guardians who listened to their children read, who encouraged their children to use the school libraries, who encouraged their children to read often, who took their children to the public library, and who talked to them about school on an ongoing basis were also likely to help with homework. Two college-related variables—the belief that their children were planning to go to college and talking to their children about college—were also positively correlated to helping with homework. The weakest correlation was between helping with homework and the rating that parents/guardians gave to the public school system (see Table 4.4).

Table 4.4
Variables That Were Correlated to Helping with Homework in the Order of the Strength of Each Correlation

Variable	Strength of the Correlation	Significance
Encouraging children to check their work	.63	p < .001
Helping children study for tests	.54	p < .001
Limiting TV viewing	.51	p < .001
Contacting teachers regularly	.47	p < .001
Buying books for children	.43	p < .001
Racism source	-.39	p < .02
Talking to children about college	.38	p < .001
Encouraging children to read	.35	p < .001
Talking to children about school	.35	p < .001
Encouraging children to use the school libraries	.30	p < .001
Listening to children read	.26	p < .003
Taking children to the public library	.22	p < .01
Believing that children were planning to attend college	.22	p < .02
School system rating	.17	p < .05

$N = 96$

Contacting Teachers on a Regular Basis

Seventy-six percent of the parents/guardians said they assisted their children academically by contacting their teachers on a regular basis. Fourteen questionnaire items were positively related to this variable. The strongest correlations were between contacting teachers and helping with homework, encouraging children to check their work, and helping them study for tests. Five correlations pertained to reading-related variables: buying books, encouraging children to use the school libraries, encouraging them to read regularly, listening to them read, and taking them to the public library. Again, two variables pertaining to college—the belief that one's children were planning to go to college and talking about college on an ongoing basis—were also correlated to contacting teachers. Limiting television viewing, talking to children about school, the value that parents/guardians placed on children's education, and parents'/guardians' gender were also positively correlated to contacting teachers. In other words, women were more likely than men to contact their children's teachers on a regular basis (see Table 4.5).

Table 4.5
Variables That Were Correlated to Contacting Teachers in the Order of the Strength of Each Correlation

Variable	Strength of the Correlation	Significance
Helping with homework	.47	p < .001
Encouraging children to check their work	.45	p < .001
Helping children study for tests	.42	p < .001
Talking to children about college	.34	p < .001
Encouraging regular reading	.36	p < .001
Taking children to the public library	.33	p < .001
Limiting TV viewing	.32	p < .001
Buying books for children	.32	p < .001
Parents'/guardians' gender	.26	p < .004
Talking to children about school	.24	p < .01
Value placed on children's education	.24	p < .01
Believing that children were planning to attend college	.23	p < .01
Encouraging children to use the school libraries	.22	p < .01
Listening to children read	.17	p < .05

$N = 98$

Talking to Children about School

Eighty-two percent of the parents/guardians said that they talked to their children about school on a regular basis. Eleven other questionnaire items were positively linked to this variable. The three strongest correlations to talking to children about school were talking about college, limiting television viewing, and encouraging children to check their work. One variable—providing "other" less frequently cited academic assistance—was inversely related. In other words, parents/guardians who talked to their children about school on a regular basis were unlikely to state that they used uncommon strategies to assist them academically. All of the other variables have repeatedly surfaced as a result of their correlations to other strategies that parents/guardians cited (see Table 4.6).

Encouraging Children to Check Their Class Work and Homework

Seventy-three percent of the parents/guardians said that they encouraged their children to check over their class work and homework. This variable was

Table 4.6
Variables That Were Correlated to Talking to Children about School in the Order of the Strength of Each Correlation

Variable	Strength of the Correlation	Significance
Talking to children about college	.47	p < .001
Limiting TV viewing	.45	p < .001
Encouraging children to check their work	.42	p < .001
Believing that one's children planned to attend college	.36	p < .001
Helping with homework	.35	p < .001
Buying books	.33	p < .001
Encouraging children to read	.30	p < .001
Helping children study for tests	.28	p < .001
The value parents/guardians placed on their children's education	.28	p < .002
Encouraging children to use the school libraries	.25	p < .004
Contacting teachers on a regular basis	.24	p < .01
Other assistance	-.19	p < .03

$N = 106$

linked to sixteen other questionnaire items, most of which have been correlated to the other strategies that parents/guardians utilized to assist their children academically. Two academic problems, however, were inversely related to this variable. Parents/guardians who encouraged their children to check over their work were unlikely to have children who struggled with science or history (see Table 4.7).

Helping Children Study for Tests

Fifty-seven percent of the parents/guardians said that they helped their children study for tests on a regular basis. A mother of a kindergartner said that she not only checked over her daughter's homework but helped her with math by giving her "practical problems" to do; took her to the library, and attended school functions. This mother stated that when helping her daughter study for tests, "I sit down with her and we sweat it out together."

Fifteen questionnaire items, most of which were associated with other strategies that parents/guardians utilized, were linked to this variable. Parents/guardians of elementary school–age children were more likely than those with older school-age children to help their children study for tests. The number of

Table 4.7
Variables That Were Correlated to Encouraging Children to Check Their Work in the Order of the Strength of Each Correlation

Variable	Strength of the Correlation	Significance
Helping with homework	.63	p < .001
Talking about college	.55	p < .001
Limiting TV viewing	.54	p < .001
Buying books for children	.51	p < .001
Contacting teachers	.45	p < .001
Helping children study for tests	.43	p < .001
Talking to children about school	.42	p < .001
Encouraging regular reading	.38	p < .001
Taking children to the public library	.33	p < .001
Listening to children read	.29	p < .001
Encouraging children to use school libraries	.28	p < .001
Science problem	-.24	p < .01
Reading to children	.23	p < .01
Believing that one's children planned to attend college	.21	p < .02
Value placed on children's education	.21	p < .02
History problem	-.21	p < .02

$N = 94$

days per week that children read to their parents/guardians was positively correlated to having parents/guardians who helped their children study for tests. Science problems, poor grades, and suspension were the only variables that were inversely related to helping children study for tests. In other words, the children of parents/guardians who helped them study for tests on a regular basis were unlikely to have these problems (see Table 4.8).

Limiting Television Viewing Time

Fifty-eight percent of the parents/guardians said that they limited the amount of television that their children watched on a daily basis. Most of the fourteen questionnaire items that were positively correlated to this variable were also correlated to other types of assistance that parents/guardians gave. However, gender was linked, indicating that women were more likely than men to limit daily television viewing. Moreover, there was also a positive

Table 4.8
Variables That Were Correlated to Helping Children Study for Tests in the Order of the Strength of Each Correlation

Variable	Strength of the Correlation	Significance
Helping with homework	.54	$p < .001$
Buying books	.49	$p < .001$
Encouraging reading	.46	$p < .001$
Limiting TV viewing	.44	$p < .001$
Encouraging children to check their work	.43	$p < .001$
Contacting teachers	.42	$p < .001$
Talking about college	.41	$p < .001$
Number of days per week children read to their parents/guardians	.29	$p < .01$
Encouraging children to use the school libraries	.28	$p < .001$
Talking to children about school	.28	$p < .001$
Taking children to the public library	.26	$p < .004$
Having elementary school-age children	.25	$p < .004$
Science problem	-.25	$p < .004$
Suspension	-.20	$p < .03$
Poor grades	-.19	$p < .03$

$N = 74$

association between this variable and the number of days per week that parents/guardians read to their children (see Table 4.9).

Talking to Children about College

Seventy-four percent of the parents/guardians said that they encouraged their children to attend college on a regular basis. This variable was correlated to numerous questionnaire items that will be discussed in Chapter 13.

Serving as a Classroom Volunteer

Only 20 percent of the parents/guardians said that they assisted their children academically by serving as a classroom volunteer. This variable was linked to five other questionnaire items. Three items were inversely related to serving as a classroom volunteer. These negative correlations suggest that parents/guardians who gave less than *good* ratings to their own academic assistance

Table 4.9
Variables That Were Correlated to Limiting Daily Television Viewing in the Order of the Strength of Each Correlation

Variable	Strength of the Correlation	Significance
Encouraging children to check their work	.54	p < .001
Helping with homework	.51	p < .001
Talking about college	.46	p < .001
Talking about school	.45	p < .001
Helping children study for tests	.44	p < .001
Encouraging regular reading	.35	p < .001
Taking children to the public library	.34	p < .001
Buying books	.33	p < .001
Encouraging children to use school libraries	.33	p < .001
Contacting teachers	.32	p < .001
Number of days per week parents/guardians read to their children	.25	p < .03
Reading to children	.22	p < .01
Parents'/guardians' gender	.21	p < .02
Listening to children read	.18	p < .05

$N = 75$

and/or to their children's elementary and high school teachers were more likely to serve as classroom volunteers than those who gave themselves and their children's teachers higher ratings. Two problems were positively associated with serving as a classroom volunteer. Parents/guardians whose children struggled with science and/or who had poor grades were more likely than others to serve as classroom volunteers (see Table 4.10).

During the interview phase of the study, several parents/guardians discussed the reasons why they did or did not serve as classroom volunteers. Some parents/guardians said that they had visited their children's classrooms to observe their children's behavior and how teachers interacted with their children, but had not necessarily offered to volunteer. However, some parents/guardians said that they had actually volunteered, but were given the impression that they were not welcome in classrooms. One interviewee, a mother of several school-age children explained:

I ask the teachers if they need any extra help. I tell them that if my kids need help, I'll be there and I will help. And do you know what the teachers tell me? "We don't need

Table 4.10

Variables That Were Correlated to Serving as a Classroom Volunteer in the Order of the Strength of Each Correlation

Variable	Strength of the Correlation	Significance
Science problem	.29	$p < .001$
High school teachers' rating	-.27	$p < .02$
Parents'/guardians' self-rating	-.20	$p < .03$
Poor grades	.19	$p < .03$
Elementary teachers' rating	-.18	$p < .04$

$N = 26$

help." But at the end of the school year, they have a problem with my kids. I think it's that I'm intimidating to the teachers because they aren't teaching fair. I don't know if they're fearful or what. I've offered my help several times. Every year, I come and I offer and they say, "Well, I don't think. . . . " They let other parents come and volunteer their services. But I have never once been asked to come and sit in the classroom. There are things that they don't want me to see, but I see a lot. I'm not prejudiced but I see a lot of non–English speaking parents in the class.

Other Ways of Assisting Children Academically

Fourteen percent of the parents/guardians said that they assisted their children in other ways besides those mentioned previously. Some said they participated in school fund-raisers; others said that they attended assemblies and other school events. Parents/guardians also mentioned serving on the School Site Council and attending PTA meetings. A few said that they had gone to the School Board with concerns. Several parents/guardians who participated in the interview phase of the study said that, while they had attempted to become involved with parent organizations at school, they soon became disillusioned and stopped attending because they felt unwelcome. A recurring theme was that the school appeared to be catering to Spanish-speaking parents. For example, one interviewee recounted:

The first day I went to the parent meeting, I was upset. I told them that I was upset and I'd never come back again, because when I went in there, they had everything for Spanish-speaking people. They didn't have anything written in English. It upset me. I asked for pamphlets in English. They had to go to the office, make some pamphlets in English, and I had to put them in order myself, and staple them, so that I could read them.

Another mother said that she stopped attending parenting classes at school because she felt insulted. She explained:

They wanted me to go to counseling. I don't need to go to no counseling! When my kids were small, they used to give those parenting classes. I used to volunteer and go. I have five kids and they have five different personalities. I wanted to learn how to deal with each one of them and each one of their personalities on an individual basis. I would volunteer my time, going to different classes and different workshops. I felt insulted when they told me to go to counseling. I really do. They must be crazy! I told them that I've been to parenting classes. I have certificates and awards. I have plaques on my walls. I told them that they could come to my house and see them.

Another frequently cited message was that several interviewees had felt compelled to contact the school board on their children's behalf. These parents/guardians believed that school officials had failed to take their concerns seriously. However, they noticed that they were taken more seriously once they'd earned the reputation of being determined to go to the school board if necessary. The two narratives that follow are based on in-depth interviews with a foster mother and a single-parent father.

IF I CAN MAKE A DIFFERENCE IN THIS LITTLE BOY'S LIFE

Although all of the parents/guardians who participated in the interview phase of the study were actively involved in assisting their children academically, none was as single-minded as Mrs. Pulver. Her own three biological children were all successful adults. One of her sons taught math and science, the other was "a computer boy," and her daughter worked as a supervisor for Child Protective Services. Now Mrs. Pulver was determined to save one second grader from failure.

When she retired from pediatric nursing, Mrs. Pulver's goal had been to open a home for drug-addicted babies. However, the process required that she first prove her capabilities by showing officials that she could successfully care for one "drug baby" before being entrusted with the care of several others. For this reason, she became the foster mother of an eight-month-old baby. His biological mother had used speed, cocaine, and LSD during her pregnancy. "That woman used it all," Mrs. Pulver declared. As a result, the baby went through withdrawals and exhibited abnormal behavior. "This kid would bang his head against the walls," Mrs. Pulver explained. "I was able to calm him down. He went from sticking three fingers down his mouth to regurgitate; I went through that and stopped that. All the little things that I could stop, I did."

Although the child had many problems, Mrs. Pulver soon decided that she wanted to keep him permanently. Instead of opening a home for many drug-addicted babies, she chose to invest all her time and effort into rearing this child. She stated:

When he was a year old, I decided that there was more that I could give him. So, I decided to keep him and I'm glad I did. When he was about three, I had him evaluated again and the little boy had an I.Q. of 127! And I said, "I have to do something with this. I can't just let it go. If I do not put it to good use, he will be the smartest thing out there on the streets. God placed the little boy here for a reason and I have to see him through."

When he came to me, his six brothers and sisters had been in and out of the foster care system. But he was the baby and nobody wanted to fool with him. I learned this from the court papers. The other relatives didn't want him because he was work. He was a little baby, so they put him in the system. When his mom went to jail, an aunt took all of the children except for him.

Later, when a biological grandmother tried to take the little boy away, Mrs. Pulver refused to give him up. "They live right around the corner from me, and they didn't try to bond with him," she explained. "They never came to see him and they never called him. I've come to the conclusion that he wouldn't survive there anyway. He really wouldn't. I want him to have secure, nice memories of his life and this is the way I try to better his life. I don't want him with a head full of foster homes."

At age four, Mrs. Pulver's foster son was evaluated again to ascertain the causes of his behavioral problems, such as "not listening, not following directions, that type of stuff." He was diagnosed with Attention Deficit Hyperactivity Disorder (ADHD) and placed on two medications. Adverse reactions to the medications caused him to be hospitalized in a mental ward of a children's hospital. Several subsequent hospitalizations followed.

At the time of her interview, Mrs. Pulver's foster son was struggling in school in several areas; he disliked reading and he rushed through his schoolwork and homework. "It's too easy for him," Mrs. Pulver said. His biggest problem, however, was with discipline. "Noise and children make him nervous," according to Mrs. Pulver, and "He doesn't respect women." She attributed his lack of respect for women to "abandonment issues" stemming from the visits that he'd had with his biological mother. Although she had relinquished her parental rights, she had told the boy that Mrs. Pulver was not his "real mother" and that she was planning to regain custody of him. She had also encouraged the boy to run away if he didn't like the way Mrs. Pulver ran her household. These messages confused the child. As a result, Mrs. Pulver forbade further visits.

In addition to being exasperated with her foster son's biological mother, Mrs. Pulver was disgusted with the school system. She felt that they had done "nothing but call me up on the telephone" to help him. Moreover, this same school district had failed to adequately prepare her own three children for college. As a result, "They had to work twice as hard in college," according to Mrs. Pulver. She strongly believed that the teachers were underqualified, had low expectations, and provided African American students with a low level of instruction. She said, "Every year I had to go to the school and change their classes. I would tell the counselors point blank, 'I want my kids in academic classes. I want them in College Prep classes.' I had to do it every year, because the classes were just about nothing!" In her foster son's case, she believed that the course work and homework were not only too easy for him, but they were repetitious as well.

One of the reasons for Mrs. Pulver's disgust with the school district was that when she compared her own K–12 schooling experiences with those of her foster son and biological children, she concluded that not only did their teachers need to raise their expectations and improve their instructional practices, but she suspected that they might not even care about African American students. Although her father had only had a third grade education, all of his children had become successful adults. Mrs. Pulver attributed their success to the positive messages about education that her father instilled in his children ("My daddy loved us but he was strict and taught us what hard work and life were all about.") and the African American teachers that they had while attending segregated Texas schools. She exclaimed:

I praise God for those Black teachers, because those kids made it! They became teachers, counselors, everything that you could imagine. We had a four-room school. Our books came from the White school, after they finished. We didn't even get typewriters until I was in twelfth grade. But all the time you had the same teachers. These Black teachers cared. They would discipline you. They would really teach you. Yes, ma'am, they sure did! Those teachers were interested in the children. Most of my siblings became educators and my nieces and nephews all went to college.

In spite of her great disappointment with her foster son's school district, Mrs. Pulver tried to compensate for the deficiencies by assisting him academically in many ways. Although she rated her foster son's school district as *needs to improve,* she rated her own assistance to his education as *excellent.* Her assistance involved strategies that she utilized at home and at his school.

At home, she read to him regularly, taught him his multiplication tables long before his teacher even introduced them to the class, checked his homework, gave him messages about the importance of obedience and respect for adults, and tried to teach him strategies that would prevent him from resorting to inappropriate behavior. For example, she said, "I teach him to chew gum when something is eating him up on the inside. He chews that gum and chews that gum and it calms him down. He's such a beautiful kid. I haven't found gum on the floor, carpets, or anyplace but the trash can." For several consecutive years, Mrs. Pulver had also taken her foster son to the Homecoming festivities at a famous historically Black college. She also took him on regular "out-of-state trips to expose him to the better things in life."

At school, Mrs. Pulver also assisted him academically. She met with his teachers on a regular basis, sat in his classrooms as an observer, and attended school functions. "I taught him and his teachers what to do when he becomes nervous," she said. Often, this resulted in the child being sent to the office so that he could do his work in a quieter environment. Occasionally, when teachers failed to do what was in his best interest, Mrs. Pulver resorted to more drastic action. For example, she insisted that her son be transferred from the classroom of his first grade teacher. Moreover, she urged his second grade teacher to provide him with a more challenging curriculum.

Despite the difficulty of rearing a child under such a challenging set of circumstances, Mrs. Pulver was steadfast about her decision to keep him with her until adulthood. She said, "I told the social worker, 'This is one little Black boy. Along with me and the Lord, he will not hit the streets. He will not go to prison. If I can make a difference in this little boy's life, I'm willing to do it. It's not an easy job, but I feel that through prayer, I can do it.' This boy has done a beautiful thing in my life. He really has." At the time of her interview, Mrs. Pulver had already started to save money for his college education and said, "I live to see him go to college."

I ALSO SPEND A LOT OF TIME STUDYING IN THE UNIVERSITY LIBRARY TO GIVE THEM A SENSE OF "HEY, THIS IS WHERE I WANT TO BE"

At the time of his interview, thirty-four-year-old Ron was completing his junior year of college. In addition to working full time as a staff member at a health care facility for the mentally and physically challenged, Ron shared custody of his three children with his ex-wife. The children, a fifth grade girl, an eighth grade boy, and a ninth grade girl, spent three months with one parent before returning to live with the other parent for another three months. However, regardless of which parent they were living with, they remained at the same school. Furthermore, Ron said that during the alternate months, when his children were living with their mother, he saw them on a regular basis and spoke with them by telephone daily. During his interview, Ron, who planned to become a middle school teacher, described his children's schooling experiences and the ways in which he assisted them academically. He was extremely proud that all his children were earning outstanding grades. Regarding specific strategies, Ron stated:

Basically, to help my kids become better students, I try to show good study habits for them. Because I'm a college student, my kids see me studying. As a single parent, they see me cooking and cleaning. I also spend a lot of time studying in the university library to give them a sense of "Hey, this is where I want to be." They love the college atmosphere, because it can be fun as well as educational. It keeps them focused and it reminds them of what they have to do in order to be prepared for college. So, I don't have that many problems with them.

Although he was not concerned about his children's grades, Ron was concerned about two problems. His youngest child, a fifth grader, was suffering from low self-esteem. Ron described his efforts to improve her self-image, as follows:

My youngest daughter has a darker complexion and she hears a lot of jokes, like "You're Black, like an African," or "You're Black, like a skillet." She hears this from other kids, mostly Black kids. I guess that is what hurts her the most. I tell her, "Black is beautiful. The darker the berry, the sweeter the juice." I explain to her, "Look at your line. Your grandmother was dark complexioned." I show her pictures of her grandmother when she was a baby and a teenager. I show her how smooth her skin is and how beautiful she is. She sees that and she sees it in me, because I'm dark skinned. I tell her, "Daddy is proud to be different from everybody." I just reassure her that there's nothing wrong with being different. She has a gift. I tell her that "a lot of times, when people make fun of you, they are only jealous of you. It's going to hurt you for a while, but you'll get through it. But there will be a special group of people, just like you, who will make you feel accepted.

The second problem that concerned Ron was that his son, an eighth grader, was having problems with several of his teachers. Ron attributed these problems to his son's outspokenness and bluntness. He stated:

He's good at math. He's good at writing. He likes to read a lot. The main problem is with his behavior. He questions the teachers' authority. If a teacher wants a certain thing done, he always asks, "Why?" and sometimes his aggressiveness gets him in trouble. He'll ask a question and then, he'll say, "That answer is stupid" or "That answer doesn't make sense. We should do it this way." He's outspoken as to what he feels is right.

According to Ron, his son had always been outspoken, but it didn't become a problem until he became a seventh grader. After a three-month visit to his mother's house, Ron noticed that his son's grades dropped and his attitude changed. Ron said, "It's just that it's becoming more noticeable now than when he was younger. I guess when he was younger, he felt that he had to give a certain respect to older people. But as he got older, maybe, he realized that he needed to say something. He's having all of these feelings inside and he wants to express them and wants to be heard."

Part of the problem was that at home, Ron, like Venisha in Chapter 1, gave his son more latitude about speaking up than certain teachers did at school. He explained:

He does question me and, with me being an open person, I don't necessarily try and put him in his place and say, "You're a child and not supposed to be saying certain things." I encourage him to ask me questions as to why certain things are, because there are certain things I want him to understand. I tell him, "When there are certain things on your mind, you need to learn to express them without hurting people's feelings or without saying the wrong things."

My grandmother once told me, "There is nothing wrong with speaking your mind, but it's the way you present it to people. You can hurt their feelings if you say it in the wrong way." So, that's what I'm trying to teach him to do now. "Son, put it in a way that's not disrespectful, so you don't hurt anyone's feelings. Then, they'll understand what you're trying to say. They can feel what you're saying a lot better without thinking you're trying to get smart with them or saying something bad about what they're doing."

Although his son's outspokenness and bluntness resulted in problems with several of his teachers, Ron noticed that his son didn't have problems with his English teacher. Ron attributed this to the English teacher's attitude toward his son and the fact that the class gave him opportunities to express himself. Ron said:

You know, I think it's funny. I think he gets along with that teacher. I think that teacher respects his position. My son is very good at explaining himself and the reasons why he feels a certain way. So, maybe it has to do with the teacher really stepping back and listening to his feelings. The teacher might be looking at it from both sides and saying, "Maybe he's right or maybe he's wrong, but let's give him a chance to express himself." Through that form of expression, my son is able to present his opinions in a respectful way.

In addition to advising his son to change his manner of voicing his opinions, Ron used several other strategies to assist him. He kept him involved in sports as "another way of occupying his idle time." Second, he met with his son's teachers and sat in his classes as an observer on a regular basis. According to Ron:

It's embarrassing to him for me to sit in class with him, because his peers are there. When I started popping up in his classes, he began to understand that he couldn't do what he used to do, because I might pop up at any time. He doesn't want to disrespect me or make me look like a bad parent who didn't teach him the right things, so he tries to behave. I sit in his classes when he's been good and I do it when he's been bad. So, that way, he can't say that I'm just paying attention to everything that he does wrong.

However, Ron's son was not the only person who was displeased about his presence at school. Ron found that teachers and school security personnel were suspicious. He stated, "They were intimidated because I'm a big African American man. When I walk on campus, I'm always asked a lot of questions by security guards and different teachers. It just seems like they're intimidated. They don't make eye contact with me, even though I dress very conservatively."

Another way that Ron attempted to assist his son was by encouraging him to read African American literature. He explained:

I had to take him away from his video games, not because I felt that the games were too violent or that they weren't good educational tools, but because it was taking too much attention away from what he was supposed to be doing. So, what I began to do was to get him self-help books, like Ben Carson's *Think Big* and Nathan McCall's *Makes Me Wanna Holler*.

He understands that I wanted him to read these books because both of the authors used to be discipline problems. I also had him read *The Autobiography of Malcolm X*. I had to teach him that it wasn't a story about race or religion, but more of a story about one person who was uneducated, considered to be an outcast, and then, who was able to educate himself. In other words, it gives him a sense of hope to see that "If my teachers can't teach me, I can teach myself."

Like Mrs. Pulver, Ron was hopeful that his efforts would pay off. He was optimistic about his son's future and believed that all of his children would eventually follow in his footsteps by going to college.

SUMMARY

This chapter described specific ways in which African American parents/guardians assisted their children academically and how they rated the quality of their assistance. The overwhelming majority of parents/guardians rated their assistance as *excellent* or *good*. Parents/guardians whose children experienced racism at school, whose children were discipline problems at school, and/or whose children were suspended were less likely than others to give themselves a high self-rating. These findings could indicate that children's negative schooling experiences might have contributed to parents/guardians' low level of involvement. However, the findings could also suggest that these parents'/guardians' lack of extensive involvement in their children's schooling might have contributed to behavioral problems and suspension. This low level of involvement could also make certain children more susceptible to racism at school. For example, it is possible that individuals—particularly adults at school—are more likely to subject children to racism when their parents/guardians appear to be uninvolved, and, subsequently, unlikely to become a visible and vocal presence at school.

Parents/guardians who rated their involvement as less than good were also more likely to have children who struggled with math, history, and/or reading comprehension problems. As illustrated by several of the narratives that have been presented, some parents/guardians feel that they are unqualified to assist their children with certain academic problems, such as math and reading comprehension difficulties. Therefore, one possibility is that low parent/guardian involvement might stem from parents'/guardians' inability to help their children in specific areas. Furthermore, these parents/guardians may have given themselves lower ratings for this very reason.

Another finding was that high parent/guardian involvement was inversely linked to having children who disliked school. One obvious explanation is that highly involved parents/guardians may have instilled a positive attitude about school in their children. (The narrative in Chapter 13 is illustrative of this point.)

The nine variables that were positively correlated to parents'/guardians' self-ratings were linked to their beliefs about teachers, administrators, the quality of education offered by the public school system, and the benefits of the course work and homework that their children received. Parents/guardians who were highly involved were more likely than others to be satisfied with the afore-mentioned aspects of their children's schooling. These findings suggest that good teaching, fair treatment by school officials, beneficial course work and homework, and a good school district are factors that are linked to high involvement for African American parents/guardians. Another finding was that the parents/guardians of children who were in G.A.T.E. during middle school were also more likely than other parents/guardians to report that they were highly involved in their children's education. The important role of children's academic track also surfaced in previous chapters. Therefore, educators and policymakers who seek to increase African American parent/guardian involvement must also seek to increase their satisfaction in these areas.

In addition to the reading-related ways that African American parents/guardians assisted their children academically (see Chapter 3), this chapter described other ways in which they assisted their children. Nearly 60 percent or more of the parents/guardians said that they talked to their children about school, contacted teachers, encouraged their children to attend college, helped them with homework, advised them to check over their schoolwork, limited television viewing, and helped them study for tests on an ongoing basis. Moreover, during the interview phase of the study, Mrs. Pulver pointed out that she routinely took her foster son to a historically Black college and that she was already saving money for his college education. Ron explained that he took his three children to the university library to study with him, sat in on his son's classes, and encouraged his son to read African American literature.

Only a small percentage of parents/guardians said that they volunteered to help in their children's classrooms. This could be attributed to time constraints, since many of the parents/guardians worked full time. However, it could also stem from the fact that some parents/guardians did not feel that they were welcome at school. For example, although he visited his son's school often, Ron sensed that teachers and school security personnel were intimidated by him. Another interviewee stated that despite the fact that she offered to assist teachers, they made it clear that her help was not wanted.

Certain strategies, such as encouraging children to check over their work and helping children study for tests were inversely related to particular problems. This indicates that providing African American parents/guardians with feedback about the most effective types of parental assistance can be extremely beneficial. Therefore, educators and policymakers who are committed to increasing parent involvement and closing the achievement gap must find ways to ensure that parent involvement becomes quality involvement. In *Family Involvement in Children's Education: An Idea Book*, the U.S. Department of Education (2001a) said that, in order to increase family involvement, schools must provide families with both support and opportunities to become involved. Families must feel welcome at school and they must also be encouraged to voice their concerns. They must be included in the decision-making process and they must be given the training that they need in order to assist their children academically.

In the same booklet, the U.S. Department of Education (2001a) described twenty programs throughout the United States that were successful in improving the relationships between families and schools, and subsequently in improving student achievement. In ten of the programs, African American students comprised a substantial percentage of the student population, ranging from 30 percent to 95 percent. The programs used a multifaceted approach to increase parent involvement. Parenting–child communication workshops, seminars, regular sessions with school psychologists, computer-literacy classes, math classes, G.E.D workshops, counseling, dental and health care, transportation services to school events, home visits from school staff, and ongoing communication with parents to elicit their viewpoints about various topics were among the services that were offered by the ten programs. Regardless of the type of program and services offered, the result was a marked improvement in student achievement. The U.S. Department of Education urged school administrators, teachers, and staff not only to broaden their conception of family involvement but to become willing to use multiple approaches to increase parent involvement.

5

Discipline, Suspension, and Expulsion

In "The 32nd Annual Phi Delta Kappa Gallup Poll of the Public's Attitudes Towards the Public Schools," Rose and Gallup (2000) described public sentiment about numerous issues. For example, the respondents were asked to identify the main problems facing public schools in their community. Lack of discipline among students and the need for more control of student behavior were the main problems that parents of public school children identified.

However, in another study, "The Sixth Phi Delta Kappa Poll of Teachers' Attitudes Toward the Public Schools," Langdon and Vesper (2000) found differences between the public's as opposed to teachers' perceptions of public schools. First of all, a higher percentage of teachers than the public gave the public schools in their community a grade of "A" or "B." Second, a higher percentage of teachers than the public felt that the schools in their community were "very safe and orderly." A third difference was that, whereas "discipline/more control/stricter rules" were the main problems that concerned the public about the schools in their community, the two main problems for teachers were "lack of parent involvement" and "more teachers/smaller class size," respectively.

Like the teachers in the Langdon and Vesper (2000) study, the majority of African American parents/guardians in the current study were more concerned about issues other than discipline, such as the academic problems that were described in Chapter 2. In fact, only 17 percent of the questionnaire respondents indicated that one or more of their children had discipline problems at school.

The low percentage of questionnaire respondents who cited discipline as a major concern was surprising because African American students—particularly African American males—have disproportionately high suspension and expulsion rates in the school district in which the majority of the children of the parents/guardians who participated in the current study attended school. The same is true of the entire county. For example, during the period from July 1, 2000, to June 30, 2001, African American children comprised 20 percent of the elementary school students in the district. However, they accounted for 47 percent of the elementary school students who were suspended from school. At the middle school level, African American students comprised 21 percent of the student body, but 36 percent of the students who were suspended. At the high school level, they comprised 20 percent of the student body, but 36 percent of the suspended students.

This chapter will examine variables from the questionnaire that were correlated to discipline problems, suspension, and expulsion. During the interview phase of the study, many parents discussed their concerns about one or more of their children's behavior at school and related experiences. A recurring theme in the narratives that have been presented thus far was that an African American child—typically a boy—had been identified as a discipline problem early in his/her schooling and soon teachers or other school officials were strongly urging the parents/guardians to have the child placed on medication for ADD or ADHD. The narratives that are included later in this chapter will illustrate how this scenario may unfold.

DISCIPLINE

Although discipline was not among the problems that most of the African American parents/guardians who completed the questionnaire identified as a concern, as noted previously, 17 percent indicated that at least one of their children had behavioral problems at school. There were correlations between discipline problems and nineteen other questionnaire items.

Fifteen variables, including several academic problems, were positively related to discipline problems. For example, parents/guardians of children who had poor grades and problems with writing, spelling, grammar, history, homework, math, science, social studies, pronunciation, and/or their reading rate were more likely to indicate that one or more of their children had behavioral problems at school. Parents/guardians who said that their children experienced racism frequently at school and those whose children disliked school were also more likely to have children who had behavioral problems at school. Moreover, parents/guardians of elementary school–age children were more likely to say that their children had behavioral problems. One perplexing correlation surfaced. Parents/guardians who believed that most teachers had treated their children fairly were also likely to mention that their children had discipline problems. Three variables that were inversely related to discipline pertained to academic track. Parents/guardians who had children in the highest-level elementary, middle, and/or high school tracks were unlikely to have children who had behavioral problems at school. The fourth inverse relationship indicated that parents/guardians who gave a high rating to their level of academic assistance were unlikely to have children who had discipline problems (see Table 5.1).

Table 5.1
Variables That Were Correlated to Discipline Problems in the Order of the
Strength of Each Correlation

Variable	Strength of the Correlation	Significance
High school track	-.50	p < .001
Middle school track	-.39	p < .001
Experiencing racism frequently	.33	p < .03
Poor grades	.32	p < .001
Science problem	.31	p < .001
Disliking school	.31	p < .001
Pronunciation problem	.29	p < .001
Parents'/guardians' self-rating	-.29	p < .001
Social studies problem	.28	p < .001
Homework problem	.26	p < .003
History problem	.25	p < .004
Math problem	.24	p < .01
Elementary school track	-.23	p < .01
Reading rate	.22	p < .01
Grammar problem	.22	p < .01
Writing problem	.21	p < .02
Parents'/guardians' perception of teacher treatment	.20	p < .03
Spelling problem	.18	p < .04
Having elementary school-age children	.18	p < .04

$N = 22$

SUSPENSION

Thirty percent of the parents/guardians who completed the questionnaire
said that one or more of their children had been suspended from school at least
once. Although 26 percent of the parents/guardians did not identify the school
level at which the suspension(s) occurred, 23 percent said they had children
who were suspended at more than one level of school, such as in both elementary and middle school, in elementary school and high school, or in both middle
school and high school. Five percent had children who were suspended at all
three levels. The highest percentage of suspensions occurred during middle
school and the lowest percentage occurred during high school. When asked
whether or not school officials had treated their suspended children fairly, 44
percent of these parents/guardians said "yes," 28 percent said "no," and 28

percent did not answer. There were correlations between whether or not a parent/guardian had a child who'd been suspended from school and eighteen other questionnaire items. Nine variables were positively correlated to suspension and nine were inversely related.

Parents/guardians whose children had been suspended from school were unlikely to believe that school administrators had treated their children fairly, and they were more likely to state that their children had experienced racism at school and/or had been expelled. Second, the more school-age children a parent/guardian had, the greater the likelihood that the parent/guardian had children who'd been suspended. Problems with reading comprehension, pronunciation, poor grades, history, and homework were also linked to suspension. Moreover, parents/guardians of children who were retained in a grade or who failed a middle or high school course were also more likely to have children who were suspended from school.

Conversely, nine variables were inversely related to suspension. For example, parents/guardians who rated their assistance to their children's education as *excellent* or *good* were unlikely to have children who'd been suspended from school. Moreover, parents/guardians who rated their children's elementary teachers as *excellent* or *good* were also less likely to have children who'd been suspended from school. Additionally, parents/guardians who had elementary school–age children, who helped their children study for tests, and who encouraged them to read on a regular basis were also unlikely to have children who'd been suspended from school. Furthermore, the parents/guardians of children in the highest elementary, middle, and high school tracks were unlikely to have children who'd been suspended from school (see Table 5.2).

EXPULSION

Whereas 30 percent of the parents/guardians had children who'd been suspended from school, only 6 percent had children who'd actually been expelled. Most of the parents/guardians who had children who'd been expelled believed that school officials had not treated their children fairly. Like suspension, expulsion was also linked to several other questionnaire items. However, the percentage of expelled students was too small to warrant correlation analyses. During the interview phase of the study, a mother of three described why her son was expelled from school during eighth grade and why she (unlike most parents/guardians in a similar predicament) believed that school officials had treated him fairly. She stated:

He had this toy gun; well, it is a cigarette lighter and it's shaped like a gun. The teacher asked him what it was and he wouldn't show it to her. One of the kids said that he had a gun. The teacher called the security guards and he wouldn't let the security guard check him. He just ran off the campus and came home. They couldn't figure out if he had a gun or not, so he was expelled. Because he's Special Ed, he has rights. He went

Table 5.2
Variables That Were Correlated to Suspension in the Order of the Strength of Each Correlation

Variable	Strength of the Correlation	Significance
Number of school-age children	.41	p < .001
Expulsion	.40	p < .001
Middle school track	-.38	p < .001
High school track	-.33	p < .01
Elementary track	-.31	p < .001
Experiencing racism at school	.28	p < .01
Beliefs about administrators' treatment	-.27	p < .01
Reading comprehension problem	.26	p < .003
Encouraging regular reading	-.26	p < .004
Pronunciation problem	.23	p < .01
Grade retention and/or course failure	.22	p < .02
Elementary teachers' rating	-.21	p < .02
Poor grades	.20	p < .03
Helping children study for tests	-.20	p < .03
Having elementary school-age children	-.20	p < .03
History problem	.19	p < .04
Homework problem	.18	p < .04
Parents'/guardians' self-rating	-.18	p < .04

$N = 39$

to a "community school" for a year and he did well. Now, they let him back in regular school. I think he was treated fairly. I tried to explain to them what he had. I showed them what he had but they didn't accept that. He should have just showed the teacher what it was, even though it was a cigarette lighter. He just made it a big mess.

The following narratives are based on interviews with two other mothers who discussed their sons' school-related behavioral problems.

MAKING UP FOR LOST TIME

When she was growing up, thirty-five-year-old Francine dreamed of becoming a nurse. Now, as a single parent of four children, she was determined to make up for the years when her own personal problems had prevented her from being the parent that she desired to be. Nearly twenty years earlier, a series of setbacks when she was in high school had changed the course of her life. Prior to that period, Francine had been earning good grades; was a member of her high school's girls basketball, baseball, and volleyball teams; was singing in the school choir; and was dating her high school sweetheart. However, as a result of the setbacks, she ended up on illegal drugs for fifteen years, including the years when she gave birth to two of her three youngest children. She explained:

I was a troubled teen. Actually, when my daughter's father passed away in my arms, that just made me kind of crazy for some years. He got shot accidentally. I was in tenth grade and we had a two-month-old baby. He was sixteen too. We were both going to the same school. We were like brother and sister. He'd drive me to school and we had classes together. When it first happened, I was scared to go to sleep because that was the first funeral I'd ever been to in my life. People would have to sit on the phone and talk to me until I fell asleep. There was really no one there for me except maybe one person. I really think my mom didn't know how to deal with me with it and my sisters never really said anything. I think maybe if somebody would have said something at the time, or tried to help me get through it, it would have been much easier. His death really messed me up for years. It really did. Right now, I got my life together and I'm trying to make it even better than what it is now. Drugs played a big part. Right now, I go to Narcotics Anonymous meetings. Before my baby's daddy died, I wasn't doing drugs.

Once she started using illegal drugs, Francine's life began to spiral out of control. During her years as a drug addict, she committed five felonies. She was sent to jail and was on her way to being sentenced to three years in prison for each felony when she ended up in a drug rehabilitation program instead. "The only time I got any type of counseling was when I went to my drug rehab program," she stated. The counseling not only changed her outlook, but it also gave her the determination to improve her life and that of her children. "I went to court every three months to show them that I was still clean," she said. "I'm not going back. Once I start something and set my mind to it, that's just it. Before rehab, I didn't know how to get clean. It wasn't that I didn't want to get clean, but I didn't know how to get clean."

"Getting clean" meant assuming full responsibility for her children who had previously been cared for by Francine's mother. At the time of her interview, Francine's children were living with her and she had been "clean" for four years. Her determination to make up for lost time manifested itself in two ways: (1) She wanted to provide her children with a stable home life; and (2) she was trying to assist them academically to the best of her ability.

Improving their home environment started with an arduous task. In order to move her children out of a crime-ridden apartment complex, Francine purchased a condemned house. She explained:

The house I live in right now was condemned and I did all the work on it. I had to. I had to move. I told the landlord, "You need me as bad as I need you. They're gonna tear your house down. You'll have an empty lot and you won't profit. So, I'll do the work and I'll move my kids in."

So, I let my kids stay with my mom for a month and I worked on this house for a month and then moved my kids here. It was tiring, but I did it. I got tired and wanted to give up many days. But I couldn't give up because my kids were depending on me. I can't let my kids down by making promises that I can't keep. If I tell them that I'm gonna do something, I'm gonna follow through with it, you know, because kids look at that.

Once she and her children were settled in their new home, Francine began to get them actively involved in maintaining the home and yards. She wanted to keep them busy so that they would not be tempted by outside pressure, and she wanted to teach them the importance of hard work, mostly through gardening. She said:

I have a garden in the backyard, where I'm growing all my vegetables and fruits. I have everything in my backyard from bell peppers to collard greens, watermelon, cantaloupe, everything! I like to let my kids see them grow. That amazes my kids. They say, "Oh wow! Mom's got pumpkins in the backyard. Let's go out and water." There's something to do here every day. If we don't do anything but go in the backyard and pull weeds, I'm out there with them. I'm not gonna make them go out there by themselves. We're all gonna do it together. I try to be there because there's a whole lot of parents out there that aren't. And years back, I didn't have time.

Although Francine believed that her efforts to provide her children with a stable home life were paying off, she was extremely concerned about the difficulties that her son, a fifth grader, was having at school. Francine described three problems—grammar, reading, and discipline—that were upsetting to her.

Whereas the grammar problem concerned her, during her interview, she spent more time discussing the reading problem and his behavioral problems. In spite of the fact that he loved to read, Francine was troubled about her son's reading rate. "He likes books but he reads slow," she explained. "At the public library, they have a program where you read a whole lot of books and you get prizes. So I'm taking all my kids up there to enroll them in the program. He likes to win prizes. He likes to read. We can walk there every day."

Whereas her son's reading problem and grammar problem bothered her, they were overshadowed by his behavioral problems, which had started early in his schooling and resulted in his being placed on medication for ADD. By the time he was in fifth grade, her son had already been suspended from school six times. Although Francine disciplined him at home by withdrawing privileges from him and had even taken him to Juvenile Hall "to scare him," she described her son as being "something else!" She attributed his behavioral problems to his quick temper and early negative labeling at school, which resulted in his being singled out as a "discipline problem" in kindergarten. Francine gave the following examples of some of her son's experiences:

Once, the teacher did something—put him on the wall or something and he didn't want to stay on the wall. When he got to the class, the teacher told him to sit down. He wouldn't sit down and he threw a pencil. They called the vice principal down because he wouldn't go to the office. He said the vice principal grabbed his arm. He fought the vice principal all the way to the office and threw an ice bottle [a bottle of frozen ice water] at him.

They suspended him, but they have a principal up there that didn't like him in the first place. She used to tell him all kinds of stuff. One day, she told him she was gonna call the police on him if he did anything else. So one day, he got suspended and we were waiting on him to walk home. He never made it home. We're driving around looking for him; he's up in the tree at home. We're riding all around the city looking for him. I had to go back up to that school and let the principal have it. I told her, "Don't tell him that. Now, he's scared, thinking that you're gonna call the police on him. He's up in the tree at home." That principal has done the same thing to a whole lot of the kids in the neighborhood where we used to live. A boy up the street is no longer there either. He can't go back to that school. And three other kids over there are changing schools this year.

Although her son was labeled as a behavioral problem by administrators and most of his teachers at both of the elementary schools that he attended, Francine noticed that two of his teachers had fewer problems with him than most. Therefore, she concluded that the teachers' classroom management styles, their gender, and their race also had some bearing on his behavior. Concerning the two teachers (a White male and an African American female), she stated:

He had a male teacher and all his other teachers were female. His male teacher wasn't having it. But he had problems there too, because I had to go up there and talk to him too. He did better with the male teacher because he's a male himself. But after he had Miss R. in fifth grade things got better. She doesn't take no mess. I have only had to call her one time this year. My son took a puzzle book or something to school and she took it away from him. When she called me and told me that she took it, I said, "Good. Keep it." She stays on him, no matter what. I really appreciate her. She doesn't take none of his mess, she don't wanna hear none of his excuses, and his homework better be done! He has pretty good grades. Yes, he does. He's very good in school, especially math. He loves math. He's doing geometry and stuff and I know geometry is hard. He does good work. I know kids that are a lot older than him that can't do geometry.

With White female teachers he thought that he could do anything that he wanted to do in their classes. I think they weren't strict enough.

He ran over the teachers. He did his homework and everything and he did his work, but every day, I went to that school to get my son for some reason or another. With Miss R., he met his match! She's done an excellent job, because she has changed my son's life.

In addition to seeing an improvement in his grades, Francine also noticed that her own efforts, the fifth grade teacher's efforts, and the efforts of a school counselor were paying off in other ways. Regarding her son, she stated:

One day, he came home and said that he was about to get into trouble at school. And he said, "You know what mom? I did what you told me to do." I said, "What's that?" He said, "I was sitting there and I was getting mad. Then, I thought about what you said, 'Think before you do it. Think before you do it.'" He said, "I thought about it and I was thinking before I did it and I said, 'No. I'm just gonna ignore him. I'm just gonna ignore him.'" I said, "Well, that's a good thing."

Even though she was pleased with her son's improved behavior in fifth grade, Francine was fearful of the long-term effects of the ADD diagnosis and the medication that was prescribed for him. One of Francine's concerns was that ADD was hereditary. She said:

I had it when I was a kid. I think he inherited it, because his father did too. I was on medication until I was in the fifth grade. Then, my mom just took me off of it, because she didn't want me to get addicted to it. That's what she told me. My son's been on medication since the third grade. It calms him down a lot. I wanna take him off it but I'm scared. They say kids will get addicted to it. I don't want him to depend on it, but he has to have it.

In the meantime, Francine planned to continue to make up for lost time by assisting her children as best she could. In addition to showing support for her children's teachers, she assisted them academically by reading to her children, listening to them read, playing word games with them, taking them to the public library, helping them with projects, and keeping them busy with positive activities. Moreover, she spoke to them candidly about her past as a means of keeping them focused. She said:

Most people are in denial. I'm not in denial about anything. I keep it as real as I most possibly can. Because when you fall into denial, that'll link you back to old, stinkin' behavior and that'll set you up to use drugs. I don't keep secrets from my kids. To me, where people mess up is hiding stuff from your kids. If you talk to your kids and make them understand, they'll respect you better than if you keep secrets from them. My kids talk to me about drugs. I tell them about drugs and that they don't ever wanna do that, because drugs will mess them up. I sit down and talk to my kids, and whatever they need to ask me, they ask and I tell them the truth.

Making up for lost time with her children was Francine's main priority, but making up for lost time with herself was another. She had enrolled in a program that would allow her to earn her General Education Diploma (G.E.D.). Afterwards she wanted to complete the course work that would enable her to become a drug counselor. "There are people around who be walkin' by, just lookin' so crazy and I say, 'Why don't you go get yourself clean?' or I just talk to them. I really want to get my credential to become a drug counselor, so we can have Narcotics Anonymous meetings every day."

I DON'T THINK HE'S CHALLENGED

Like numerous parents/guardians who participated in the study, Elise, a divorced mother of two, was worried about how her son, a third grader, was faring in school. Starting in kindergarten, her son had demonstrated a high aptitude, which resulted in his being "promoted to first grade within three weeks. And when he was in second grade, they thought of promoting him to third grade." In spite of his ability to excel academically, Elise's son was quickly labeled as a discipline problem. Consequently, discipline, instead of academics, was the predominant theme during Elise's interview. Although she said that her son's problems were "not really the school's fault," her comments indicated that she felt that the school system, her son, and his father all shared culpability.

In Elise's opinion, the school system was partly to blame for her son's problems because they promoted him from kindergarten to first grade after merely three weeks of school without ascertaining whether or not he was emotionally mature enough for the move. "Mature-wise," she stated, "I think he wasn't ready for it. I think that's what happens as far as his discipline problem goes." She also believed that teachers had failed to challenge him academically. "I think he's bored," she stated. "I don't think he's challenged." However, Elise also felt that her son had contributed to his own problems. She explained:

He's characteristically always in a rush to get things done. He has to be first, first, first! He talks too much; he talks out of turn; he wants to be the first to answer, so that's how he gets in trouble. He never does his homework. He says that he does, but he doesn't do it, and I called his teacher and she says that he turns it in every day. So, he rushes through everything and just gets done. I know that he's difficult to handle. And as much as I tell him that the school is too busy for them to have to worry about one or two children, that's still his thing.

Throughout the years, teachers began to suggest to Elise that her son might have ADD. "At one point, I was really upset, because a teacher told me that I should put him on medication, but I didn't think that was their call," Elise stated. When her son became a third grader, the pressure to have him tested and placed on medication intensified. The pressure came from his third grade teacher. According to Elise:

Last year, all of his tests—everything he did—was in the 90th percentile. His third grade teacher said, "He's not doing as well as he did last year." She wanted him to stay more focused and she felt like his behavior was getting in the way of his academics. I told her that I'd consider having him tested for ADD and I did take him to the doctor because I don't want them to feel like I'm not doing anything about it.

Despite the fact that the doctor did not diagnose her son with ADD, Elise decided to become more informed about the disorder. She read about ADD and became convinced that her son displayed some of the symptoms. Elise stated:

I think he has a lot of the tendencies as far as at home, like his attention span, his compulsiveness, and his impatience. You know, I have a book or two about ADD and he's kind of a high-need child. But academically he does great. Some days, I would like to put him on medication. He lies a lot. The ADD book said that lying is real convenient because they can't come up with a reason why they didn't do anything, so they just use excuses. I find him doing that a lot.

Because her frustration with her son's behavioral problems was growing, Elise had recently begun to give more thought to allowing him to be placed on ADD medication. In fact, she had already begun the process, which involved the school and paperwork that she was required to complete. Her son had been getting Referrals to the office from his third grade teacher. Elise explained:

He gets Referrals for pushing and horse playing. I think once it was for using profanity, which we don't use in our household at all. He'll tell me that he didn't say it, but I believe he did say it, whether he learned it from other kids or not. It's just the way our society is. I monitor the songs on the radio that they think they want to hear. They're learning things in society, which is natural, but I try and teach them right from wrong. I talked to the doctor about two months ago. His teacher and I have both done the survey that's required for him to get put on medication.

When Elise's ex-husband attempted to become more involved in her son's life, an obstacle arose. Her son had been enrolled in a before- and after-school program. When his father wanted to start picking him up after school in order to spend more time with his son, Elise was given an ultimatum by the school principal: Her son either had to be a participant in both the before- and after-school segments of the program or he had to drop out completely. Elise said:

As a single parent, I needed the before-school care and the principal wasn't willing, even for a month, to let his dad step in and try and spend time with him, because he wasn't following the program, which was before and after school. If he wasn't in the after-school care program, then he would have to be out of the program altogether. Since his dad hasn't been in his life that much, I thought that was kind of unfortunate.

In her effort to get her son placed on medication, Elise consulted another doctor, but at the time of her interview, medication had not been prescribed for him. At school, the psychologist consulted with him for a short period. For her part, Elise tried to find ways to channel her son's energy in positive directions. "He's very active," she stated. "He's very gifted athletically. He got those genes from his dad, who was a professional athlete. He's on two basketball teams, he plays the drums, he did karate, and we keep him really involved in activities."

SUMMARY

This chapter presented feedback from the African American parents/guardians about their children's behavioral problems, and suspension and expulsion from school. The two related narratives presented additional information about these topics. Although the percentages of parents/guardians whose children experienced these problems are small, this chapter uncovers information that can be useful and illustrates the need for additional related studies with larger samples of African American parents/guardians.

The results indicate that numerous negative schooling factors are associated with discipline problems. In addition to various academic problems, discipline problems were correlated to experiencing racism frequently at school. These findings suggest that academic problems can lead to behavioral problems or behavioral problems can result in academic problems. However, both Elise and Venisha (in Chapter 1) believed that their children's discipline problems were linked to a lack of academic challenge. As a result, boredom led to unacceptable classroom behavior. Both mothers mentioned that their sons would rush through their schoolwork and have idle time on their hands.

Once again, academic track turned out to be an important factor in schooling experiences. Parents/guardians of elementary, middle, and high school students in the highest tracks were less likely than those of children in lower tracks to have children who were perceived as discipline problems at school.

One surprising variable—parents'/guardians' perception of teacher treatment—was also linked to discipline problems. In other words, parents/guardians who believed that their children's teachers had treated them fairly were also likely to have children who had behavioral problems at school. However, some of the narratives revealed a different finding. Several parents/guardians, including Francine, Elise, and Venisha, believed that early negative labeling by teachers and school administrators caused their children to become identified as having discipline problems. This finding is similar to that of Sbarra and Pianta (2001), who found that, starting in kindergarten, the teachers who participated in their study were more likely to label African American children as discipline problems than White children.

Whereas 17 percent of the questionnaire respondents stated that their children had behavioral problems at school, 30 percent stated that their children had been suspended from school at least once, which is indicative of the high suspension rate among African Americans in the primary school district in which most of the respondents' children were enrolled. Like discipline problems, suspension was correlated to experiencing racism at school and several academic problems.

Another finding was that suspension was negatively correlated to parents'/guardians' perception of how school administrators had treated their children. Those who believed that their children had been treated unfairly were also more likely to have children who'd been suspended from school. This finding is similar to comments by some of the parents/guardians who participated in the interview phase of the study. For example, Francine described an administrator who appeared to target children living in a certain neighborhood for unfair treatment. She also cited examples of behavior by two administrators—a vice principal who grabbed her son's arm and a principal who threatened to call the police on her son—that actually exacerbated situations. In *Bad Boys: Public Schools in the Making of Black Masculinity*, Ferguson (2001) described numerous schooling practices that set African American boys on a cycle of failure that starts in elementary school. The stories from some of the parents/guardians in the current study are similar to those in Ferguson's research.

The number of school-age children in the household was also linked to suspension. Children in larger families were more likely than those in smaller families to have been suspended from school. Conversely, parents/guardians who reported a high level of involvement in their children's formal education, who helped them study for tests, and who had children in the highest academic tracks were unlikely to have children who'd been suspended from school. However, several of the narratives clearly show that even highly involved parents, such as Venisha and Francine, may have children who end up getting suspended multiple times.

Only a tiny percentage of the parents/guardians stated that their children had been expelled from school. As was expected, suspension was the strongest correlate to expulsion. However, parents'/guardians' perception of teacher and administrator treatment was also significant. Parents/guardians of children who were expelled were also likely to believe that their children had been treated fairly by most of their teachers, but they were unlikely to believe that administrators had treated their children fairly. These findings can be attributed to the fact that administrators, not teachers, make the decision to expel children from school. The parents/guardians of G.A.T.E. elementary students and the parents/guardians who stated that they placed a high value on their children's education were unlikely to have children who were expelled from school.

One of the clearest messages that has surfaced from the narratives in this chapter and in previous chapters is that not only do schools appear to be ill-equipped to address the needs of African American children whom they perceive to be difficult, but they may also contribute to discipline problems (Ferguson, 2001; Thompson, 2002). Francine believed that her son misbehaved in the classes of teachers he perceived to be weak. "He thought that he could do anything that he wanted in their classes," Francine stated, but he was less problematic in the classroom of his one and only male teacher and he was actually well-behaved in the classroom of Miss R. According to Francine, Miss R., an African American teacher, "doesn't take none of his mess." She described Miss R. as being strict, having high expectations, and being consistent in her behavior. Delpit (1995) described the characteristics of teachers that African American children deem worthy of respect as opposed to those they do not respect. Teachers who fail to "act with authority" or like a friend instead of an adult in a position of authority, were perceived to be unworthy of respect. Conversely, teachers deemed worthy of respect demonstrate that they (1) have strong classroom management skills; (2) have positive interpersonal relationships with students; (3) believe that all students can learn; (4) challenge students to meet their high expectations; and (5) use a communicative style that can hold African American students' attention.

Another clear message is that teachers and other school officials appear to be quick to suggest that "problematic" African American children are suffering from ADD or ADHD. This appears to be a widespread practice and a source of great consternation for African American parents/guardians. For example, Francine stated that both she and her boyfriend had been diagnosed with ADD during their childhoods. When school officials tell African American parents/ guardians that their children might have these disorders, the parents/guardians want to show that they are not only concerned about their children's welfare but that they are also receptive to the advice of school officials. Elise stated, "I did take him to the doctor, because I don't want them to feel like I'm not doing anything about it." Several parents/guardians mentioned that because of school officials, they had their children tested by a doctor, only to be told that their children did not have ADD. The parents/guardians who did allow their children to be medicated were fearful of the long-term effects of the drugs that had been prescribed. Jocelyn (in Chapter 3) for example, mentioned that she telephoned the school numerous times to see how Ritalin was affecting her son before deciding after just one day, that it would be too stressful for her to keep him on the medication. Because ADD and ADHD are still considered by some to be questionable diagnoses (Armstrong, 1995), and because several of the parents/guardians were ambivalent, fearful, and doubtful about the diagnosis and the effects of the treatment, educators, researchers, and policymakers will have to devote more attention to this issue. In the meantime, teacher training institutions and school districts must do a better job of equipping teachers and administrators with effective skills to improve the schooling experiences of "problematic" children. The U.S. Department of Education (2000a) reported that the majority of new teachers are unprepared to meet the needs of students from nonmainstream backgrounds, and Gordon (1999b) said that classroom management is a major problem for new teachers. However, the current study suggests that the problem may even be prevalent among veteran teachers.

Part II

African American Parents/Guardians Discuss the Education System

6

Beliefs about Teachers

Like parents, teachers fulfill one of society's most important roles: They are responsible for providing the formal education of children who will one day control the nation's political and economic future. Being a teacher is not an easy job. After completing college requirements, many new teachers enter the workforce only to learn that they have been underprepared, and that they are underrespected and underpaid in comparison to other professionals. Moreover, new teachers are often given "the most challenging students, asked to teach multiple subjects, assigned the responsibility of extracurricular activities, and asked to teach classes for which they are not certified" (U.S. Department of Education 2000a, p. 23). These factors contribute to job dissatisfaction, which prompts many new teachers to quit during the first three years.

Among the teachers who stay are resilient individuals who strive to become exemplary educators in spite of the obstacles (Haberman, 1995). Others struggle along, year after year, without ever unlocking the secret to becoming exemplary teachers. One reason is that there are so many models of good teaching that it can give teachers conflicting messages. For example, Cruickshank and Haefele (2001) described ten types of good teachers that have been identified, but said that there has been no consensus on a prototype. According to Ladson-Billings (2001) "Even those who have chosen teaching as a profession have naive and poorly formed notions of what it means to teach" (p. 25).

One of the main problems that many new teachers face is dealing with students who come from backgrounds that are different from their own (Delpit, 1995; Ladson-Billings, 2001). Students of color comprise nearly 40 percent of the nation's school-age population, but the overwhelming majority of teachers are White. Moreover, the majority of new teachers are unprepared to meet the needs of students from nonmainstream backgrounds (U.S. Department of Education, 2000a).

Researchers and policymakers have devoted numerous years and much effort to the topic of improving teacher quality. Throughout U.S. history, many researchers have tried to blame the low academic achievement of African American students on their aptitude, home environment, cultural "deficiencies," socioeconomic status, and the like. In recent years, however, a large body of research has underscored the important role of the teacher in improving academic achievement.

For example, the National Center for Education Statistics (1996) looked at the effects on student achievement of small classes and schools; parent education; other background factors, such as poverty, language, and family characteristics; and teacher qualifications. The U.S. Department of Education concluded that small classes and schools were the least important of the categories. Parent education accounted for 24 percent, and "other background factors" accounted for 26 percent. However, teacher qualifications accounted for 40 percent. In another report, the U.S. Department of Education (2000a) stated that the quality of teaching that students receive is the most important "in-school factor" affecting student achievement. Nevertheless, 30 percent of new public school teachers in the United States "are hired without full certification" and expectations for students are often greater than expectations for their teachers. Furthermore, "Basic literacy, content knowledge, and skill levels that many states require of teachers are significantly below what they require of students on high school graduation tests" (U.S. Department of Education, 2000a, p. 13).

In addition to improving the efficacy of teacher preparation programs and decreasing the number of underqualified teachers in schools, there is a need to provide in-service teachers (teachers who are already working in classrooms) with more professional development. In the past, teachers have not received adequate professional development. Previous professional development programs devoted "too little attention to real-world problems teachers face" and failed to adequately prepare teachers "to address the needs of diverse students and those with disabilities, and to integrate technology into instruction." Additionally, the professional development that teachers received was not long enough. "While approximately 85 percent of teachers report receiving less than eight hours a year of professional development in a specific area, teachers report, and research confirms, that professional development of longer duration is more effective" (U.S. Department of Education, 2000a, p. 17).

In *African American Teens Discuss Their Schooling Experiences* (Thompson, 2002), a theme that surfaced throughout the study was that African American students want better relationships with their teachers. The eight characteristics that half or more of the students associated with outstanding teachers were (1) explaining things well; (2) making the course work interesting; (3) giving extra help; (4) patience; (5) fairness; (6) friendliness; (7) humor; and (8) challenging students academically. The least valued practices and characteristics were giving lots of homework, strictness, and giving rewards.

In the county in which the majority of parents/guardians who participated in the current study resided, there were nearly 18,000 public school teachers during the 2000–01 school year. Whereas children of color comprised 63 percent of student enrollment, teachers of color only comprised 20 percent of the teaching force. Moreover, although African American students comprised 12 percent of the students in the county, African Americans only accounted for 5 percent of the teachers (California Department of Education, 2001).

There were more than twice as many female teachers as males in the county. For example, for the three largest racial/ethnic groups in the county, the ratio of White female teachers to males was 9,881 to 4,220; for Hispanics there were 1,496 female teachers but only 640 males; and for African Americans, there were 630 females but only 269 male teachers (California Department of Education, 2001).

In the county in which the majority of the study's participants resided, the average public school teacher had taught for nearly twelve years and had taught for nine years in his/her current school district; both of these percentages were slightly lower than state averages. There were more than 1,500 first-year teachers in the county and more than 1,200 second-year teachers. Nearly 13 percent of the teachers in the county were teaching with an Emergency Credential, which was slightly higher than the state average of 11.5 percent. Statewide, 86 percent of the public school teachers had a full Teaching Credential in 2000–01, but in the aforementioned county, 83 percent did (California Department of Education, 2001). This chapter presents the results of feedback from the African American parents/guardians who participated in the current study regarding their beliefs about their children's teachers. A related narrative will provide additional information.

DO MOST TEACHERS CARE ABOUT STUDENTS?

Sixty percent of the parents/guardians who completed the questionnaire said that most teachers care about their students. One mother said that she believed that most teachers care about their students because "They're very responsive when you have questions. I also sit in on my kids' classes to make my presence known, and let them know that I am concerned." A grandmother said that she also believed that most teachers care about students. "I think it's like a partnership," she explained. "The kids have to take something in there. They have to show the teacher that they want to learn. I think if you do this, you get a more receptive attitude from the other party. The teachers and the parents need to show that they are interested." In explaining why she was convinced that most teachers care about students, a mother of two said:

I have come to know some of the teachers as friends. I think it takes special people to work with children. I think that some people do it for the paycheck and some people do it just to do it. I'm not a kid person. I could never be a teacher. So, when I look at it that way, I would hope to think that people who are doing it are doing it because it's important to them.

However, a mother of six school-age children in elementary, middle school, and high school wrote on her questionnaire:

I wish that the teachers really liked their jobs and were interested in the welfare of the children, instead of feeling like "This is my job, I have a degree in teaching, and I'm gonna get paid if these kids learn or not." It is not fair to the kids and this is something that's been an ongoing problem in society for years. It is a shame that racism still exists and the victims are the kids.

An interviewee, a mother of several school-age children, also believed that most teachers do not care about African American students. She said:

Kids know good, and they know bad, and they know when somebody doesn't like them. And they know when a teacher has favorites, and a lot of teachers do. They do have their favorites. They favor the kid that dresses better or the kid with a working mom, or whatever. I used to work in a convalescent home as a certified nurse's aide. And when I did work, it was the eleven-to-seven shift. If I liked changing patients in a convalescent home, teachers should love their job. It's not like you have to go change bowels movements. These teachers do not wanna teach. I mean at 3:30, they hit the door, just like the kids. Stay until 4. Thirty minutes is not going to hurt you. Before school, some of the teachers are here, but they have their doors locked and will not let you in. So why are you here at eight, if you don't wanna be bothered? The kids are lined up.

Another parent, the mother of two children, said that she did not believe that most public school teachers care about their students because "They don't show it. They don't spend enough time. They don't care if you learn or not. They need to spend more time and explain things better. Teachers are not really into helping the kids learn."

A parent of three school-age children said that she wasn't sure whether or not most teachers care about students. "I have mixed feelings," she stated. "But I do know that I've met some who'd go the last mile to help their students in any way."

The variable representing parents'/guardians' beliefs about whether or not most teachers care about students was correlated to nineteen other questionnaire items. The two factors that were inversely related to parents'/guardians' beliefs about whether or not teachers care about students were (1) children experiencing racism at school, and (2) the racial climate in the school district. In other words, parents/guardians whose children had experienced racism at school and those who believed that racism was common in the school district were unlikely to believe that teachers care about students. Most of the variables that were positively related to parents'/guardians' beliefs about whether or not teachers care about students pertain to how they perceived administrators, how they rated their own involvement in their children's education, and the ratings that they assigned to teachers, course work, and homework. However, the school district's location also had some bearing on parents'/guardians' beliefs about whether or not teachers care. In some districts they were more likely to believe this than in others (see Table 6.1).

HOW TEACHERS TREAT AFRICAN AMERICAN STUDENTS

Seventy-three percent of the parents/guardians said that most of their children's teachers had treated their children fairly. One parent said that the main reason why most teachers had treated her children fairly was this: "They knew

Table 6.1
Variables That Were Correlated to Parents'/Guardians' Beliefs about Whether or Not Most Teachers Care about Students in the Order of the Strength of Each Correlation

Variable	Strength of Correlation	Significance
High school teachers' rating	.60	$p < .001$
Parents'/guardians' beliefs about whether or not administrators care	.56	$p < .001$
Elementary teachers' rating	.55	$p < .001$
Public school system rating	.50	$p < .001$
Parents'/guardians' beliefs about administrators' treatment	.49	$p < .001$
Benefits of middle school homework	.48	$p < .001$
Benefits of middle school course work	.47	$p < .001$
Benefits of high school homework	.42	$p < .01$
Benefits of high school course work	.41	$p < .01$
School district racial climate	-.40	$p < .001$
Benefits of elementary school homework	.39	$p < .001$
Experiencing racism at school	-.39	$p < .001$
Benefits of elementary school course work	.35	$p < .001$
School district location	.33	$p < .001$
Children's attitude about school	.33	$p < .001$
Middle school track	.28	$p < .02$
Parents'/guardians' self-rating	.28	$p < .004$
Value placed on children's education	.22	$p < .03$
Listening to children read	.19	$p < .05$

$N = 129$

they would have had to deal with me. They knew that I'd go to the school board." A father said that he believed that his daughter's teacher treated her fairly, because the teacher "doesn't single certain ones out and give them more attention than others. Everybody that's in her class is treated the same." A mother of three secondary school students said that teachers had treated her children fairly because she was actively involved in her children's education. She explained, "From the start, I showed interest in my children's education. I get to know my kids' teachers and keep the lines of communication open with them." A mother of four, who believed that most of her children's teachers had treated them fairly, said:

I think they give them all opportunities to change, and if the attitude or behavior continues, they apply the discipline. They also give them meaningful tasks as far as homework assignments and things that they send home. They keep parents involved in the kids' homework assignments. Whenever I've asked for anything, it's been taken into consideration and they've acted upon it. I've never felt that when I sat down and spoke to them about my kids that they were unfair.

A mother of two said she believed that her children had been treated fairly, but felt that some teachers have less patience with children than others. She stated:

When my son gets in trouble, I think he's treated fairly. But then again, when he was in kindergarten and first grade, he had teachers that I had been in contact with when his sister was younger. But, I think when he came to second grade, he just became more of a problem and that particular teacher didn't have as much patience for him. And I know that with different personalities, be it good or bad, that it's easier to pick on someone that you may not care for, for one reason or another.

A father said that he and his children were at odds over whether or not most teachers had treated them fairly. He stated:

I think they treated them fairly and I can honestly say that my kids will disagree. But as a parent, I understand that kids have to understand the chain of command. They have to understand that there are certain things that you do at school, and there are certain things that you're not supposed to do. If you don't understand an assignment, fine. But, if you are giving the teacher a hard time, then, that's a problem.

Six questionnaire items were related to parents'/guardians' beliefs about teacher treatment of children. Parents/guardians whose children were discipline problems and/or who had problems with homework were still likely to believe that most of their children's teachers had treated them fairly. Surprisingly, children's elementary, middle, and high school academic tracks were inversely related to their parents'/guardians' beliefs about how teachers treated them. For some reason parents/guardians who had children in the highest-level tracks were less likely than others to believe that teachers had treated their children fairly. Furthermore, parents'/guardians' rating of their children's high school teachers was also inversely related to their beliefs about teacher treatment. In other words, parents/guardians who gave a high rating to the quality of their children's high school teachers were unlikely to believe that most teachers had treated their children fairly (see Table 6.2).

RATING ELEMENTARY TEACHERS

Sixty-eight percent of the parents/guardians rated most of their children's elementary school teachers as *excellent* or *good* (see Table 6.3). One father rated his daughter's kindergarten teacher as *good* because "When I was in elementary school, a lot of teachers didn't care. They weren't calling home.

Table 6.2
Variables That Were Correlated to Parents'/Guardians' Beliefs about Whether or Not Most Teachers Had Treated Their Children Fairly in the Order of the Strength of Each Correlation

Variable	Strength of Correlation	Significance
High school track	-.30	$p < .03$
Middle school track	-.26	$p < .03$
Elementary track	-.25	$p < .01$
High school teachers' rating	-.25	$p < .04$
Homework problem	.22	$p < .02$
Discipline problem	.20	$p < .03$

$N = 129$

Table 6.3
How African American Parents/Guardians Rated Their Children's Elementary School Teachers

Rating	Percent
Poor	2
Needs to improve	12
Fair	16
Good	42
Excellent	26
No answer	2

$N = 129$

They would just let things go. But my daughter's teacher knows what she's teaching." Another parent rated most of her children's elementary school teachers as *good* because "I can think of some who were really good, enthusiastic, who encouraged them to read, and urged the parents to come into the classroom. Of course, there were a few who had the attitude that they really didn't wanna be there." A mother of four said:

I was very impressed with my kids' elementary teachers. They always talked to me about any problems or concerns that they had and my kids enjoyed them. One of my daughters recommended that her brother go through the same teacher that she had in the sixth grade. That was the main teacher who helped my son make progress. She was down to earth and open with the students, and she let them know exactly what was expected of them.

The rating that parents/guardians gave to most of their children's elementary school teachers was correlated to twenty-three questionnaire items. Three of the variables that were inversely related to how they rated their children's elementary school teachers pertained to racism. Parents/guardians who believed that racism was common in their children's school district, whose children had experienced racism, and/or whose children experienced racism frequently at school were more likely to assign a lower rating to their elementary teachers. The number of school-age children per family, whether or not parents/guardians had served as classroom volunteers, whether or not children had been suspended from school, had poor grades, and/or had problems with homework were also negatively linked to how parents/guardians rated elementary teachers. In other words, these parents/guardians were unlikely to believe that their children's elementary teachers had done an *excellent* or a *good* job. Moreover, children's attitude about reading was also inversely related to how their parents/guardians rated their elementary teachers in that those whose children disliked reading were more likely to give a low rating to elementary school teachers. Parents'/guardians' high school teachers' rating and their beliefs about whether teachers care about students were the strongest positive correlations to how they rated elementary teachers. Three reading-related variables were also positively associated with the ratings of parents/guardians. Parents/guardians who bought books for their children, who read to their children frequently, and whose children read frequently at home were more likely than others to assign a high rating to most of their children's elementary school teachers. Furthermore, parents/guardians who had children in G.A.T.E. elementary classes were more likely than others to assign a high rating to elementary teachers (see Table 6.4).

RATING MIDDLE SCHOOL TEACHERS

Sixty-six percent of the African American parents/guardians who had children who were currently in or who had been in middle school at one time,

Table 6.4
**Variables That Were Correlated to How Parents/Guardians Rated
Elementary Teachers in the Order of the Strength of Each Correlation**

Variable	Strength of Correlation	Significance
High school teachers' rating	.67	p < .001
Beliefs about whether or not teachers care	.55	p < .001
Public school system rating	.55	p < .001
Benefits of elementary school homework	.47	p < .001
Experiencing racism at school	-.41	p < .001
Beliefs about administrators' treatment	.40	p < .001
Benefits of elementary course work	.39	p < .001
Experiencing racism frequently	-.39	p < .01
Beliefs about whether or not administrators care	.34	p < .001
Benefits of middle school homework	.32	p < .01
Poor grades	-.32	p < .001
School district racial climate	-.32	p < .003
Parents'/guardians' self-rating	.31	p < .001
Benefits of middle school course work	.30	p < .02
Number of days per week children read	.25	p < .02
Number of days per week parents/guardians read	.25	p < .03
Disliking reading	-.23	p < .01
Suspension	-.21	p < .02
Number of school-age children	-.21	p < .02
Buying books for children	.20	p < .03
Elementary track	.20	p < .03
Homework problem	-.19	p <. 03
Serving as a classroom volunteer	-.18	p < .04

$N = 129$

rated their children's middle school teachers as *excellent* or *good* (see Table
6.5). One parent said that she had a high opinion of elementary school teachers,
but both middle school and high school teachers were in need of improvement.
"When kids get out of elementary school," she stated, "most teachers just want
to be paid." Conversely, a mother of four who rated her children's middle school
teachers as *good* said, "I had an opportunity to volunteer at the middle school
which they are currently at. I liked the teachers' attitudes, their expectations,
and how I saw them behave." A grandmother said she rated her granddaughter's middle school teachers as *good*, because "They seem to take time with
her. I didn't hear any complaints out of her." A mother of two daughters who

Table 6.5
How African American Parents/Guardians Rated Their Children's Middle School Teachers

Rating	Percent
Poor	3
Needs to improve	8
Fair	23
Good	49
Excellent	17

$N = 96$

attended a highly rated public college preparatory middle school, stated, "Some middle school teachers stand out as being really good to me, and some had an attitude that I didn't like. They were the ones who made negative comments, not necessarily to my kids, but to other kids. They don't belong in the classroom. They don't build kids up or make them better students." A grandmother stated that, although she believed that most of her grandchild's middle school teachers were doing a good job, one middle school teacher, who taught literature, stood out as being exceptionally bad. She described her visit to his classroom as follows:

I walked into the room and this man is so disoriented, it's pathetic. He's all bad. He had an odor. I said, "I want to know why you gave my granddaughter an 'F.'" He said that she got an "F" because she deserved an "F." So, he goes and gets her folder and brings it over. There is nothing in her folder. My granddaughter told him, "You know I handed in some things." He had to go and hunt around the room for something. He brought two sheets of paper that she had done for the whole period. My granddaughter said, "Grandma, I handed in more than that." The teacher said my granddaughter had requested that he move her, but my granddaughter said he had never moved her. She told him, "I would ask you questions and you would not answer me. You would send me back to my seat." I told the teacher, "This is very disheartening to see, not just because of my child, but any child who comes to you for help. This is what you're being paid for." He said, "If she wasn't talking in class. . . . " I said, "I don't care what she was doing. When she comes to you for help you're supposed to help her. If she's being bad, send her to the office."

The teachers want to sit and talk to us like we're dummies, like we don't know anything. So I told a school board member about it, but he didn't do anything. I wanted him to go to the classroom and see what a state of disarray this man is in. I don't think he should be teaching. He couldn't find anything. It was deplorable! I'm not saying that everything was his fault. My granddaughter has areas where she needs to improve. But I know we worked on one of the things that he said she didn't turn in.

Seven questionnaire items were positively correlated to how parents/guardians rated their children's middle school teachers. The variables that produced the strongest correlations were the ratings that parents/guardians gave to their children's high school teachers, the level at which students were retained or failed courses, and the benefits of their children's middle school and high school course work and homework. The parents/guardians who were most satisfied with their children's high school teachers, and who believed that their children had received beneficial middle school and high school course work and homework, were also most likely to believe that their children's middle school teachers had done an outstanding job. The same was true, however, of parents/guardians who had children who failed middle school and/or high school courses. This might suggest that they equated course failure with academic rigor or that they attributed it to a lack of effort on their children's part. Furthermore, the location of the school district in which children attended school was related to the ratings that parents/guardians gave. Certain districts appeared to have better middle school teachers than others (see Table 6.6).

RATING HIGH SCHOOL TEACHERS

Forty-nine percent of the African American parents/guardians rated their children's high school teachers as *excellent* or *good* (see Table 6.7). However, a mother of four rated most of her children's high school teachers as *fair* because teachers "have so many unruly kids, they don't know what to do. They're trying to protect themselves." A mother of three rated her son's high school teachers as *excellent* because "I've seen them give their all to him and to the others. I've seen them go way beyond the call of duty to make sure that

Table 6.6
Variables That Were Correlated to How Parents/Guardians Rated Middle School Teachers in the Order of the Strength of Each Correlation

Variable	Strength of Correlation	Significance
High school teachers' rating	.76	p < .001
Grade retention/course failure level	.70	p < .001
Benefits of high school homework	.55	p < .001
Benefits of middle school homework	.50	p < .001
Benefits of middle school course work	.48	p < .001
Benefits of high school course work	.43	p < .003
School district location	.22	p < .03

$N = 96$

Table 6.7
How African American Parents/Guardians Rated Their Children's High
School Teachers

Rating	Percent
Poor	7
Needs to improve	13
Fair	31
Good	33
Excellent	16

$N = 77$

he excelled to the point that he was able to excel." Another mother rated all
of her daughter's high school teachers, except for one, as *good*. She stated, "I
would say, except for her biology teacher, they've been really good. I just think
he's one of those teachers who just piles the work on you with no real reason,
just busy stuff." A mother of an eleventh grader rated her daughter's high
school teachers as *good* because:

I've seen her do well on tests. She puts her thoughts together well. She seems pretty
well rounded and understands quite a bit. I have listened to other parents say that they
have daughters or sons that are 4.0 students. My daughter's probably a 3.1 or something
like that. And hearing them talk and seeing them interact, I feel that my daughter is a
lot higher intelligence-wise than they are, and she has had better classroom experiences.
I think she's better prepared.

How parents/guardians rated high school teachers was correlated to twenty-
three other questionnaire items. Three of the variables pertained to reading.
Parents/guardians of children who disliked to read and/or who had a problem
comprehending what they read were unlikely to assign a high rating to high
school teachers. However, parents/guardians who read to their children were
likely to assign a high rating. Parents'/guardians' beliefs about school administrators and elementary and middle school teachers were also linked to this
variable, as was the value that parents/guardians placed on elementary, middle,
and high school course work and homework. Those with favorable impressions
of teachers, administrators, and their children's course work also tended to have
a favorable view of most of their children's high school teachers. For some
reason, children's elementary track, but not their middle school track, was
positively correlated to how parents/guardians rated their children's high
school teachers. The school levels at which children were suspended and three
variables related to racism were inversely linked to this rating. Therefore, the
parents/guardians of children who had been suspended during middle school

and/or high school, those whose children experienced racism at school, and those whose children attended school in a district in which racism was common tended to give low ratings to high school teachers. Moreover, as previously noted, parents/guardians who gave a high rating to their children's high school teachers were unlikely to believe that most teachers had treated their children fairly. One possibility is that the mistreatment might have only pertained to middle school and elementary school teachers (see Table 6.8). In the following narrative, a mother describes her son's schooling experiences and illustrates how she viewed teachers and related factors.

Table 6.8
Variables That Were Correlated to How Parents/Guardians Rated High School Teachers in the Order of the Strength of Each Correlation

Variable	Strength of Correlation	Significance
Middle school teachers' rating	.76	p < .001
Elementary teachers' rating	.67	p < .001
Benefits of high school homework	.67	p < .001
Parents'/guardians' beliefs about whether teachers care	.60	p < .001
Benefits of high school course work	.56	p < .001
Public school system rating	.55	p < .001
Suspension level	-.53	p < .001
Parents'/guardians' beliefs about administrators' treatment	.49	p < .001
Experiencing racism	-.45	p < .001
Parents'/guardians' self-rating	.41	p < .001
Benefits of middle school course work	.41	p < .004
Experiencing racism frequently	-.41	p < .02
Benefits of middle school homework	.39	p < .01
Parents'/guardians' beliefs about whether administrators care	.36	p < .01
Reading comprehension problem	-.32	p < .004
Benefits of elementary school course work	.31	p < .01
Benefits of elementary school homework	.29	p < .01
Children's attitude about school	.29	p < .01
School district racial climate	-.29	p < .04
Disliking reading	-.28	p < .01
Elementary school track	.25	p < .03
Parents'/guardians' beliefs about teacher treatment	-.25	p < .04
Reading to children	.24	p < .04

N = 77

THEY NEED TO CARE MORE ABOUT THE KIDS

Of all the parents/guardians who agreed to be interviewed, Trishina, a mother of six school-age children, was the only one who'd become so exasperated with the school system that she had resorted to homeschooling two of her sons. As a recreational aide at the elementary school that three of her children attended, she routinely heard conversations and observed practices that most parents/guardians never hear. She had noticed recurring problems of underqualified teachers, low standards, and low expectations at the schools that her children attended. Although she felt that most of her children's elementary school teachers had done a good job, she was extremely displeased with their middle school and high school teachers. As a result of her children's schooling experiences and her own observations, she had concluded that most teachers and administrators do not care about students. Trishina stated:

They're just letting them go through the system and not really working with them. Most teachers, but not all teachers, don't care about the kids. They need to care more about the kids to make sure they get a good education, instead of just putting them through the system to get them out of the way, especially the problem kids. Just because they don't want to be bothered, they just let them go through.

However, Trishina was pleased that her children's elementary teachers had been willing to work with her children and that they had utilized different strategies as a result of consulting with Trishina. One teacher's high expectations and refusal to settle for substandard work resulted in Trishina's son winning a writing award in fifth grade. Trishina said, "He's really a smart kid, but he wants to do just whatever to get through. He had a teacher that wouldn't accept that and made him do his best. She knew he could do better and because she wouldn't accept it, it helped him."

Conversely, Trishina rated the middle school teachers in her children's school district as *needs to improve,* and the high school teachers as *poor.* Regarding the middle school and high school teachers, she said:

They wouldn't go the extra mile to make sure the kids caught on. Pretty much when you get to junior high and high school, you're going to the next grade anyway. They don't hold you back; you just go on. Especially in high school, you'll be in the tenth grade with ninth grade credits and still go on to the next grade. Then, by the time you're in twelfth grade, everybody has tenth grade credits. One teacher told me that my son wasn't comprehending what he was reading and didn't know what he was doing, but she gave him an "A."

When she saw a pattern of failure from her twelve-year-old and fourteen-year-old sons, Trishina pulled them out of the public school system and decided to homeschool them. She explained:

They were getting bad grades and I figured, with the homeschooling, I could really help them. I want them to get their high school diploma. I'm going to keep homeschooling them until they're ready to graduate. I keep telling them that being a Black male, they'll have it hard anyway. They need that high school diploma.

My tenth grader likes to play sports, so he has to keep his grades up to play sports. The other two just like to horse around and play, I guess. When I had them tested to get into the homeschooling program, my ninth grader tested real high, but he gets straight "F's." My seventh grader tested at grade level. They said the teachers wouldn't help them if they wanted them to. And I tell them, "If you guys ask a teacher to help you and if that teacher doesn't want to help you, then you come talk to me, and I'll go talk to that teacher. But if you're not letting me know, then there's nothing I can do for you." I think that they didn't want to do the work, but now they have to do it, because I'm here with them to make sure they're doing it. They're turning their work in and getting good grades.

SUMMARY

This chapter presented feedback from the African American parents/guardians about numerous issues pertaining to their perceptions of teachers. The majority of the parents/guardians who completed the questionnaire said that they believed that most teachers care about students. Parents/guardians whose children had experienced racism at school, and who believed that racism was common in their children's school district were unlikely to believe that teachers care about students. Conversely, those who believed that the quality of teaching and the quality of course work, and homework that their children received was *outstanding* were more likely to believe that teachers care. Positive student treatment by administrators was also positively correlated to the belief that teachers care about their students.

The majority of the parents/guardians also believed that most of their children's teachers had treated their children fairly. Surprisingly, parents/guardians of children who were discipline problems and/or who had homework problems were likely to believe that most of their children's teachers had treated them fairly. However, the parents/guardians of children in the highest elementary, middle school, and high school tracks were less likely than those who had children in lower level tracks to believe this. One possibility is that because African American children tend to be underrepresented in the highest tracks, their parents/guardians might have felt that their children were not treated as well as their non-Black classmates. In Chapter 10, for example, a parent stated that she even had to fight the school system in order to have her daughter tested for the G.A.T.E. program. Furthermore, in *African American Teens Discuss Their Schooling Experiences* (Thompson, 2002), some students said that they felt uncomfortable in the G.A.T.E. program so they left the program voluntarily. This finding warrants further investigation.

Nearly 70 percent of the parents/guardians rated their children's elementary teachers as *excellent* or *good*; 66 percent rated their middle school teachers as *excellent* or *good*; and only 49 percent of those who had children in high school rated their high school teachers as *excellent* or *good*. Children's experiences with racism at school and parents'/guardians' beliefs about the prevalence of racism in the school district, as well as other negative schooling experiences, appeared to have an effect on how they rated teachers. Again, parents'/guardians' beliefs about the benefits of course work and homework were also related to how they rated teachers. A theme that has surfaced in numerous narratives is that some African American parents/guardians measure good teaching by comparing and contrasting their children's schooling experiences with their own schooling experiences. Another interesting finding was that parents/guardians who had served as classroom volunteers were more likely than those who had not to assign a low rating to elementary school teachers. Perhaps these parents'/guardians' observations during their visits gave them a negative view of elementary teachers. However, several parents/guardians mentioned that they felt a stronger connection to elementary teachers than to middle school and high school teachers. Another way of interpreting this finding is that parents/guardians who gave high ratings to elementary teachers were unlikely to serve as classroom volunteers. Perhaps these parents/guardians felt no need to do so, since they believed that their children's teachers were doing an *excellent* or *good* job.

Like the majority of the parents/guardians who completed the questionnaire, Trishina, whose narrative was presented in this chapter, was pleased with the quality of instruction that was provided by her children's elementary school teachers. She was displeased, however, with their middle school and high school teachers. During Trishina's interview she mentioned that working at a school gave her the opportunity to hear conversations that indicated that most teachers do not care about students. She also saw evidence that teachers had low expectations, were unwilling to help students, and were underprepared to meet the needs of some students. Her sons' downward academic spiral prompted her to resort to homeschooling. She complained about grade inflation and high school teachers passing unprepared students to the next grade level. For example, she stated, "One teacher told me that my son wasn't comprehending what he was reading and didn't know what he was doing, but she gave him an 'A.'" Trishina also said that teachers were unwilling to give her sons the extra help that they requested, an accusation that has surfaced numerous times throughout this study.

These findings indicate that some teachers are ineffective with African American students, because they fail to utilize the strategies and possess the characteristics that African American students equate with good teaching. Among these characteristics are the ability to make the subject matter comprehensible, a willingness to give extra help, patience, and academic rigor (Thompson, 2002)—qualities that African American parents/guardians also appear to equate with outstanding teaching.

One of the strongest messages emanating from the data in this chapter is that many African American parents/guardians are pleased with the job that some teachers, particularly elementary teachers, are doing. However, the data also indicate that there is room for improvement in the form of improving teachers' attitudes, strengthening teachers' skills, and providing ongoing professional development that will better equip teachers with the information and resources that they need to work effectively with African American parents/guardians and their children.

7

Course Work and Homework

Research has shown that certain instructional practices have more of a positive impact on student achievement than others. For example, according to the National Center for Education Statistics (2001), "Students at grade 8 whose teachers reported spending between two-and-one-half hours and four hours on mathematics instruction had higher math scores than those whose teachers reported four hours or more" (p. 151). Three other classroom practices were also linked to mathematics achievement. For fourth graders, doing math problems from a textbook frequently, talking with others about solving math problems on a monthly basis, and using a calculator on a monthly basis were positively related to higher math scores. In other words, moderate as opposed to daily use of these practices appeared to be more beneficial to students. However, for eighth graders and twelfth graders, the converse was true. Students who engaged in certain practices, such as doing textbook math problems daily and using a calculator frequently, had higher math scores.

Research has also shown that certain homework practices appear to be more beneficial than others. For younger children, too much homework can be counterproductive. For example, "fourth grade teachers who reported that they assigned 45 minutes of mathematics homework had students with lower average scores than teachers who assigned less homework" (National Center for Education Statistics, 2001, p. 153). In fact, fourth graders whose teachers reported that they assigned no mathematics homework at all had higher average scores than fourth graders whose teachers reported assigning fifteen, thirty, forty-five minutes, or one hour of mathematics homework per day. Moreover, the average student score decreased with each increase in the amount of daily mathematics homework that was assigned. For example, whereas the average score was 231 for students who received no mathematics homework, it was 227 for those who received thirty minutes of mathematics homework, and 212 for those who received forty-five minutes of daily mathematics homework

(p. 152). However, for secondary students, more homework was equated with higher mathematics scores than less homework or no homework at all.

This research indicates that teachers must be knowledgeable about the types and amounts of homework that are most conducive to student achievement. However, in "How Much Is Too Much? Homework Problems," Vail (2001a) stated that, often, parents are at odds with educators over homework practices. For many families the amount of homework that is assigned can be a great source of stress that results in conflicts between parents and their children. Vail also noted that some homework practices also result in parents actually doing the work for their children. Consequently, some states have actually abolished homework during certain eras. Vail concluded that more research is needed about the effects of homework on students' learning.

In *African American Teens Discuss Their Schooling Experiences* (Thompson, 2002), the high school seniors rated the benefits of their elementary, middle, and high school course work and homework. Most students gave a high rating to the quality of course work that they received, but students in upper-level academic tracks were more likely than those in lower-level tracks or students who were retained in elementary school to rate it as *excellent* or *good*. As noted earlier, a higher percentage of students failed high school courses than elementary grades or middle school courses. The math curriculum was particularly problematic for many students. A similar message has surfaced in the current study. Throughout the current study, African American parents'/guardians' beliefs about the benefits of the course work and homework that their children received have been linked to numerous variables. This chapter will provide more information from questionnaire and interview data about course work and homework.

ELEMENTARY SCHOOL COURSE WORK

Seventy-two percent of the parents/guardians who completed the questionnaire said that most of the elementary school course work that was assigned to their children was beneficial (see Table 7.1). Parents/guardians who believed that the course work was beneficial tended to state that it had prepared their children for middle school and taught them important skills. A mother of six said that she believed that her children's elementary school course work was beneficial "because it teaches them things, like some things they didn't know, especially science. We played and talked about science, but in class they learned more about what could happen and what's true and untrue." A mother of three said that her children's elementary school course work was beneficial, because "It was a challenge for them." A father said that he saw the positive results of his daughter's course work. "When we're on the computer, she can answer all the questions. Without a lot of that school work, she couldn't answer anything like that." A mother of an eight-year-old said that her daughter's course work

Table 7.1

How Parents/Guardians Rated Their Children's Elementary School Course Work

Rating	Percent
Not beneficial	1
Somewhat beneficial	17
Beneficial	72
No answer	10

$N = 129$

was beneficial because "She'll always use it. Everything that she's being taught, she'll use. She's been getting that good foundation."

Few parents/guardians believed that the course work had *not* been beneficial. Those who did, however, believed that it was merely busy work, that it was not challenging, or that it failed to provide their children with important reading and math skills, as indicated by some of the parents/guardians whose narratives have been shared in previous chapters. Conversely, several parents/guardians believed that their children's elementary school course work needed improvement. These parents/guardians felt that some aspects had been *beneficial*, but not all. For example, a grandmother said that her grandchildren's course work was only *somewhat beneficial*, because it failed to teach them critical thinking skills. She stated:

They can get book knowledge from the school, but if they don't have any common sense, what good is it going to do them? If they were really doing as well as they could be doing in school, it seems to me they would think more readily than they do. It's like routine. They know the procedure, but they don't think about how they got from point A to point B. So what you've got is a lot of educated fools out here. And to me, some of the things they do are just stupid. I don't know any other word for it. It's just stupid.

Another grandmother said that her granddaughter's elementary school course work was only somewhat beneficial "because she wasn't getting what she needed."

Parents'/guardians' beliefs about the benefits of elementary school course work were correlated to fifteen other questionnaire items. Reading comprehension problems, math problems, and experiencing racism at school were inversely related to this variable. Therefore, the parents/guardians of children who had these problems were unlikely to believe that their children's elementary school course work was *beneficial*. Beliefs about administrators, whether or not teachers care about children, how parents/guardians rated elementary and high school teachers, and parents'/guardians' self-rating were positively related to how they rated their children's elementary school course work. In other words, satisfaction with these aspects of their children's schooling was related to satisfaction with elementary school course work. However, the strongest correlations were between parents'/guardians' beliefs about the benefits of elementary school course work and their beliefs about the benefits of their children's elementary school homework and their middle school and high school course work and homework. Satisfaction in these areas increased the probability of parents'/guardians' satisfaction with their children's elementary school course work (see Table 7.2).

MIDDLE SCHOOL COURSE WORK

Seventy-five percent of the parents/guardians who had children who were currently in middle school or who had previously been in middle school said

Table 7.2
Variables That Were Correlated to How Parents/Guardians Rated Their Children's Elementary School Course Work in the Order of the Strength of Each Correlation

Variable	Strength of Correlation	Significance
Benefits of elementary school homework	.66	p < .001
Benefits of middle school homework	.56	p < .001
Benefits of middle school course work	.54	p < .001
Benefits of high school homework	.53	p < .001
Benefits of high school course work	.47	p < .001
Public school system rating	.39	p < .001
Elementary teachers' rating	.39	p < .001
Beliefs about whether or not teachers care	.35	p < .001
High school teachers' rating	.31	p < .01
Parents'/guardians' beliefs about administrators' treatment	.29	p < .004
Parents'/guardians' beliefs about whether or not administrators care	.27	p < .01
Parents'/guardians' self-rating	.23	p < .02
Experiencing racism	-.23	p < .03
Math problem	-.21	p < .02
Reading comprehension problem	-.21	p < .02

$N = 129$

that most of the course work that was assigned was *beneficial* (see Table 7.3). Most parents/guardians who believed that the course work was *beneficial* said that it had prepared their children for high school. One mother said that the skills that her son learned from his middle school course work resulted in him winning a scholarship in high school. Another mother liked the projects that were related to her daughter's middle school course work because they helped her to prioritize and they taught her how to do research, skills that she would use throughout her life. A mother of a seventh grader said that her daughter's middle school course work "offered a lot of variety and gives her a well-rounded education."

On the other hand, some parents/guardians believed that their children's middle school course work was *not beneficial* or only *somewhat beneficial.* Those who found the middle school course work less than beneficial, like those who believed that the elementary school course work was less than beneficial, thought that it was busy work, that it was nonchallenging, or that it failed to equip their children with the preparation that they needed for high school. This was particularly true of parents/guardians whose children were struggling academically. A mother of two middle school boys said that, unlike their elementary school course work, her children's middle school course work was *not beneficial* because "They're not really teaching the children the way they should. The kids are really on their own, but they're not able to figure it out themselves. So, they're not really learning."

Fifteen questionnaire items were linked to the variable representing how parents/guardians rated their children's middle school course work. Retention/course failure was inversely related, indicating that parents/guardians whose children were retained or who failed courses were unlikely to be satisfied with their children's middle school course work. Surprisingly, the number of days per week that children read to their parents/guardians and that parents/guardians read to their children increased the likelihood of parents'/guardians' dissatisfaction with their children's middle school course work. Parents'/guardians' beliefs about the benefits of their children's middle school homework, high school course work, and high school homework were the main

Table 7.3
How Parents/Guardians Rated Their Children's Middle School Course Work

Rating	Percent
Not beneficial	3
Somewhat beneficial	22
Beneficial	75

$N = 65$

factors that were related to how they rated their children's middle school course work. Those who were most satisfied were also more likely to find their children's middle school course work to be beneficial (see Table 7.4).

HIGH SCHOOL COURSE WORK

Sixty-eight percent of the parents/guardians who had children in high school rated most of the course work that was assigned as *beneficial* (see Table 7.5). One mother said that her daughter's high school course work was *beneficial* because it helped her to grow. Another mother said that her son's high school course work prepared him for life, taught him to become independent, and "it stretched his mind."

Thirteen questionnaire items were correlated to the variable representing how parents/guardians rated their children's high school course work. Parents'/

Table 7.4
Variables That Were Correlated to How Parents/Guardians Rated Their Children's Middle School Course Work in the Order of the Strength of Each Correlation

Variable	Strength of Correlation	Significance
Benefits of middle school homework	.82	p < .001
Benefits of high school course work	.72	p < .001
Benefits of high school homework	.68	p < .001
Benefits of elementary school homework	.57	p < .001
Benefits of elementary school course work	.54	p < .001
Middle school teachers' rating	.48	p < .001
Number of days children read to parents/guardians	-.48	p < .001
Beliefs about whether or not teachers care	.47	p < .001
High school teachers' rating	.41	p < .004
Number of days parents/guardians read to children	-.35	p < .04
Public school system rating	.32	p < .01
Children's attitude about school	.30	p < .02
Elementary teachers' rating	.30	p < .02
Retention/course failure	-.29	p < .02
Children's attitude about reading	.26	p < .05

$N = 65$

Table 7.5
How Parents/Guardians Rated Their Children's High School Course Work

Rating	Percent
Not beneficial	12
Somewhat beneficial	20
Beneficial	68

$N = 46$

guardians' perception of the racial climate in the school district was the only variable that was inversely related to how they rated high school course work. Those who believed that racism was common in the school district were unlikely to state that their children's high school course work was *beneficial*. Parents'/guardians' beliefs about the benefits of their children's high school homework, middle school course work, middle school homework, and their high school teachers' rating had the strongest bearing on how they perceived their children's high school course work (see Table 7.6).

ELEMENTARY SCHOOL HOMEWORK

Sixty-eight percent of the parents/guardians rated most of the homework that was assigned to their children during elementary school as *beneficial* (see Table 7.7). The main reason why certain parents/guardians believed the homework was *beneficial* was they thought that it "reinforced what their children learned in class." For example, one mother said the homework "gave them structure and the basics." A mother of two said that her children's elementary school homework was *beneficial* because "I think it teaches them discipline." Another mother said that her daughter's elementary school homework was *beneficial* because it offered a lot of variety in math, science, and English; it gave her a well-rounded curriculum; and she was given more than one day to complete the work. A mother of six said the homework "helps them with things that they struggle with in class. When they bring it home, if they are not catching on to the way that the teacher is teaching, maybe me or one of the kids will teach them, and they will learn it." Several interviewees stated that they liked the fact that their children were given homework packets that were due at the end of the week, thereby giving the students more time to complete the work. However, this was one of the main criticisms from parents/guardians who believed that their children's homework had only been *somewhat beneficial*. For example, a mother of four said, "I've been against those homework packages, because you give a child a homework package, and they can complete it in a matter of a day or two. Then, they've got all this free time, and I think

Table 7.6
Variables That Were Correlated to How Parents/Guardians Rated Their
Children's High School Course Work in the Order of the Strength of Each
Correlation

Variable	Strength of Correlation	Significance
Benefits of high school homework	.76	p < .001
Benefits of middle school course work	.72	p < .001
Benefits of middle school homework	.66	p < .001
High school teachers' rating	.56	p < .001
Public school system rating	.50	p < .001
Benefits of elementary school course work	.47	p < .001
Beliefs about whether or not administrators care	.47	p < .003
Benefits of elementary school homework	.43	p < .002
Middle school teachers' rating	.43	p < .003
Parents'/guardians' beliefs about whether or not teachers care	.41	p < .01
School district racial climate	-.40	p < .01
Children's attitude about school	.32	p < .02
Value of children's education to parents/guardians	.32	p < .03

N = 46

Table 7.7
How Parents/Guardians Rated Their Children's Elementary School
Homework

Rating	Percent
Not beneficial	2
Somewhat beneficial	21
Beneficial	68
No answer	9

N = 129

it's just rushed and really not thought about." Another mother said the home-work was only *somewhat beneficial* because "They aren't allowed to bring textbooks home." Some adults complained about the quality of the homework. One grandmother said she had to supplement her grandson's homework and referred to his homework as "that little mess they sent." She stated, "The only thing this child has ever gotten from first grade, all the way up to fourth and fifth grade, is ten to fifteen spelling words that they do a week. I've never seen anything they sent that's an explanation of how you punctuate and how you use grammar correctly." Another common complaint among the parents/guardians who believed that the homework was only *somewhat beneficial* was that teachers failed to collect the homework.

The rating that parents/guardians gave to their children's elementary school homework was correlated to fourteen other questionnaire items. Their rating was inversely related to poor grades and experiencing racism at school. In other words, the parents/guardians of children who'd had these types of negative experiences at school were unlikely to rate the elementary school homework that was assigned as *beneficial*. The factors that had the strongest links to their rating were based on how they rated their children's elementary teachers and elementary course work, and their middle school and high school course work and homework (see Table 7.8).

MIDDLE SCHOOL HOMEWORK

Sixty-one percent of the parents/guardians rated most of the middle school homework that was assigned to their children as *beneficial* (see Table 7.9). Parents/guardians who believed that their children's middle school homework was *beneficial* tended to believe that it prepared them for high school and strengthened their skills. One mother said that her children's middle school homework "introduced them to the bigger things in life." Several parents/guardians also believed that the homework was *beneficial* if it was something that their children could do independently. Parents/guardians who believed that the homework was only *somewhat beneficial* tended to state that it was not challenging, particularly those who had children in Special Education classes. A mother who worked at a school said that her children's middle school home-work was *not beneficial* because "Their math homework from high school and junior high school had every other answer—the odd numbers—in the back of the book. So most of the kids just go to the back of the book and write the answer down, and the teachers accept that, instead of having them show their work."

Seventeen questionnaire items were linked to how parents/guardians rated their children's middle school homework. Parents/guardians who believed that racism was common in their children's school district, whose children experienced racism at school, and whose children experienced racism from adults on campus or from multiple sources were unlikely to believe that their children's

Table 7.8
Variables That Were Correlated to How Parents/Guardians Rated Their
Children's Elementary School Homework in the Order of the Strength of
Each Correlation

Variable	Strength of Correlation	Significance
Benefits of middle school homework	.67	p < .001
Benefits of elementary course work	.66	p < .001
Benefits of middle school course work	.57	p < .001
Benefits of high school homework	.53	p < .001
Elementary teachers' rating	.47	p < .001
Benefits of high school course work	.43	p < .002
Parents'/guardians' beliefs about whether or not teachers care	.39	p < .001
Public school system rating	.30	p < .001
High school teachers' rating	.29	p < .01
Parents'/guardians' self-rating	.29	p < .002
Experiencing racism	-.27	p < .01
Poor grades	-.22	p < .02
Encouraging children to read	.19	p < .04
Value placed on children's education	.19	p < .04

$N = 129$

Table 7.9
How Parents/Guardians Rated Their Children's Middle School Homework

Rating	Percent
Not beneficial	9
Somewhat beneficial	30
Beneficial	61

$N = 67$

middle school homework was *beneficial.* The strongest factors that were related
to parents'/guardians' beliefs about the benefits of middle school homework
were their beliefs about the benefits of middle school course work, and elementary school and high school course work and homework. As noted previously, some parents/guardians had children at multiple levels of school and

some had children who had already graduated. Therefore, the correlations were indicative of these circumstances (see Table 7.10).

HIGH SCHOOL HOMEWORK

Sixty-one percent of the parents/guardians who had children in high school rated most of their high school homework as *beneficial* (see Table 7.11). Parents/guardians who were pleased with high school homework tended to believe that it strengthened their children's skills and reinforced the course work. For example, one mother stated that the high school homework "showed what to focus on." Those who were displeased thought that it was busy work or nonchallenging. This was particularly true of parents/guardians whose

Table 7.10
Variables That Were Correlated to How Parents/Guardians Rated Their Children's Middle School Homework in the Order of the Strength of Each Correlation

Variable	Strength of Correlation	Significance
Benefits of middle school course work	.82	p < .001
Benefits of high school homework	.78	p < .001
Benefits of elementary school homework	.67	p < .001
Benefits of high school course work	.66	p < .001
Benefits of elementary school course work	.56	p < .001
Middle school teachers' rating	.50	p < .001
Parents'/guardians' beliefs about whether or not teachers care	.48	p < .001
Source of racism	-.44	p < .02
Parent's/guardians' beliefs about whether or not administrators care	.41	p < .003
High school teachers' rating	.39	p < .01
Elementary teachers' rating	.32	p < .01
Encouraging children to read	.30	p < .02
Experiencing racism	-.30	p < .03
School district racial climate	-.29	p < .04
Public school system rating	.28	p < .03
Encouraging children to use school libraries	.26	p < .03
Children's attitude about school	.25	p < .04

$N = 67$

Table 7.11
How Parents/Guardians Rated Their Children's High School Homework

Rating	Percent
Not beneficial	14
Somewhat beneficial	25
Beneficial	61

$N = 46$

children left regular public high schools for continuation schools (special public schools for students who have academic or behavioral problems) to make up course credits.

Sixteen questionnaire items were correlated to this variable. Parents/guardians of students who had been suspended at more than one level of school, as well as parents/guardians who believed that racism was common in their children's school district, and those whose children had experienced racism at school were unlikely to rate the high school homework as *beneficial*. However, those who gave high ratings to their children's high school course work, high school teachers, and middle school course work, homework, and teachers were more likely to believe that the homework was *beneficial* (see Table 7.12).

SUMMARY

The majority of the African American parents/guardians who completed the questionnaire believed that their children's elementary, middle, and high school course work and homework were *beneficial*. Those who were dissatisfied with their children's elementary school course work tended to have children who suffered from problems with reading comprehension and math, and/or who had experienced racism at school. This suggests, as noted in previous chapters, that negative schooling experiences can be related to parents'/guardians' negative perception of other aspects of their children's schooling. Moreover, problems with reading comprehension and math might give parents/guardians the impression that the curriculum is problematic. Several narratives have indicated that, often, the parents/guardians of children who are struggling academically are frustrated with teachers' inability to rectify these problems. Therefore, they may also blame the curriculum as well. Another finding was that parents/guardians who were pleased with their children's elementary school course work also tended to be satisfied with their middle school and high school course work and homework. However, quotes from the interviews showed that this was not always the case. Another finding was that parents/guardians who were least satisfied with their children's middle school course

Table 7.12
Variables That Were Correlated to How Parents/Guardians Rated Their Children's High School Homework in the Order of the Strength of Each Correlation

Variable	Strength of Correlation	Significance
Benefits of middle school homework	.78	p < .001
Benefits of high school course work	.76	p < .001
Benefits of middle school course work	.68	p < .001
High school teachers' rating	.67	p < .001
Middle school teachers' rating	.55	p < .001
Benefits of elementary school course work	.53	p < .001
Benefits of elementary school homework	.53	p < .001
Suspension level	-.50	p < .03
Parents'/ guardians' perception of administrators' treatment	.47	p < .002
School district racial climate	-.46	p < .004
Parents'/guardians' beliefs about whether or not teachers care	.42	p < .01
Parents'/guardians' beliefs about whether or not administrators care	.42	p < .01
Public school system rating	.41	p < .004
Encouraging children to read	.36	p < .02
Experiencing racism	-.35	p < .03
Children's attitude about school	.29	p < .04

$N = 46$

work also had children who failed courses or who were retained in elementary school. This is another example of how negative schooling experiences can be related to parents'/guardians' perception of other schooling factors. Like elementary school course work, parents'/guardians' beliefs about the benefits of their children's high school course work was linked to racism. Those who believed that racism was common in the school district were unlikely to believe that the course work was *beneficial.*

Parents'/guardians' beliefs about the benefits of their children's elementary, middle, and high school homework were also linked to several negative schooling factors. For example, those whose children had poor grades and/or who had experienced racism at school were unlikely to believe that their children's elementary school homework was *beneficial.* Those who believed that racism was common in their children's school district, whose children had experienced racism at school, and/or who had experienced racism from adults on campus were unlikely to believe that their children's middle school homework was beneficial. Parents/guardians who believed that racism was common in their children's school district, whose children had experienced racism, and/or whose children had been suspended from more than one school level were unlikely to state that their children's high school homework was *beneficial*. Chapter 10, as noted previously, will examine other schooling factors that are associated with racism.

8

Beliefs about Administrators

In every organization, leadership sets the tone for acceptable and unacceptable behavior, and the vision and goals of the organization emanate from its leaders. Educational leaders are no different. Although school district officials, local school boards, and state education officials have an impact on school practices, the site-based administrator—the principal—is the organizational leader who has a tremendous amount of influence on the school's culture and climate, and on other school administrators, teachers, staff, students, and parents. According to Tirozzi (2001) "Excellence in school leadership should be recognized as the most important component of school reform. Without leadership, the chances for systemic improvement in teaching and learning are nil" (p. 438).

However, just as there are barriers to the preparation, recruitment, and retention of qualified teachers, there are also barriers to the recruitment and retention of qualified principals. Furthermore, just as there is a widespread problem of providing new teachers with the support that is necessary to ensure success, there is often little support for new principals. According to the U.S. Department of Education (2000a), there are six major barriers to the development of effective school leaders: (1) ineffective training programs; (2) weak bureaucratic requirements; (3) inadequate compensation and authority; (4) little focus on recruiting qualified principals into high-needs schools; (5) unclear and overwhelming responsibilities; and (6) a lack of professional support. Other researchers have stressed that the changing role of the school principal has compounded these problems. As a result, job stress reduces the pool of qualified applicants. For example, Newsom (2001) wrote, "A generation ago, a principal's main duties were to make sure the students behaved, the building stayed clean, and the buses ran on time. Principals also hired staff and performed annual job evaluations. Today, principals have all of these duties and more" (p. 31).

Another barrier to the preparation, recruitment, and retention of qualified principals appears to stem from the confusion surrounding what the primary purpose of a school principal should be. Whereas principals are being trained to be managers, they should be trained to be effective instructional leaders instead. Moreover, principal training institutions are using outdated methods to train them (Tirozzi, 2001). However, Fink and Resnick (2001) said that daily demands make it difficult for principals to serve as instructional leaders as opposed to "generic managers." They wrote, "Their days are filled with the activities of management: scheduling, reporting, handling relations with parents and the community, and dealing with the multiple crises and special situations that are inevitable in schools" (p. 598). As a result, these duties make it unlikely for principals to have time to spend in classrooms and time to discuss instructional practices with teachers. Furthermore, many principals are "unsure [about] what to look at or how to intervene when they visit classrooms" (p. 599). The U.S. Department of Education (2000a) reported that "Despite the key role that instruction plays in increasing student achievement, only 10 percent of all teachers 'strongly agreed' that their principal talked to them frequently about instructional practices" (p. 27). Today the need for principals to become effective instructional leaders instead of merely serving as managers is all the more pressing because of the growing racial/ethnic mismatch between public school students and school personnel. The fact that the number of children of color in public schools is expected to grow, even as the teaching force continues to be overwhelmingly White has been well-documented (U.S. Department of Education, 2000a). But the racial/ethnic gap between principals and students has been reported less frequently. For example, while the number of female elementary school principals has increased over time, African Americans, Hispanics, and Asian Americans "combined account for only about 15 percent of principals in elementary schools where rapidly growing minority populations are expected to reach 55 percent nationwide by 2004" (Ferrandino, 2001, pp. 440–441).

Therefore, recruiting more qualified educators of color to accept principalships is crucial. However, preparing current and future principals to become effective instructional leaders is equally as important. Tirozzi (2001) said that training principals to improve "the academic achievement and social and emotional well-being of students" (p. 435) should become paramount. For these and other reasons, some researchers have already begun the process of identifying the systemic and individual factors that result in school leadership that actually has a positive effect on student achievement.

Fink, a school superintendent, and Resnick, a school psychologist (2001), described how their urban school district created a pattern of successful leadership that contributed to student achievement for more than a decade. They reported that the district's success rested on the foundation of "nested learning communities." Each school became a learning organization that, under the principal's leadership, started an ongoing quest to improve its ability to teach children. The resulting "culture of learning" required principals to possess the requisite knowledge that enabled them to differentiate between effective and ineffective teaching practices, and to provide teachers with beneficial professional development opportunities.

In another study, Reitzug and Patterson (1998) described how one urban middle school principal, Debbie Pressley, empowered students through her leadership style. Unlike many principals in urban schools, Pressley, an African American, chose not to use a leadership style that sought to "control" students. Instead, her empowerment model was based on a "healthy child" concept that required her to make a personal investment in students' academic, social, and emotional welfare. Reitzug and Patterson identified five themes that characterized Pressley's leadership style: (1) She chose to focus on her interactions with students, instead of focusing primarily on her interactions with adults on campus; (2) she honored students' voices by legitimizing their opinions and concerns; (3) she showed students that she was concerned about them by focusing on academics and sharing her personal expectations with them; (4) she helped students connect to their communities by explaining community expectations and standards to them; and (5) she helped students search for alternative courses of action and alternative possibilities for problem-solving (p. 167).

As researchers, policymakers, and educators continue to address issues pertaining to the preparation, recruitment, and retention of qualified school principals, there is a need for African American parents/guardians and students to enter the discussion. Feedback from both groups might add new insights that could alleviate these problems. In *African American Teens Discuss Their Schooling Experiences* (Thompson, 2002), the students were not asked to discuss their experiences with school administrators. However, some of the interviewees described their experiences with principals as being very limited. For example, one student stated that students rarely saw their high school principal and that he seemed disconnected from them. When the students were asked about specific ways in which public schools could better prepare students for college, nearly 60 percent of the respondents said that more counseling about college was necessary and several interviewees complained about their high school counselors, a topic that will be addressed in further detail in Chapter 13.

In the county in which the majority of parents/guardians who participated in the current study resided, there were more than 1,400 administrators during the 2000–01 school year. Seventy-nine percent were White; 12 percent were Hispanic or Latino; 8 percent were African American, and less than 1 percent were American Indian or Alaskan Native, Asian, Pacific Islander, or Filipino. Although students of color comprised more than 60 percent of the students in the county's public schools, non-Whites only accounted for 21 percent of the administrators. For most of the racial/ethnic groups, there was a higher number of female administrators than males. For example, whereas there were 608 White female administrators, there were 550 White male administrators; whereas there were 96 Hispanic/Latino female administrators, there were only

70 male administrators; and whereas there were 73 African American female administrators, there were only 36 African American male administrators in the public schools in the entire county (California Department of Education, 2001). This chapter will present feedback from the African American parents/guardians who participated in the current study regarding their beliefs about school administrators. Related quotes from the interviews will be included.

DO ADMINISTRATORS AND COUNSELORS CARE ABOUT STUDENTS?

Nearly 60 percent of the African American parents/guardians who participated in the study said that they believed that most school administrators and counselors cared about students. In explaining why she believed that most school administrators cared about students, one parent said that she had reached this conclusion as a result of the quality of the curriculum and classes in which her children were placed. Furthermore, she thought that administrators were effective in working "with a parent if you have a concern about a teacher or counselor." However, 16 percent of the parents/guardians said that most administrators did *not* care about students and one-fourth said they did not know, or they refused to answer this question. For example, a mother of two stated that she didn't know whether or not school administrators cared about students, but "I would like to think so." A mother of three, who participated in the interview phase of the study said that although she believed that most administrators had treated her children fairly, she was uncertain about whether or not they actually cared about students. She remarked, "Out here, the principal only recognizes the kids who are bad, that get sent to the office, or who get suspended. Maybe the principal needs to recognize the students who are doing good, like they did at my kids' other school. And the principal and staff should show that they care more." Conversely, a mother of six said that she did not believe that most public school administrators cared about students, because they appeared to have a deficit mindset (the mindset that students come from deficient backgrounds and the belief that they have a limited aptitude) about students. She stated, "Maybe, it's the way they talk, talking about how the kids need different things. It's just like they're only there to get a paycheck and they have a 'whatever' attitude. I hate to say it, but it's true." Like several parents/guardians, a grandmother said that her contact with school administrators, such as principals and vice principals, was so limited that she couldn't answer the question.

Many parents/guardians also made comments about school counselors. A mother of three school-age children said that she believed that her son's elementary school counselor cared about students "because she sits down with him and then goes to his class with him. Instead of pulling him out of class or sending him to another class when he misbehaves, she helps him in class with his work." Another mother said she believed that counselors cared about students, but she also made an effort to stay in touch with them. "We call them, and if they don't call us back," she stated, "we have sources that will get involved and they tell us exactly what we need to know regarding what our children are or are not doing, and I like that." Like several other interviewees, the mother of a ninth grader and a seventh grader expressed concern about the relationships between school counselors and students. However, she placed the onus on her daughter. She said:

As far as counselors are concerned, I only know the ones who deal with my kids. If you look at the high school, there are so many kids that the counselors don't even get to know the kids really. That's why I've been encouraging my daughter that it's her responsibility to get in there and meet the counselor and ask questions. She's not a problem kid. So, it's not like she's gonna be in the counselor's office all of the time because she's in trouble. If she wants to get to know the counselor, she's going to have to make an effort to go in there, let the counselor know who she is, so when it's time to get scholarships and all of those things, the counselor will know her.

A mother who worked in an elementary school library said that she was concerned that counselors were unable to provide true counseling to students. She explained:

Some of them, I can't really give them that much credit. When you're a counselor, being a psychology major, you have to take the kids' problems and issues seriously and work with them one-on-one. In middle schools, where it's needed more than ever, a lot of counselors give kids who need one-on-one help, the cold shoulder. That's where the transition takes place between trying to grow up and still being a child. I find that middle schools need to have more professional counselors or they need more of something else. There's something missing and I can't put my finger on it.

Fourteen questionnaire items were correlated to the variable representing parents'/guardians' beliefs about whether or not administrators and counselors cared about students. Parents/guardians whose children had been suspended during middle school and/or high school, as well as those who believed that their children's school district was racist, were unlikely to believe that administrators and counselors cared about students. Moreover, the parents/guardians of students who disliked school and/or who disliked reading were also unlikely to believe that most counselors and administrators cared about students. The main factor that was related to parents'/guardians' beliefs about whether or not administrators and counselors cared about students was their belief about how their children had been treated by administrators. The second strongest positive correlation was between whether parents/guardians believed that administrators and counselors cared and their beliefs about whether most teachers cared about students (see Table 8.1).

Table 8.1

Variables That Were Correlated to Whether or Not Parents/Guardians Believed That Most Counselors and Administrators Care about Students in the Order of the Strength of Each Correlation

Variable	Strength of Correlation	Significance
Parents'/guardians' beliefs about administrators' treatment	.63	p < .001
Parents'/guardians' beliefs about whether or not teachers care	.56	p < .001
Suspension level	-.51	p < .02
Public school system rating	.48	p < .001
Benefits of high school course work	.47	p < .003
Benefits of high school homework	.42	p < .01
Benefits of middle school homework	.41	p < .003
High school teachers' rating	.36	p < .01
Elementary teachers' rating	.34	p < .001
School district racial climate	-.30	p < .01
Disliking reading	-.29	p < .01
Benefits of elementary school course work	.27	p < .01
Disliking school	-.25	p < .01
Parents'/guardians' self-rating	.22	p < .03

$N = 96$

HOW ADMINISTRATORS TREAT AFRICAN AMERICAN STUDENTS

Sixty-seven percent of the parents/guardians said that most school administrators had treated their children fairly. A mother of three school-age children said that she believed that administrators had treated her children fairly because "Most of the ones I've come in contact with have shown concern about my children." Another mother said that she believed that most administrators had treated her children fairly because "I've never had any run-ins with them. They're really in charge of the curriculum and seeing that the school is well kept." A mother of two-school age children said that "If there were any issues, the administrators handled them very well." A mother of six believed that school administrators had treated her children fairly because they feared her. "Actually, they knew me and knew what I was capable of doing," she stated. "The principal told me that he appreciated that I would go to him before going to the school board, but most parents would go to the board first."

However, 17 percent of the parents/guardians said that administrators had not treated their children fairly, and 16 percent said that they did not know or they refused to answer this question. Like many parents/guardians, a mother of four said, "I don't know. I don't speak to the administrators. I don't have any contact with them, just the teachers and counselors." Another mother said that, whereas she believed that most administrators at her children's middle school had treated them fairly, "At the high school, I would say that they don't even know my daughter."

The variable representing parents'/guardians' beliefs about administrator treatment was correlated to fourteen other questionnaire items. Six questionnaire items were inversely related to parents'/guardians' beliefs about how their children had been treated by administrators. Parents/guardians who believed that racism was common in their children's school district and/or whose children experienced racism at school were unlikely to believe that administrators had treated their children fairly. The same was true of parents/guardians whose children disliked school, whose children had been suspended from school, and those whose children had been expelled. Furthermore, parents/guardians whose children were enrolled in certain school districts were more likely than others to believe that their children had been treated unfairly by school administrators.

The strongest positive correlations pertained to parents'/guardians' perception of other adults on campus. For example, as mentioned previously, those who believed that administrators cared about children were also likely to believe that administrators had treated their children fairly. Those who believed that most teachers cared and those who rated their children's elementary school and high school teachers as *excellent* or *good* were also likely to believe that administrators had treated their children fairly. The rating that parents/guardians gave to the public school system, and their children's high school homework, elementary course work, and their beliefs about whether or not their children planned to attend college were also positively correlated to their beliefs about administrators' treatment of their children (see Table 8.2).

SUMMARY

The majority of the African American parents/guardians who completed the questionnaire said they believed that most school administrators and counselors cared about students and had treated their children fairly. Those who were disinclined to believe that administrators cared about students also tended to have children who had been suspended from secondary school or from more than one level of school. They also were more likely to believe that racism was common in their children's school district. Moreover, their children tended to have a negative attitude about reading and about school.

Five negative schooling factors were linked to parents'/guardians' beliefs about how administrators had treated their children. The parents/guardians of

Table 8.2

Variables That Were Correlated to Whether or Not Parents/Guardians Believed That Most Administrators Had Treated Their Children Fairly in the Order of the Strength of Each Correlation

Variable	Strength of Correlation	Significance
Parents'/guardians' beliefs about whether or not administrators care	.63	p < .001
High school teachers' rating	.49	p < .001
Parents'/guardians' beliefs about whether or not teachers care	.49	p < .001
Benefits of high school homework	.47	p < .002
Experiencing racism	-.46	p < .001
Public school system rating	.45	p < .001
Expulsion	-.43	p < .001
Elementary teachers' rating	.40	p < .001
School district racial climate	-.31	p < .01
Benefits of elementary course work	.29	p < .004
Suspension	-.27	p < .01
Disliking school	-.24	p < .01
Believing that children planned to attend college	.23	p < .02
Specific school district	-.21	p < .03

$N = 108$

children who had been suspended, expelled, and/or who experienced racism, were unlikely to believe that administrators had treated their children fairly. These factors might be linked. For example, it is possible that the parents/guardians of children who had been suspended felt that their children were suspended because of racism, and they might have concluded that the administrators in charge had behaved in racist ways and/or had treated their children unfairly. Because African American children are disproportionately represented among suspended students in the school district in which the majority of parents/guardians had children enrolled, this might be the case. The parents/guardians of children who disliked school were also unlikely to believe that administrators had treated their children fairly. In a previous narrative, a mother described how children from certain neighborhoods were singled out for negative treatment by an elementary school principal. She also stated that an administrator had grabbed her son's arm and a principal had threatened to call the police on him. In another narrative, a mother said that her son had been singled out and labeled as a discipline problem at one school. However, when she transferred him to a different school, the principal attempted to focus on his good qualities. These examples shed light on why there might be a link between children's attitude about school, negative schooling experiences, and parents'/guardians' perception of administrator treatment.

Another finding was that the specific school district in which children attended school was correlated to their parents'/guardians' beliefs about whether or not administrators had treated their children fairly. This suggests that certain school districts have administrators who are more likely than others to be perceived as treating African American children fairly. Fink and Resnick (2001) described how one entire urban school district created a leadership program that had a positive impact on students. Reitzug and Patterson (1998) explained how one principal, Debbie Pressley, empowered students. Goldberg (2001) described the results of interviews that he had conducted with forty-three eminent educational leaders since 1989. Five important qualities surfaced: (1) Each leader had a strong belief in the importance of his/her work; (2) each leader was courageous enough to maintain his/her beliefs even when they became unpopular; (3) each possessed a social justice consciousness that included the belief that issues relating to racism and poverty must be addressed; (4) each had high standards and was willing to invest years of service in his/her causes; and (5) each "exemplified situational mastery, the happy marriage of personal skills and accomplishment" (p. 757).

The results from this chapter and the aforementioned examples from research strongly suggest that (1) it is possible for principals to become effective school leaders; and (2) effective school leadership should have a positive impact on student achievement. If it isn't affecting student achievement in a positive way, it is ineffective. Moreover, the feedback from the African American parents/guardians can be utilized to improve the recruitment, preparation, and professional development of school leaders who work with African American children.

9

Improving the Public School System

For decades researchers and policymakers have searched for ways to improve public schools. However, most school reform efforts have failed to make widespread and lasting improvements (U.S. Department of Education, 1998). In its "Tools for Schools" study, the U.S. Department of Education (1998) examined twenty-seven school reform models that were funded by the National Institute on the Education of At-Risk Students. The researchers found that effective reform models are flexible; they are based on current research; they involve all aspects of the school organization—not only academic standards, but social relations as well; and they offer guidance, technical assistance, and instructions on implementing the model so that reform can occur at multiple school sites. The newest education reform legislation, "The No Child Left Behind Act," (2002) promises to make sweeping changes that are designed to close the persistent achievement gap (U.S. Department of Education, 2001b)—something no previous reform effort has yet accomplished. In the meantime, however, the widespread belief that public schools are in need of improvement remains popular.

There are many reasons why there is a common perception that public schools are in need of reform. The most obvious is the fact that the achievement gap continues to persist. Children of color, particularly African Americans and Hispanics, and poor children in public schools tend to lag behind their peers of other racial/ethnic groups (National Center for Education Statistics, 2000, 2001). A second reason is that a high percentage of the public believes that numerous aspects of schools are in need of improvement. For example, in "The 33rd Annual Phi Delta Kappa/Gallup Poll of the Public's Attitudes Toward the Public Schools," Rose and Gallup (2001) reported that when asked to grade the public schools in their communities, 51 percent of the respondents gave them an "A" or "B." However, a higher percentage (62 percent) of parents of public school students than respondents with no children in public schools (47 percent) did so (p. 43). Conversely, when asked to grade the public schools "in the nation as a whole," only 23 percent of the respondents gave them an "A" or "B." Moreover, a smaller percentage of nonpublic school parents did so. Nevertheless, when asked whether reforming the existing public school system was better than creating an alternate system, 72 percent of the respondents wanted the existing system to be reformed. They did not want to see an alternate system instituted (p. 44).

In its annual report, "Quality Counts" (2001), the editors of *Education Week*, graded American public schools in many states on five categories: standards and accountability; improving teacher quality; school climate; adequacy; and equity. In the category of "standards and accountability," 47 percent of the states earned an "A" or "B" and 41 percent earned a "D" or "F." In the category of "improving teacher quality," no state earned an "A" and only 8 percent earned a "B." However, 44 percent earned a "D" or "F." Of the thirty-five states that received a grade for "school climate," no state earned an "A" and only 3 percent earned a "B." However, 65 percent earned a "D" or an "F." In the category of "adequacy of resources," nearly half the states earned an "A" or "B" and only 16 percent earned a "D" or "F." In the last category, "equity," 18 percent of the fifty states earned an "A" or "B," but nearly 40 percent earned a "D" or "F" (p. 89).

The aforementioned examples underscore the fact that public schools are in need of improvement in numerous areas. As policymakers, educators, and researchers search for solutions, inviting parents/guardians into the discussion can be beneficial. Throughout this book, thus far, data from African American parents/guardians who participated in the study pertained to various aspects of their children's and their own schooling experiences. This chapter presents feedback from the parents/guardians about specific ways in which they would like to see the public school system improved, and how they rated the public school system. A related narrative is included.

HOW AFRICAN AMERICAN PARENTS/GUARDIANS RATED THE PUBLIC SCHOOL SYSTEM

When asked to rate the public school system, 57 percent of the parents/ guardians who completed the questionnaire rated it as *excellent* or *good*. However, nearly one-fifth gave it a low rating (see Table 9.1). A mother of two said that she rated the public school system as good because:

I feel that the curriculum that they're being taught and especially a particular principal at their elementary school made it a priority that the kids do their very best. They had some requirements that I may not have been happy with. I may have thought that some of the teachers were too strenuous, but, then, when the principal left, those requirements became options. Then, I felt like what the kids were given wasn't that much.

Another mother of two rated the public school system as *good*, because it gave her children "the materials that they need to be competitive with private

Table 9.1
How Parents/Guardians Rated the Public School System

Rating	Percent
Poor	2
Needs to improve	17
Fair	22
Good	32
Excellent	25
No answer	2

$N = 129$

schools and with the outside world." A mother who worked at an elementary school rated the public school system as *excellent*, because "It's easy for me to have access to the teachers. I volunteer my time during my lunch break, and I go in there and help the teachers with whatever they need help with. I read to the kids, help them write, and help them make projects. I consider that an excellent thing." Another mother who worked at an elementary school also gave the public school system an *excellent* rating, explaining, "When the kids are down, they help them build themselves up." An interviewee explained why she rated her children's school district as *fair:*

I've seen better schools. My seventh grader had a teacher in Los Angeles who had every kid in her class knowing how to read before they finished that kindergarten class. But I noticed in this district, the kindergarten students didn't know how to read when they finished kindergarten. I said, "That must have been one good teacher for her to have the whole class reading." I mean everybody in that classroom knew how to read. My son knew how to read very well when he was in kindergarten and first grade. But my nephew didn't learn how to read in kindergarten in this district. He had a good teacher, but he didn't know how to read. He was reading a little bit when he finished first grade, but not as good as he should have been. If this district had better teachers, like some that I've seen in the past, I would have rated it as *good*, but I don't think the teachers are that good.

The rating that parents/guardians gave to the public school system was correlated to twenty-five other questionnaire items. Six variables were inversely related to how they rated the public school system. Four of the six pertained to racism at school, indicating that parents'/guardians' belief that racism was common in the school district and their children's experiences with racism had a negative impact on how they rated the school system. Parents/guardians whose children had problems with reading comprehension or who had been suspended from more than one school level were also unlikely to give a high rating to the public school system.

Of the variables that were positively correlated to how parents/guardians rated the public school system, the strongest factors were how they rated elementary and high school teachers, whether they believed that teachers and administrators cared about students, and their beliefs about the benefits of their children's high school course work. Their public school rating was also linked to whether or not they believed that their children had been treated fairly by administrators. However, two problems—problems with reading rate and with writing—were also positively correlated, indicating that the parents/guardians of children who were struggling in these areas still had a high opinion of the public school system (see Table 9.2).

AFRICAN AMERICAN PARENTS'/GUARDIANS' RECOMMENDATIONS FOR IMPROVING THE PUBLIC SCHOOL SYSTEM

Sixty-six percent of the parents/guardians who completed the questionnaire wrote recommendations about how the public school system could be improved. These recommendations can be divided into nine categories (see Table 9.3). Each suggestion will be discussed below, along with related comments.

Improve Teachers' Attitudes, Instructional Practices, and Their Relationships with Students

Thirty-three percent of the parents/guardians who answered the question said that the public school system could be improved if teachers' attitudes, instructional practices, and/or their relationships with students were better. Many parents/guardians emphasized the need for teachers to provide more assistance to students during class time. They said that teachers should be willing to offer more one-on-one help for struggling students, and they should do periodic checks to ensure that students understand the subject matter. A parent of two elementary school children wrote on the questionnaire, "The public school system could be improved if teachers spent more time on a particular subject during the course of one week. Instead of studying several subjects in one day, let kids study one subject three to four days." During the interview phase of the study, another parent made a similar comment. She stated, "I would like to see more focus on singular subjects as opposed to everything at once. I think they need to spend more time, instead of jumping from subject to subject." A mother who also participated in the interview phase of the study criticized the education system for putting too much pressure on children. She explained:

I think a lot of work needs to be done with all this testing that's taking place. A lot of teachers feel frustrated, because, basically, what they're doing is teaching the test, and I don't think that's necessarily good for the kids. If they're just teaching the test, then

Table 9.2

Variables That Were Correlated to How Parents/Guardians Rated the Public School System in the Order of the Strength of Each Correlation

Variable	Strength of Correlation	Significance
Elementary teachers' rating	.55	p < .001
High school teachers' rating	.55	p < .001
Parents'/guardians' beliefs about whether or not teachers care	.50	p < .001
Benefits of high school course work	.50	p < .001
Beliefs about whether or not administrators and counselors care	.48	p < .001
Parents'/guardians' beliefs about administrators' treatment	.45	p < .001
Experiencing racism	-.43	p < .001
Racism source	-.43	p < .01
Benefits of high school homework	.41	p < .004
Benefits of elementary school course work	.39	p < .001
Experiencing racism frequently	-.38	p < .01
Benefits of middle school course work	.32	p < .01
School district racial climate	-.32	p < .003
Parents'/guardians' self-rating	.31	p < .001
Benefits of elementary school homework	.30	p < .001
Benefits of middle school homework	.28	p < .03
Reading rate problem	.27	p < .003
Buying books for children	.26	p < .003
Reading to children	.26	p < .004
Listening to children read	.21	p < .02
Reading comprehension problem	-.21	p < .02
Writing problem	.19	p < .03
Children owning books	.19	p < .04
Value placed on children's education	.19	p < .04
Suspension level	-.19	p < .04

$N = 126$

there's probably a lot of learning that's not taking place. The kids are all stressed out about passing the test and there's not really any freedom to just be a student and just learn or explore. It's always to pass a test.

Another interviewee urged teachers to "go the extra mile for the kids. If the kid is not catching on, make sure they catch on, and don't move them on to the next level when they don't know the first level. Because they're not going to learn the next step without knowing the first one." A stepparent urged

Table 9.3
African American Parents'/Guardians' Recommendations for Improving the Public School System

Recommendation	Percent
Improve Teachers' Attitudes, Instructional Practices, and Their Relationships With Students	33
Other/Miscellaneous Recommendations	27
Improve After School Programs	25
Improve Relationships With Parents/Guardians	18
Provide Students with Better Equipment, Materials and Supplies	14
Reduce Class Size	13
Improve the Curriculum	6
Treat Children Fairly	5
Improve Homework Practices	5

$N = 85$

teachers to raise their expectations and to stop letting kids who can't read graduate. Another mother spoke at length about how the public school system could be improved, stating:

I think that teachers need to take more interest in each individual child if they can. If enough teachers pulled together and cared, then maybe we could get the help that the kids need, because a lot of the kids aren't getting this from home. And some of them aren't ever gonna be able to get it from home. But teachers still have a responsibility to the community to teach our children. I do not believe that it's the teacher's job to teach your child morality; that should start at home. I understand too that when the teachers have to deal with discipline problems—children who are not being instructed at home, who do whatever they want to do at home, and feel they can come to school and do the same thing—that's double work. It's not the teachers' job to raise your child morally. But it is their job to find that little niche maybe that the child needs, the interests they have, the potential that they have. Don't just go there and get paid, and do your day's work and let the child be neglected as far as his education. More teachers need to be interested in what that child needs.

Another parent said, "I think that if teachers showed that they cared a little more, the system would improve. I have never really rated teachers as being bad, but I've seen teachers in other districts who care more about students than the teachers do here. It makes a big difference and it affects how much kids learn."

In explaining why she believed that teachers needed more training, one mother said, "Sometimes you may have a teacher that's good in one subject or one phase of math, but may not have expertise in another. That teacher will have the tendency to skip over that subject. Then, your child is missing an important part of his education that is needed for the next year. So teachers need opportunities to gain more knowledge about other subjects."

A grandmother summarized the sentiments of many of the interviewees by saying, "You can't keep a bad teacher around, because the future of our children is at stake. If you have a lot of complaints about a teacher, you know that there is something wrong."

A father wanted teachers to take students' individual needs and desires into consideration. He explained:

The teachers want the curriculum to be noticeable through the students. They're presenting the kids with questions and all the answers, but they're not listening to the child. The child might say "That's boring. I can't understand it. Could you give me something else to read?" Most teachers are so firm about their educational background that they just force these kids into doing things that are not a part of who they are. Everybody can't be a mathematician. Everybody can't be an English teacher or a chemist. Some kids have a vocational skill that will enable them to take the simplest thing apart and put it back together. Sometimes, I think some teachers are so systematic that they don't give kids credit for the same thing that they are trying to teach. For example, one kid might not be able to express himself in English well, but if you get him to sing it to music or try and paint a picture of it, it can say the same thing in a different form. I don't think the teachers understand the form in which most kids present their education or how educated kids are.

This same father also wanted teachers to consider individual learning styles and personality differences among students as well as sociocultural and socioeconomic differences as well. He stated:

The school system needs to improve because there is such diversity in the kids' backgrounds. You have some who come from urban areas and others who come from suburban areas, and their struggles could be different. For kids in rural areas or in the ghetto, it is hard because they have to overcome a lot of obstacles as far as drugs, a new dad in the home, and not having the material things that someone else has. They deal with a lot of struggles, and a lot of those struggles take on repressed feelings. They hold a lot of that in, and a lot of times they try to take it out on others or lash out these frustrations in school.

If some of the teachers can have a heart to understand their struggles and just spend a little time with them, I think that will be great. Teachers should be patient and know that it's going to take time to sink in. The more patience the teacher has with them, the better the relationship will be between the kid and the teacher. With that relationship, the child has a mentor that he can look up to. Maybe they'll say, "Mrs. So-and-So says that, in her quiet time, she reads a book. Or when she gets frustrated, she sits down and reads poetry." Maybe, these kids can take on those same personality traits and maybe it can help the teachers as well.

Improve After-School Programs

Twenty-five percent of the parents/guardians who made recommendations suggested that more after-school programs be offered and that the quality of existing programs be improved. Many parents/guardians spoke about creating, expanding, or improving after-school tutorial services. Others suggested that more programs be added, including sports programs starting in elementary school. A father said he wanted a longer school year and better after-school programs. "I would like to see it improve in the time they give to kids," he stated. "I think there should be after-school activities that will allow the kids to make a choice. Will it be fun to stay at school or go home? I think they should go to school ten months, because it takes some kids longer to catch on to what they're trying to teach them."

Improve Relationships with Parents/Guardians

Eighteen percent of the parents/guardians who made recommendations said that the public school system would improve if relationships between parents/guardians and school personnel improved. Three themes emerged: (1) African American parents/guardians want better communication with school personnel; (2) administrators and teachers must actively seek to improve parent/guardian involvement at school; and (3) parents/guardians themselves must take the initiative to become more involved in their children's education.

Many of the parents/guardians who rated their own level of participation in their children's education as *excellent* or *good*, were critical of other parents/guardians and blamed them for not being more actively involved in their children's education. One interviewee said:

Most of the kids don't have parents at home doing anything for them. I see third and fourth graders get up in the morning and dress themselves. Where are these parents? I see grandparents raising these kids. It's not the grandparents' job to raise these kids. So, that's why a lot of people say, "Well, the parents don't care." Well, maybe a few don't care. It's on the parents, but a lot has to do with the teachers.

A mother of two who rated her own involvement in her children's education as *good*, also discussed why parents should become more involved in their children's education. She stated:

I think that parent involvement is essential in today's world, and we don't have enough of it. Kids who don't have it will have to have an inner will to succeed, because without parental assistance, they will have to want to succeed. If they don't want to, they won't. There is nothing like getting it from home. In the new millennium, we have households where most parents are working and they think that the material things are enough and that is not the case. We need to spend more time, quality time. Even if you're working, quality time is important.

A mother of six children who rated her own academic assistance to her children as *good*, criticized her neighbors for their lack of involvement in their children's education. She said, "Where we live, no parents are concerned. They're hooked on drugs or drinking and the school knows that. So that's why a lot of times they take advantage and don't support the kids like they really should. They don't have to, because nobody is going to the school board. Nobody is going to do anything about it."

Another mother said, "I think parents need to know that they should insist that their child gets what they came to get from the school. If they can't read, then that is on both the parent and the school to make sure that they can. Don't wait until the last minute for them to send something home saying your child is failing. Parents and teachers need to work together, so each can know what's going on."

Whereas some parents/guardians blamed other parents/guardians for their lack of involvement, most who made recommendations pertaining to parents/ guardians placed the onus on school personnel. For example, many parents/ guardians urged administrators and teachers to communicate with parents/guardians in a timely manner about their children's progress, particularly about discipline problems, poor grades, and possible grade retention. One parent wrote on her questionnaire, "The public school system could be improved by making sure the kids are understanding what is being taught to them and if the kids are having problems, contact the parents. Some parents still care, but you never know until you go that extra mile." Several parents/guardians wrote that teachers should invite parents/guardians into the classroom to observe during class hours. A stepparent said that "Parent meetings should be held at more convenient times." Another parent said that if schools provided transportation for parents/guardians who wanted to attend school functions but had no transportation, more African Americans would attend.

Provide Students with Better Equipment, Materials, and Supplies

Fourteen percent of the parents/guardians who made recommendations said the public school system could be improved if schools had better equipment, supplies, and/or materials. Many parents/guardians mentioned that more books and a wider variety of books were needed. Others wanted more computers for students. Still others stated that school buildings needed renovation. One mother remarked, "I would like to see more computers put in, because technology is advancing. This is the thing of the future and our young Black kids need to know about it. They need to know more about computers. This will improve their lives. So, yes, I would like for them to invest more money into putting more computers in the school and into training the children to use them."

Reduce Class Size

Thirteen percent of the parents/guardians who made recommendations said the public school system could be improved if students had smaller classes. Many respondents felt that overcrowded classrooms were detrimental to their children by preventing teachers from being able to provide students with the individualized attention the students needed. A mother of four stated, "I look at my one son who is in the Resource Specialist Program and I feel like there shouldn't be more than ten kids in that class, because those kids need additional help."

Other Recommendations

Twenty-seven percent of the parents/guardians made "miscellaneous" recommendations. Among these recommendations were more field trips. Some parents/guardians emphasized the importance of field trips to colleges and businesses to provide children with exposure to life outside their community. Some parents/guardians said that "dress code" policies should be improved. One wrote, "There should be more teaching and less concern about the way kids dress." However, another believed that the dress code should be stricter. Many parents/guardians also said that the school system would benefit if discipline practices and school safety issues were improved. A recurring recommendation was that school personnel should pay more attention to students' problems. Several parents/guardians also said that "year-round" schools (a system that was implemented in California to reduce overcrowding) were disadvantageous to their children and they called for a return to the traditional September–June academic calendar. Some parents/guardians also criticized the standardized testing system, saying that it set children up for failure. Among the other recommendations were (1) increase church involvement in schools; (2) increase administrators' and counselors' involvement with students and parents; (3) provide students with internships leading to possible employment opportunities; and (4) increase the number of teachers' aides and tutors in every classroom.

Six percent of the parents/guardians recommended that the curriculum be improved. Several stressed the need for a culturally relevant curriculum to which African American children could relate. Others suggested that courses be improved in general and some said that the technology component of the curriculum should be strengthened, by giving students more time to use computers. One parent said that the curriculum should include more music, art, and theater.

Five percent of the study participants said that the public school system would improve if adults at school treated children more fairly. One parent urged teachers to "be fair to all students, especially when giving out awards."

Another parent wrote, "We need more educated teachers who accept our Black children and their differences."

Five percent of the respondents also suggested that homework practices be improved. One parent wrote, "I would love to see the public school system improved by teachers making sure that kids understand the homework when they send it home, instead of giving them homework and asking parents with no knowledge of it to do it." The narrative that follows is based on an interview with a foster father who explained his recommendations for improving the public school system in detail.

ALL OF THEM HAVE BRIGHT IDEAS

During his interview, Mr. Brown, a fifty-eight-year-old who co-owned a daycare center with his wife, discussed the positive and negative aspects of the public school system by sharing examples from his adult children's and his three school-age foster sons' schooling experiences. Like Mrs. Pulver, the foster parent whose narrative was presented in Chapter 4, before becoming foster parents, Mr. Brown and his wife had successfully reared their own biological children. Two were undergraduates at historically Black colleges. Mr. Brown attributed his children's academic success to his and his wife's commitment to their education. He stated:

When I grew up, there were no college graduates in my family. We didn't have the chance to go to college because we had to work. When we had our children, we stressed education, knowledge, assertiveness, dedication, and having a good character. We took our children to school every day from kindergarten on. We were interested in every aspect of their education. We've always instilled in them that "Education is first and foremost." We bought a phonics program when it first came out. On top of that, we went to every meeting that had anything to do with improving our children's education.

I wasn't the kind of parent that always looked for an "A." If you made "A's" fine. But doing your best was what I was concerned about. My daughter was valedictorian in junior high and high school. So, I'm proud of that, and I'm proud of me and my wife.

At the time of his interview, Mr. Brown was applying the same mindset and strategies that he and his wife had utilized in rearing their own children to their three foster sons. He'd had custody of each of the boys, two kindergartners and a third grader, for more than five years. Because their biological mothers had abused alcohol and/or drugs, each of the boys suffered from learning and developmental disabilities that required them to be placed in the Special Education program. Moreover, although they had not been officially diagnosed as suffering from ADD, Mr. Brown believed that each boy suffered from it.

Because he was pleased with some aspects of how the public school system had assisted his foster sons academically, Mr. Brown rated it as *excellent* and his children's elementary teachers as *good*. He was mostly pleased with the classroom management capabilities of teachers. He stated, "Most of the kids in my sons' classes don't have behavior problems. They keep those kids under control." Mr. Brown was also pleased that he had a good rapport with his sons' teachers and that the teachers were willing to coordinate their efforts with those of Mr. and Mrs. Brown's program for the children. According to Mr. Brown:

You have to give these children things to do; keep them busy. My granddaughter, who is in kindergarten, is very bright. She'll sit down with them and try to work with them on letters. Then, they go to school and the school tries to reinforce that. We talked to the teacher about it. She has her own curriculum with her staff, and they try to reinforce the same things that we try to do here.

Conversely, Mr. Brown was displeased with some aspects of the boys' schooling. One aspect concerned the way in which teachers perceive and communicate with parents, and teachers' attitude about teaching. He explained:

I think a lot of teachers have to be reeducated, and then, on top of that, not just be there for the paycheck. If you're dealing with children, especially in an area that has a high rate of one-parent families, the families themselves don't have an education past twelfth grade. Teachers have to learn how to deal with those parents, in order to get their attention and to have those parents start working with their children. Those teachers need to learn how to communicate with people. They should not be standoffish and they should not put anybody down, because I'm sure it has probably happened. And I'm not talking about coming in with your credentials, because you guys have a bad habit of coming in and saying, "I have a Ph.D. in this. I'm a psychologist in that." Just come in and act like a normal person.

The second source of Mr. Brown's displeasure pertained to the number of underqualified teachers and substitute teachers in the school system. He stated:

Sometimes situations and people have a tendency to suppress a child from being able to give out that gift that he or she really has. That's unfortunate. I would love to see teachers give a child that looks like me, a shot. Bring out the best in them. All of them have bright ideas and all of them are bright. But, right now, it's quite easy to get a teaching job. That's the bad part of it, because sometimes, you get anybody. That's what the children have been suffering with. There are pedophiles and people who are only there for a paycheck. The kids who come to my daycare center after school tell me things. They're in fourth and fifth grade. I would ask them what homework they had. They would say, "Nothing." I would ask, "Well, what did they have you do in school today?" They would say, "Sit in the classroom, doing nothing." That so-called teacher that is only there for three to five days is not really being beneficial or living up to the creed or the code that he or she is supposed to.

The third source of his displeasure pertained to teachers' attitudes and expectations about students. He wanted them to have a more positive attitude about children and to find ways to identify their strengths. He stated:

All children have something to offer. The sad part is that nobody really sits down with them one-on-one to help develop their potential. If teachers can help develop it, they will see a major turnaround in how we deal with each other and how our children deal with others. But there are backlashes against our children. People look at you from the outside. They don't look at you from within. If a child comes from a bad home, he or she has three strikes against him. Then, when he goes to school, the first thing they look at (because I've seen it in my children's classes) is the type of clothes that he's wearing and whether or not his hair is combed. Whether this child has potential or not, they've already labeled this child. Now, when you start labeling a child, that label will stick. That means that teachers have a problem child on their hands. The school system leaves a lot to be desired and a lot of things are wrong. There are some good teachers, but the environment has a lot to do with it. Cruel kids have a lot to do with it. Parents, teachers, and administrators need to learn how to distinguish between what the child looks like and how that child acts, as opposed to what that child might really bring to the world. Who knows, you might have a president there, or maybe, someone who can save somebody's life.

SUMMARY

This chapter presented feedback from African American parents/guardians regarding specific ways in which the public school system could be improved. Like the public school parents in Rose and Gallup's poll (2001), a high percentage of the African American parents/guardians rated the public school system as *excellent* or *good*, but 41 percent rated it as less than good. Parents'/guardians' level of satisfaction with the public school system was positively linked to their level of satisfaction with teachers, course work, and homework. It was also positively related to their beliefs about whether or not most teachers and administrators cared about students, as well as their own self-rating, and certain strategies that they utilized to assist their children academically. Conversely, negative schooling factors pertaining to racism, suspension from school, and having children who had a reading comprehension problem were linked to lower levels of parent/guardian satisfaction with the public school system. Also like the parents in Rose and Gallup's poll, in which more than 70 percent wanted the existing system reformed rather than creating an alternate system, the African American parents/guardians wanted to see the existing system improved, instead of scrapping it entirely. None said that it was hopeless or that it should be eradicated.

There were two main ways in which a fourth or more of the parents/ guardians wanted to see the public school system improved. More than a third said that teachers' attitudes, instructional practices, and their relations with students are in need of improvement. Problems related to these issues have surfaced repeatedly in many of the narratives in previous chapters. Some parents/guardians have complained that their children were subjected to low expectations and low standards, and were singled out as discipline problems early in their schooling. Several parents/guardians also believed that many teachers were unwilling to give their children the extra help that they needed. In this chapter, Mr. Brown was critical of teachers who judge African American children solely on the basis of their physical appearance. He wanted teachers to realize that all children "have bright ideas" and potential.

One-fourth of the parents/guardians recommended that after-school programs be improved and that more after-school programs be offered. Some parents/guardians wanted high-quality tutorial programs to assist students after school. Others wanted after-school programs to offer fun activities that would give students positive options.

This chapter added the voices of African American parents/guardians to the ongoing discussion of how the public school system can be improved. Just as many narratives and quotes from the interviews indicate that there are problems to be addressed, they also clearly show that African American parents/guardians believe in the potential of the existing system.

Part III
African American Parents/Guardians
Discuss Other Issues

10

Racism

Racism and issues pertaining to racism have been studied extensively. Nieto (2000) differentiated between institutional racism and individualized racism. Individualized racism is targeted at a specific individual. In schools, institutional racism can surface through common practices, such as ability tracking, low expectations and standards for certain students, and the percentage of under-qualified teachers in certain schools. Some researchers have even argued that the institutional racism that is embedded in the American public school system is set up to perpetuate class differences that predispose certain racial/ethnic groups to remain at a lower socioeconomic status.

In her study of factors contributing to the poor achievement of five African American males, White-Johnson (2001) found that although the students felt that they were treated differently than other students by adults on campus, they did not consider this to be racist behavior. Moreover, the students appeared to be unaware of the manifestations and even the existence of institutional racism. In *African American Teens Discuss Their Schooling Experiences*, Thompson (2002) reached a similar conclusion. Although the majority of the teens said that they had not experienced racism at school, 43 percent said that they had. Moreover, nearly 60 percent said that they knew another student who had experienced racism at school and the majority believed that, although it was uncommon, racism existed at their high school. For example, several students said that racial slurs were so common at their high school that they had learned to ignore them. Students who had been retained during elementary school or placed in the Special Education program during elementary school were more likely than others to say that they had experienced racism at school. Most of the students who stated that they had experienced racism at school said that the culprit was another student. However, nearly one-third said that the culprit was an adult on campus. Despite the fact that questionnaire data and some of the narratives in Thompson's study revealed examples of institutional racism, few students associated these practices with racism. It appeared that their definition of racism tended to be limited to individual as opposed to institutional racism. This chapter presents the results of feedback from the African American parents/guardians regarding several issues pertaining to racism at school. Three related narratives from interviews are also included.

EXPERIENCING RACISM AT SCHOOL

Twenty-eight percent of the parents/guardians said that their children had experienced some type of racism at school. However, although 44 percent of the parents/guardians said that their children did *not* experience racism at school, another 28 percent did not answer the question. Therefore, the number of parents/guardians whose children experienced racism at school might have been higher. According to the parents/guardians, children were more likely to experience racism during elementary school as opposed to middle school or high school. However, 27 percent of the parents/guardians indicated that their children experienced racism at more than one level of their schooling. The majority of the parents/guardians said that the racism occurred rarely or occasionally, but 14 percent of those whose children had experienced racism at school said that it occurred frequently.

Experiencing racism at school was correlated to seventeen other questionnaire items. The majority were inversely related to this variable, and only six were positively related. The questionnaire items that were positively related to this variable indicate that the parents/guardians of children who were suspended and/or expelled from school were more likely to state that their children had experienced racism at school. The number of school-age children in a home and parents'/guardians' perception of the school district's racial climate were also linked to having children who experienced racism at school. Moreover, parents/guardians of students in certain school districts were more likely than others to say their children experienced racism at school.

Questionnaire items that were inversely related to experiencing racism at school indicate that parents/guardians who believed that school administrators had treated their children fairly were unlikely to have children who experienced racism at school. The same was true of African American parents/guardians who believed that their children's elementary school and/or high school teachers and the public school system had done an *excellent* or *good* job. Parents'/guardians' beliefs about the benefits of their children's elementary school homework and course work, and middle school and high school homework were also negatively related to having children who experienced racism at school. Those who believed that the work was *beneficial* were unlikely to have children who experienced racism at school. Furthermore, parents/guardians who rated their own academic assistance to their children as *excellent* or *good* and those whose children liked to read were also unlikely to have children who experienced racism at school (see Table 10.1).

Table 10.1
Variables That Were Correlated to Experiencing Racism at School in the
Order of the Strength of Each Correlation

Variable	Strength of Correlation	Significance
Parents'/guardians' beliefs about administrators' treatment	-.46	p < .001
High school teachers' rating	-.45	p < .001
Public school system rating	-.43	p < .001
Elementary teachers' rating	-.41	p < .001
School district racial climate	.40	p < .001
Parents'/guardians' beliefs about whether or not teachers care	-.39	p < .001
Experiencing racism frequently	.37	p < .02
Benefits of high school homework	-.35	p < .03
Number of school-age children	.32	p < .002
Benefits of middle school homework	-.30	p < .03
Suspension	.28	p < .01
Benefits of elementary homework	-.27	p < .01
Children's attitude about reading	-.25	p < .02
Parents'/guardians' self-rating	-.24	p < .02
Expulsion	.23	p < .03
Benefits of elementary school course work	-.23	p < .03
Specific school district	.22	p < .04

$N = 36$

THE SOURCES OF RACISM

More than half of the parents/guardians who stated that their children experienced racism at school said that the source was other students, but nearly
40 percent said the source was an adult on campus, such as a staff member, a
teacher, or an administrator. Teachers were more than twice as likely as staff
members or administrators to be cited. Nine percent of the respondents whose
children experienced racism said that it came from both students and adults on
campus.

One mother said she noticed that racism among students was much more
prevalent in the previous school district in which her children had attended
school. She explained:

When we first moved out here from Los Angeles, we lived in _____ and we were in a Mexican area. My kids experienced prejudice. That is something that I never experienced. I see it on TV, but my kids actually experienced it. The Mexican kids were calling them "Niggers," and telling them, "I don't want to sit next to you Nigger," and all kinds of stuff. They would also treat them badly when they would be walking home from school. My kids really experienced some terrible prejudice when we lived there and I had to get them out of that school.

I took action. We had a meeting. It wasn't just one kid; it was several different families. We all talked about it. My daughter used to come home crying because in class, they would be doing an activity, and everybody would have to pick a partner. She would be somebody's partner and everyone else in the class would have a partner. Then, one Mexican kid would say, "You're going to be partners with that Nigger?" So then, because one Mexican kid said that, the girl that my daughter was partners with wouldn't want to be her partner anymore. They were calling my daughter "Nigger," and she would be the only little girl without a partner, because she was the only Black kid in class. I said, "Oh no! My kids can't be experiencing this. I don't believe this."

I asked her what the teacher said, and she said the teacher knew. Then, my other girls would come home telling me what happened to them in class. They were all experiencing prejudice at that school. And their principal was a Black woman!

So, I drove around to find a new place to live. I wanted them to go to a school where there are Black kids, Whites, all different races of kids. I grew up with Mexicans. I lived with Mexicans. Mexicans were my best friends. We ate at their house. They ate at our house. I grew up in East Los Angeles and they would never call us "Nigger." Now, my kids are in a good school. There are Black kids, White kids, Chinese kids, Mexican kids, and all kinds of kids. They have the best teachers, and my kids are always getting awards. I love that school.

The source of racism and whether or not students experienced racism from more than one source was correlated to nine other questionnaire items. Only one was positively related to this variable. Parents/guardians whose children experienced racism from adults or from both students and adults on campus were more likely to offer "other" types of academic assistance to their children than the most frequently cited types of assistance (see Chapter 4). The inverse relationships indicate that the children of parents/guardians who placed less value on their education and whose parents/guardians assigned low ratings to their children's middle school homework and the public school system were more likely than others to experience racism from adults on campus or from both adults and students. These parents/guardians were also less likely than others to take their children to the public library, to encourage them to read, to buy books for them, to help them with homework, and to believe that their children planned to go to college (see Table 10.2).

TYPES OF RACISM

Offensive name-calling and derogatory comments were the most commonly cited types of racism that were perpetrated by other students. For example,

Table 10.2
Variables That Were Correlated to the Source of Racism in the Order of the
Strength of Each Correlation

Variable	Strength of Correlation	Significance
Benefits of middle school homework	-.44	p < .02
Public school system rating	-.43	p < .01
Helping with homework	-.39	p < .02
Assisting children in other ways	.37	p < .03
Value placed on children's education	-.37	p < .03
Believing that children planned to attend college	-.37	p < .04
Encouraging children to read	-.36	p < .03
Taking children to the public library	-.36	p < .04
Buying books for children	-.35	p < .04

$N = 36$

several parents/guardians said that their children had been called the "N word" at school. Some parents in racially mixed families said their children were subjected to racism from other students because of their biracialism. The mother of a light-skinned boy said that he "was frequently called 'White boy' at school" by other students. Another mother said that during elementary school, "Some White girl told my daughter that she was Black and ugly."

Although a few parents/guardians said their children were also called racially offensive names by adults on campus, most examples of racism from adults took a different form than that perpetrated by children. For example, the parent of a high school student said that her child experienced racism from both teachers and students during all three levels of his schooling. In the case of teachers, however, the racism was perpetrated through "low expectations, negative perceptions, and preconceived ideas," she stated. Other parents/guardians said that adults on campus displayed racism through unfair disciplinary procedures. A mother of two said that her son was falsely accused of stealing a teacher's cellular phone. "When the student who took the phone admitted that he had done it," she explained, "my son, along with three other students, received the same punishment as the student who took the phone." Another parent said that teachers exhibited racist behavior by "not fairly giving the African American children the awards that they deserve. At the end of the school year, my daughter's GPA was 4.0. She did not receive any awards." Some parents/guardians were offended by culturally insensitive or blatantly racist comments from teachers. For example, one mother said that a teacher told her daughter not to touch a little White girl's hair "because she might get grease on it." A grandparent of three elementary school–age children said that they experienced racism occasionally from staff members and teachers. "Sometimes, I think this is one of the reasons why they are having problems in school," she said.

REPORTING RACISM

Sixty-four percent of the parents/guardians who stated that their children experienced racism at school said that they reported it. However, some said they chose not to report it because no one would take them seriously. "You have to prove it," one grandparent said. Among the individuals who reported to a teacher or administrator that their children had experienced racism, some were satisfied with the results and others were dissatisfied. One mother said that she was dissatisfied because the administrators "made excuses for their teachers." One mother was so displeased with how school administrators reacted when she said that her child's first grade teacher was exhibiting racist behavior that she transferred her child to another school. However, a number of parents/guardians were pleased at the outcomes after they reported that their children had experienced racism at school. Some administrators held conferences to rectify the problem. In other cases, children who exhibited racist behavior were disciplined. However, a recurring theme appeared to be that administrators were more likely to address racial problems when the culprit was a student as opposed to an adult.

THE SCHOOL DISTRICT'S RACIAL CLIMATE

Whereas 16 percent of the parents/guardians said that racism did not exist in their children's school district, 30 percent said that it did exist, but it was uncommon, and 22 percent said that it was common. Because 32 percent of the participants failed to respond to this questionnaire item, the numbers in any of the three categories could be higher. For example, one parent said that racism was common in her children's school district, but "it's covered up."

Parents'/guardians' beliefs about the existence of racism in their children's school district were correlated to twelve other questionnaire items. Factors that were positively correlated to their beliefs were related to whether or not their children had experienced racism at school and the frequency with which they experienced it. Furthermore, as noted previously, parents/guardians who encouraged their children to use school libraries were likely to believe that racism was common in their children's school district.

Conversely, parents/guardians who believed that administrators and teachers cared about students and that administrators and counselors had treated their children fairly were unlikely to believe that racism was common in their children's school district. Those who believed that racism was rare or that it didn't exist in the school district also tended to believe that their children's elementary school and high school teachers, and the public school system, had done an *excellent* or *good* job of educating their children. They also were more likely to believe that their children's middle school homework and their high school course work and homework were beneficial (see Table 10.3). The three narratives that follow are based on interviews with parents/guardians who described their children's experiences with racism.

THE TEACHERS ARE NOT GOING TO TELL YOU, "WELL, I DON'T LIKE YOUR CHILD BECAUSE HE IS BLACK"

At the time of her interview, Martina, a fifty-year-old grandmother of three school-age children, had been a dialysis patient for a year. Nevertheless, she was committed to assisting her grandchildren, particularly her ten-year-old grandson, in any way that she could. Before she became ill, Martina had been the primary guardian of her grandchildren. As a result of her illness, however, she and the children's mother shared parenting duties, but they had different styles of parenting, which often led to conflicts. "They were teenage parents, and she was doing a lot of ripping and running," Martina said of her daughter.

Table 10.3
Variables That Were Correlated to Parents'/Guardians' Perception of the School District's Racial Climate in the Order of the Strength of Each Correlation

Variable	Strength of Correlation	Significance
Benefits of high school homework	-.46	$p < .004$
Experiencing racism	.40	$p < .001$
Benefits of high school course work	-.40	$p < .01$
Parents'/guardians' beliefs about whether or not teachers care	-.40	$p < .001$
Experiencing racism frequently	.34	$p < .04$
Public school system rating	-.32	$p < .003$
Elementary teachers' rating	-.32	$p < .003$
Parents'/guardians' beliefs about administrators' treatment	-.31	$p < .01$
Parents'/guardians' beliefs about whether or not administrators care	-.30	$p < .01$
High school teachers' rating	-.29	$p < .04$
Benefits of middle school homework	-.29	$p < .04$
Encouraging children to use the school libraries	.27	$p < .01$

$N = 87$

"It's not that she was on drugs or drinking, or anything like that. But she was doing a lot of ripping and running." Although Martina felt that her daughter had made a lot of progress in her child-rearing practices, she wanted her to become stricter in enforcing bedtime rules and limiting television viewing. "Their bedtime is 8:30," Martina explained. "We'll eat anywhere between six and seven. It depends on what I've prepared. I let them watch a little TV, they do numbers, and they read all through the day, so they really don't have homework activities at night. But at their mama's house it's different. And I kept telling her it shouldn't be different. They say I'm old-fashioned, but some things never change, like the amount of sleep that kids need."

Despite their differences in parenting styles, Martina and her daughter tried to work as a team to turn around the negative schooling course down which her fifth grade grandson was headed. Martina attributed his problems to three factors: (1) the aforementioned conflict between her and her daughter's parenting styles; (2) labeling at school; and (3) racism from teachers.

Martina described her grandson as a boy who had been targeted for failure by the school system. She believed that the school system had spent so much time criticizing his personality that they overlooked his academic needs. His earliest report cards characterized him as "unsatisfactory in personal growth and classroom work habits." She explained:

Basically, his citizenship has always been unsatisfactory. They say he doesn't organize his work, and he doesn't work independently. I think they started labeling him in first grade. It's the same way with a person that's been in and out of jail. Even though they served their time, and even though they paid their debt to society, it's really not paid, because when they come out, they've still got that problem and that label. This has been one of my primary concerns. I've been telling him and telling him that "This is going to follow you if you don't change it. You have got to get your act together and cooperate with your teacher." He says he understands and then he'll say, "I'm sorry." He has broken down into tears, telling me he's trying. They were giving him smiley faces at the end of the week when he was younger, and he would be so proud of it. Then Monday, he might go in and do okay, and then Tuesday, he might have a slow day, and before he gets home, he's crying and saying "I was trying."

Whereas Martina believed that some of the criticism of her grandson's behavior was warranted, she also believed that the early labeling of him as a discipline problem, pettiness, and differential treatment by teachers toward African American children exacerbated the situation. She said:

Sometimes, I don't know if they just got frustrated with him or what it was, but it would be petty stuff. They were about to drive my daughter and me crazy—mad—about every little bitty thing. Sometimes, they say, "He's having a bad day today. He doesn't want to talk." He has days where he's not very talkative. If he's sitting in class, he's not bothering anyone, he's not talking back to you, he's not running all over the place, but he won't talk—well, leave him alone. That's part of the problem. They say he's disrupting the class, and he isn't. Is he doing his work? "Well, he's just not responding." But is he doing his work? Then, I say, "Well, what's going on? Why is this so major? Either you're going to discipline him by putting him out of the class if he's done something so disruptive. You're either going to suspend him for one or two days or something." But it's like, "We'll give him a break." If you can just give him this many breaks, why constantly call and complain about the same thing? Some teachers may call a problem a disciplinary problem. Another teacher may not call it the same thing. When my grandson cries and says, "I didn't do nothing, but I got put on the wall," or "I got punished," I tell him to speak up for himself. Don't disrespect them, but you speak up. If you didn't do anything, say you didn't do it." But then he says, "They don't believe me." Well, he's got a record too. That hurts him. He's got a history of doing bad. It kind of makes changing hard.

When Martina began to visit her grandson's classroom on a regular basis, she noticed that certain children, particularly White children, could disrupt class with impunity. Martina made the following comments about her observations when she visited one of her grandson's classrooms:

He's never had a Black teacher. There's only a few Black kids in his class. I've gone and observed. The teacher just lets those kids do what they wanna do in there. Trevor was one in particular that I usually go and observe. That child, a White boy, would talk back and do what he wanted to do. But I'm always getting these calls about my grandson talking or doing this or doing that. I couldn't understand the way these children were acting in class. And I'm trying to keep an open mind and I'm saying, "Well, what's the difference in what these kids are doing and what my grandson is doing?" Maybe I was wrong, because I didn't confront the teacher about it openly.

When her grandson was in third grade, a school counselor told Martina that she suspected that he had Attention Deficit Hyperactivity Disorder (ADHD) and should be tested by a doctor. "I think it's a bunch of bull, but I could be wrong," Martina stated. The diagnosis resulted in her grandson being required to take Ritalin several times a day, but Martina didn't believe that the medication helped him. "It's like he's just hyper, hyper, hyper," she said. "He just has mood swings where he might want to sit and not say anything, and then there are days where he's gonna run off at the mouth, or he's constantly going to be moving. He has some problems with that, but it's usually been after school."

Martina was even more vocal in expressing her disappointment about a pattern of teacher attitudes and treatment that she perceived to be racist. She said:

I think some of the teachers are racist. They may not say it, but we see it. When we went to Math Night, there was a two-hour session. I thought it was gonna be a training thing. They had computers and different things, and they asked questions. I told my grandson's teacher, "I have been out of school a long, long time. I couldn't do the math he was bringing to me." The teacher said, "Well, this is new math." But I could just tell by his expression that what I was saying was just a bunch of junk to him. He gave me a look that said, "You're probably just stupid and don't know math anyway." Math was not my greatest subject. I was average in math. When I asked the teacher if he could give me some pointers that would help me help my grandson, he just cut me off short.

Because of her grandson's problems with math, his teacher recommended that he be retained in fifth grade. According to Martina, she and her daughter planned to fight this recommendation.

My grandson's teacher tells us that he needs to study his algebra and geometry more. We weren't even aware that he was taking algebra and geometry. We were not even aware that he had these weak points in his math. His report card said that he has satisfactory skills in all reading areas. He knows his basic math, but he needs to work on geometry, algebra, and on math problem-solving. So, my first question was, "Why didn't they let us know he was even supposed to have geometry and algebra? Who told us that that was a new requirement?" I decided to get him into tutoring, but they didn't have any more openings at the school. They put him in a special class for behavior. If the teacher could always catch him acting up in class, how come he couldn't get on the phone to tell me he needed help with his math? The calls we get are about him not cooperating in class, but nobody mentioned a math problem.

I'm not a racist, but being Black, there are some things I can't close my eyes to. I was raised in the South, but I've been called "Nigger" more here in California than I ever was there. I was raised not to dislike people, because of the color of their skin. My mother taught me that was ignorant. I saw my mother being much older than a lot of people that she worked for, doing domestic work, calling people "Yes, ma'am" and "Yes, sir" up to the day she died. But she did not teach me to dislike people because of the color of their skin, and I stuck to that. I treat people the way they treat me, regardless of their color. But when a situation arises, then the conversation changes a little bit. If I were to go up there and ask my grandson's teacher right now, "Do you have a problem with my grandson because he's Black, or is it because of his disciplinary problems?" If I asked him, "Would you really put an effort into helping him try to make a change in his behavior problems, because I see that this child is really trying to make an effort to change, but he's getting opposition?" You think that man is going to be honest enough and say that he doesn't like him because he's Black? You think he's going to tell me that? Of course not! So, why would I be fool enough to ask him?

Martina concluded her remarks about racism in her grandson's school district by saying that racism is common in the entire region in which the school district is located. She had personally experienced racism while searching for employment. She also felt that it was futile to report the racism to which her grandson was subjected to school officials. "I can't just go up there and tell them that the teacher is mistreating my grandson because he's Black. Because my grandson has been labeled a disciplinary problem, I would basically have to sit in his classroom every day and document things.

THEY NEED TO PUT HIGHER EXPECTATIONS ON OUR CHILDREN. . . . THEY SHOULD DEMAND MORE OF THEM

At the time of her interview, thirty-eight-year-old April had recently begun working on a Teaching Credential. After earning a bachelor's degree in communications, she had moved her daughter, a third grader, to California from Wisconsin. Although these states are far from each other geographically, April noticed similar problems in their education systems. In both states, she had to fight to ensure that her daughter would be treated fairly.

Fighting for her daughter was just one of the many ways in which April assisted her academically. "I've been with her from the beginning," she said. "I've been with her 100 percent. I've taken her to the library; we use the Internet; we pick fun subjects to learn about. I started her out young, just reading to her. I've always been active with her school. I've worked in her class, been the Class Mom, and gone on field trips."

When her daughter started school, she was already reading. Soon, April began to teach her how to write in cursive. Because her daughter's teacher had not introduced cursive writing to the rest of the class, this led to a conflict. April explained:

I was doing cursive and bought books, so my daughter could get comfortable doing cursive. The teacher hadn't taught cursive to the class yet. They were team teaching and one of the teachers started giving my daughter extra credit for the cursive she was doing. One day when that teacher was absent, the other teacher brought my daughter in front of the class, confronted her, and told her that she wasn't going to get her extra credit, and that her mother couldn't teach her how to write. Well, I got on the phone with the principal right that day and the principal arranged a meeting with the teacher. I gave her my opinion. She had to apologize in front of the class like she had embarrassed my daughter in front of the class. I insisted on it. What she did was totally wrong.

Although "they tried to label my daughter," April said, she was eventually placed in G.A.T.E., the Gifted and Talented Education Program. As a result, she had to ride a bus to her new magnet school. Because she was the only African American child on the bus, White children began to harass her. "They were telling her that she didn't belong on the bus," April explained. "I got on the phone and I talked to the teacher, to the principal, and the bus driver." However, because April felt that there were higher expectations at the magnet school and that her daughter would receive a better education there, she chose to keep her at that school. "She could read what most of the kids couldn't read in first grade, and they would slow her down in the regular school system," April stated.

When her daughter was in third grade, April moved to California. She was dismayed that although her daughter had been identified as a G.A.T.E. student in Wisconsin, California school officials not only refused to place her in G.A.T.E., but they also refused to retest her to see if she qualified for the G.A.T.E. program. According to April:

They didn't even want to put her in G.A.T.E. They said they didn't feel she was a G.A.T.E. student. They did not want to test her, but I made them test her. I went straight to the principal and I said, "How do you know she doesn't qualify for G.A.T.E. unless you test her?" The parent can demand that. They tested five students. Only two of them passed and guess which one was mine?

Even though April succeeded in getting her daughter placed in the G.A.T.E. program in California, she soon realized that her daughter was not being challenged enough. "She was getting straight 'A's' in middle school," April explained. "I said, 'This must be too easy for her. We need to put her in an accelerated class.'" At first, they didn't want to do it, and I had to insist and insist. Basically, I had to call the principal again and the counselor."

April believed that fighting to get her daughter into a magnet school that had an accelerated program was worthwhile. "My daughter doesn't need help," she said proudly. "My daughter has a 3.9 GPA. The only problem would be math. She's in Honors math and she's got a good teacher. I think he demands for her to do her best, and that helps her."

During her interview, April spoke repeatedly about the low expectations that public school teachers often have, particularly for African American students. She also stressed that despite the fact that she was pleased with the curriculum and expectations at her daughter's magnet school, she felt that other children were equally deserving of a challenging curriculum and high expectations. April said:

I know that my daughter is going to get a better education at the magnet school. The teachers expect more from them. They have expectations of her, and they demand that she does her best. She's no smarter than any other child. You just need to demand it from her. If you tell someone they're stupid all their life, eventually, they're going to believe it. If you tell them they're smart, eventually, they'll be that too. At the magnet school, they encourage that.

The public school system would improve if they put higher expectations on our children. I think they should be doing college-level math in seventh and eighth grade. There is no reason not to. They could be reading Shakespeare. They should demand more of them. When parents see that their children aren't being treated fairly, they need to step in and deal with the teacher.

I THINK MY CHILDREN NEED TO SEE ROLE MODELS AT ALL LEVELS

In Chapter 3, Jocelyn's concerns about her son's problems at school were described. During her interview, she also spoke about racism at school. Like many parents/guardians, even though her four children had not experienced any overt racism at school, Jocelyn believed that racism did exist in their school district. Moreover, like many of the other study participants, her reason for this belief was rooted in her own schooling experiences.

Jocelyn described her elementary school years in Oklahoma as being "very positive." According to Jocelyn, "Reflecting back upon it now, that was during the time of segregation. All of my teachers but two were Black. The whole school was a Black school, and my neighborhood was Black. Your librarian could go to your same church and you saw those people in the neighborhood. That was a very good experience."

Conversely, her middle school years were negative. Jocelyn was bused to a predominantly White school. Although she had been looking forward to this new experience, she soon found that she was "always in trouble." She stated:

Oklahoma used to be Black on one side and White on the other. So, they were trying to break the school boundaries by bringing some of the Black children into the White school. In sixth grade, I got bused about thirty-five to forty miles away from home. The school was very nice, but I was like my son is now, always in trouble. I was combative.

I have always been the type of person who would tell people how I feel. I probably was not using tact when I had conversations with teachers. If something happened, I told the truth and I didn't try to sugar-coat it. Then, I was always in little fights with White kids. I was always in trouble.

My mom was up at the school trying to keep me from getting suspended. I remember my mother telling me that they wanted to suspend me for dancing, because we were doing the bump and grind or something like that, and they weren't used to that.

Jocelyn's high school years were an improvement. "I got over the fighting in my junior high phase and I started to really get along with everybody." Nevertheless, she decided to leave the school at the end of eleventh grade. "I wanted a change," she stated. "I wanted to graduate from an all-Black school." She believed that the curriculum at the Black school was not only as good as that at the White school, but also that having Black teachers was more advantageous for her. "We didn't really have that much interaction with the White teachers other than during class," Jocelyn said. "But with the Black teachers, it was different."

Years later, the positive memories that Jocelyn retained of her African American teachers convinced her that the lack of African American teachers in her children's school district indicated that racism was prevalent in the district. Whereas she strongly believed that most of the teachers—the majority of whom were White—had done a good job of educating her children, she also believed that the district needed to hire more African American teachers. Jocelyn explained:

I can tell that racism exists in this district by just my own basic experiences, and just knowing how systems work. I look at the classes, the school culture, and the people that are there. I think that if you want to give a child the best education and have the child become well-rounded, you should have a staff that reflects that. This district is not reflective. I look at my daughter's high school. There are only two Black teachers and no Black administrators. At the middle school, I think there is one or two, and the elementary school is the same. In order to become well-rounded students, I think my children need to see role models at all levels.

SUMMARY

Throughout this study, problems pertaining to racism have been negatively linked to children's schooling experiences. In this chapter, the feedback from the African American parents/guardians shed more light on their children's experiences with racism, and the parents'/guardians' beliefs about the racial climate in their children's school district. Nearly 30 percent of the parents/guardians said that their children had experienced racism at school, and it was mostly from other students. Conversely, in *African American Teens Discuss Their Schooling Experiences* (Thompson, 2002), 43 percent of the teens said they experienced racism at school. The lower percentage of parents/guardians might stem from two factors. First, because 28 percent of the parents/guardians did not respond to this questionnaire item, it is possible that the percentage was higher. This is especially likely since 52 percent of the parents/guardians believed that racism did exist in their children's school district. A second possibility is that many parents/guardians may have been unaware that their children had experienced racism at school.

Most of the parents/guardians who said that their children experienced racism said that it occurred during elementary school, and it mostly came from other students, in the form of racial slurs and derogatory comments. In cases where the culprits were adults on campus, the racism usually manifested itself through low expectations, negative perceptions of African American students, preconceived notions, and unfair disciplinary practices. Throughout the study, each of these problems has surfaced repeatedly.

For example, Martina felt that school officials had spent so much time criticizing her grandson's personality that they overlooked his academic needs. "I think they started labeling him in the first grade," she stated, and she compared her grandson's schooling experiences to that of an ex-con. Like Venisha, in Chapter 1, Martina also believed that her grandson was presumed to be a liar, even when he was telling the truth. Moreover, Martina said that she noticed that her grandson's White classmate, Trevor, was able to behave in ways that her grandson was not. What was most exasperating to Martina was this: "If the teacher could always catch him acting up in class, how come he couldn't get on the phone to tell me he needed help with his math?" Informing parents/guardians about academic problems in a timely manner was recommended previously as one of the ways in which public schools could be improved.

April was upset that she had to force school officials to test her daughter, who had already been placed in the G.A.T.E. program in another state. Later, she had to fight to get her daughter into an accelerated middle school because she was not being challenged enough at her previous school. April was extremely concerned about teachers' low level of expectations for African American children. On the other hand, Jocelyn believed that the small number of African American teachers in her children's school district was a sign that racism was prevalent throughout the school district. Although some of the correlations that pertained to racism suggest that further research is needed, a clear message is that racism at school is linked to other negative schooling factors. As Thompson (2002) concluded, issues pertaining to institutional and individualized racism must be addressed if the public school system is ever going to successfully close the achievement gap.

11

School Safety

In *Black Boy*, Richard Wright (1998) shared numerous stories from his child-hood. After being abandoned by his father, Wright, his younger brother, and their mother moved to a new neighborhood. Because Wright was older than his brother, when his mother began to work outside of the home, he was required to assume new responsibilities, such as grocery shopping. One day, his mother gave him money for groceries and sent him to the store. On the way, Wright was accosted by a group of bullies who attacked him and took the money. When he returned home in tears, his mother gave him neither shelter nor solace. Instead, she sent him back to the store and told him not to come home empty-handed. When Wright began to beg and plead for mercy and compassion, his mother gave him an ultimatum: Either he learn to defend himself against the bullies or he would have to take a beating from her. Wright was shocked. However, a quick mental calculation convinced him that it would be better to take his chances with the bullies than with his mother. Whereas he could attempt to defend himself against the bullies, he knew he was no match for his mother. So Wright left home fearful but determined to come home with the groceries. As he expected, when the bullies spotted him, they converged on him with the goal of beating him and taking his grocery money again. This time, however, Wright fought with all his might. Afterwards, he boasted that he won the rights to the streets of the city on that day.

In *Fist Stick Knife Gun: A Personal History of Violence in America*, Geoffrey Canada (1995) told numerous stories about violence from a parent's, teacher's, administrator's, and counselor's perspective. One story that he told was similar to that of Richard Wright. In 1976, his six-year-old daughter was a participant in the court-ordered desegregation of Boston's public schools. One day, she was bleeding when she returned from school and stated that another girl had raked her fingernails across her face. Outraged, Canada telephoned school officials and demanded that they take action. Their responses indicated that, while they would attempt "to do their best," they could not guarantee that his daughter would be safe from future attacks. Out of frustration, Canada did what Wright's mother had done some four decades earlier. "So I did what so many parents do across this violent nation," Canada stated. "I sat my daughter down and told her she was never again to let any boy or girl attack her without fighting back" (p. 7). He went on to say that, although he had taught his children that fighting was wrong, his aversion to having them become victims was much stronger than his desire for nonviolence.

During his years as a teacher and later as an administrator at a predominantly White school for "emotionally disturbed" students in Boston, Canada had an opportunity to study violence at school. One of his conclusions was that "Schools in America are dangerous places" (p. 29). Canada found that many students—particularly those who come from communities or situations that cause them to feel powerless—learn to rely on violence as a coping strategy. When these students act out in school, the way in which educators respond is extremely important. When educators ignore violent behavior, intimidation, and bullying, other students get the message that it is okay to act out. Moreover, the students who are the victims of such behavior learn that since school officials will not protect them, they must resort to violence to protect themselves. Today, school violence continues to concern the nation, especially as a result of high-profile cases such as the "Columbine Tragedy." Moreover, many parents, like Canada and Wright's mother, find it unrealistic and even dangerous to teach their children to be nonviolent.

In *African American Teens Discuss Their Schooling Experiences* (Thompson, 2002), the students shared their thoughts about school safety. Most of the students who participated in the interview phase of the study said that they felt safe most of the time at school, but a higher percentage of students felt safer in elementary school than in middle school or high school. In the current study, "school safety" was not selected as one of the original topics to be explored. However, during the interview phase of the study, this topic surfaced as a major concern for many parents/guardians. Their concern stemmed from two sources: Either their children had already been subjected to violence and/or the parents/guardians themselves had experienced violence at school when they were growing up and worried that their children might have similar experiences. A recurring theme was that girls—particularly girls who were perceived to be attractive—were targeted for violence by other girls. This finding also surfaced in Thompson's (2002) study of African American high school seniors. This chapter will present related information from the interviewees. The first narrative shows how a stepmother's own schooling experiences affected her outlook and actions pertaining to her stepchildren's schooling experiences.

I BELIEVE IN WALKING MY BABIES TO SCHOOL

Although resiliency surfaced as an important factor in the lives of many of the interviewees, the stories that Sandra told about her childhood and young adulthood were among the most memorable examples of resiliency. She had been successful in helping her son, a nineteen-year-old who had recently joined the Navy, complete his K–12 schooling. Now, at forty-one, she was determined to improve the quality of her two stepchildren's lives by ensuring that they received a good education. These biracial children (half-White and half–African American) had been abandoned by their White biological mother and now lived with Sandra and their father.

Sandra's stepson, a fifth grader, was struggling with reading, writing, spelling, and math, and Sandra was upset that he only had the skills of a second grader. Her stepdaughter, who was repeating third grade, was being picked on by other children. Sandra's determination to help them academically and to protect them from harm was extremely personal because she had experienced similar problems during her own schooling. During the interview, as she described her past and the effort that she was investing in her stepchildren's education, she cried frequently.

Sandra's painful journey started before she entered kindergarten. She and her siblings were taken from their parents, because the parents were heroin addicts. The children went to live with an aunt and uncle who were "only in it for the money." Thereafter, Sandra was subjected to emotional, physical, and sexual abuse. When she entered kindergarten in Los Angeles, she was ostracized for being "a skinny, ugly girl with long hair." Before long, her schoolmates were chasing her to and from school. On many occasions, to escape the bullies, Sandra would run into a laundromat near the school, curl herself into a ball, and hide in one of the clothes dryers until she felt safe enough to leave.

As if being a social outcast were not enough, at school she failed academically as well. "I was in Special Ed and had a speech impediment," she explained. "I failed all the way to fifth grade; then I was retained." During fifth grade, the source of Sandra's speech impediment and academic problems was finally identified. "I was deaf in one ear, and partially deaf in the other ear," she stated. "They just thought I was dumb."

When she reached junior high school, Sandra's schooling experiences improved. "I was maturing," she stated. "I got more interested in activities." These activities included "gang banging." As a person who had long been ostracized by her peers, Sandra's need to belong led her to join a gang. She had finally found social acceptance, but her home life was deteriorating. In addition to beating her, her aunt often locked her outside at night. Then, her uncle would let her in from the cold night air to resume his sexual abuse. When Sandra finally told her aunt, the aunt blamed her, and had her placed in a mental institution. Five months later, she was released to her aunt and uncle's custody, and the cycle of abuse resumed. It continued until Sandra was in eleventh grade, when at age sixteen, she ran away from home.

Sandra ended up in an extremely abusive marriage. When her son was three years old, she left the marriage and started a new life. She earned a General Education Diploma (G.E.D.) and began working as an aide in a convalescent home. She went to junior college and tried to improve herself. When she met her current husband, she became committed to becoming a good mother to his two children.

Because the children had been abandoned by their mother, their father had been lax in holding them accountable for their schoolwork and homework. Sandra, however, created a routine that was designed to improve their skills. "I have high expectations," she said. "I read to them, I listen to them read, I give them spelling drills, and I volunteer to go on field trips with them. I attend school functions and I make them redo sloppy work." In an effort to improve her stepson's reading skills, she enrolled him in an after-school literacy program. She also consulted with teachers regarding strategies to help both children. She was pleased that her stepdaughter's teacher had given Sandra new ideas to use at home as she worked with the children.

However, she was displeased that her concerns about the safety of her stepchildren at school were not being taken seriously. Because they were biracial children, both had been subjected to harassment from other children. As her fifth grade stepson grew bigger, he was better able to defend himself, but her stepdaughter was smaller and less powerful. This troubled Sandra. "I still walk my babies to school," she said. However, her attempts to get the principal to take action were futile. "I asked to see her, but she was always busy," Sandra stated.

SHE TOLD ME THAT SHE WAS GOING TO CUT MY BABY

School safety was also a major concern that surfaced repeatedly during Lynette's interview. Starting in middle school, both of her daughters had been in fights that had resulted in suspensions from school. Lynette understood their dilemma because she'd had similar experiences during her own schooling. In her case, she felt that she had brought the problems on herself. In her daughters' cases, however, she felt that, although they might have contributed to their problems, peer pressure and jealousy were the main causes.

During her own adolescence, Lynette moved to California from Kansas. In Kansas, she had been a popular cheerleader. When she tried out for the cheerleading squad at her new high school in California, however, she failed to make the squad. "My eleventh grade year was sad for me," she stated, "because I didn't know anybody. I wanted to be a cheerleader, but they only picked one Black person. She was a cheerleader until she graduated." Soon, things changed. Lynette made friends and began acting out at school. "I met two girls and school started to be fun," according to Lynette. "I was pretty rowdy. I was always wanting to fight boys. I don't know why. I was the loudest thing on the campus. I talked a lot and I was always in somebody's business. I was always getting into a fight. I have no idea why I was like that."

Lynette was equally candid in describing her two daughters' problems at school. Both girls were good elementary school students, but began to flounder academically during middle school. Moreover, the older of the two girls began to have social problems. Lynette explained:

My oldest daughter had some trouble in middle school with fighting. I think she's just like I was. She has a big mouth, and when she talks too much she can't back it up. See, that's where she's different from me. When I used to talk all that stuff with my big mouth, I could fight. My daughter can't fight. She gets her butt kicked. I told her, "Don't run your mouth, because you can't back yourself up." My mama always told me, "Girl, that big mouth is going to get your tail beat!" And my daughter is just like me. She has a big mouth and she's always getting her butt kicked. I said, "Girl, stop talking so much."

When she was an eleventh grader, Lynette's oldest daughter and a former friend became enemies. In this case, Lynette believed that her daughter was totally innocent. As a result, Lynette's entire family became involved. She recounted, "When that girl moved into our neighborhood, my daughters brought her to our house and introduced her to me and my husband. She's not a good-looking girl. She's big and husky like a boy. But my girls liked her. I wanted her to feel comfortable about hanging out with them. Since I have a cosmetology license, I fixed her hair, showed her how to apply make-up and I made her look pretty."

Therefore, Lynette and her daughters were shocked when this girl assaulted Lynette's oldest daughter after she got off the school bus one day. Because the fight did not occur at school or on the bus, school officials failed to take action. "They didn't do anything," Lynette complained. "But I wrote a long letter. I c.c.'d it to the principal, to the assistant principal, to the school district, and to the school police. So they all have a copy of what happened."

The next week, Lynette's younger daughter, a tenth grader, decided to take matters into her own hands. After "mad dogging" her sister's enemy all week, she started a fistfight with the girl. "She was mad, because that girl had jumped on her sister," Lynette explained. Because this incident actually took place on the school bus, school officials were forced to take action. Both girls were required to do "community service." Lynette, however, felt that further action was necessary. By this time, she feared that her daughters might actually be killed.

The girl told me that she was going to cut my baby. She said that she wished that she had a gun and she would have shot them. She told me, "If I was in L.A., you all would have got shot." I wrote all this down and I told the principal, "You all better keep your eye on her, because if this girl kills one of my babies or cuts one of my babies and makes them bleed, I'm going to sue your butts!" I said, "I'm going to sue the school district! I'm telling you beforehand what this girl is saying, what she has, and what she has done, and you guys better watch her. I will sue the pants off of your butts!"

When Lynette and her husband had a conference with the principal, the principal explained why the girl had turned against Lynette's daughters. According to Lynette:

The principal said the girl actually told him that she was jealous, because my girls dress better and they always have their hair done, always had make-up and the way they dressed. She was jealous of the way they dressed and that me and my husband have jobs. My husband and I were shocked. I told the principal, "I took this girl into my home. I did her hair. We made her look pretty, so she could feel comfortable with my girls, and then she went and jumped on my girls." He said that with that type of person, they can't deal with it. They want to live your life. She wants your life and wishes that she lives the way that we do. She doesn't just want to see it; she wants to live it.

At the time of her interview, Lynette was still dissatisfied with the outcome of this situation. Her daughters were required to do "community service," and they had also been required to pay a $62 dollar fine for fighting and to attend Anger Management classes. The other girl, however, was not held accountable at all. Lynette said:

I don't know what they did to her, but she started coming back to school. I called the principal and asked if she had gone to court. He said, "No, she didn't go, but we're going to get her." As far as I know, they didn't do anything to her. Nothing happened to her. She didn't go to court and I don't think she paid any fine. She kept coming to school, and then she tried to be my daughters' friend again. She would ask them for lunch money, but my girls just ignored her. She just wanted to keep on talking to them. She kept going wherever they went. She wouldn't leave them alone. She just wanted to be their friend. I said, "Don't let me catch her in the dark; I will put a bag over her head and knock her out!"

THE SCHOOL HAS OUR CHILDREN IN THEIR HANDS EIGHT HOURS A DAY: WE'RE ENTRUSTING OUR CHILDREN IN THEIR HANDS

Like other parents/guardians, Mary was extremely concerned about her daughter's safety at school. Prior to seventh grade, her oldest daughter had mostly positive experiences at school. Thereafter, ongoing harassment from other girls, not only at school but at nonschool events as well, had a negative effect on her daughter's schooling. Mary believed that jealousy over her daughter's beauty was the primary reason that other girls had started to target her during junior high school and continued to do so through her senior year of high school. According to Mary:

She was on Honor Roll. I was getting calls to attend different awards programs. But when seventh grade hit, that's when it all changed. In seventh grade, it became a problem with girls wanting to fight her, but she really didn't make it known to me until years later. I think it's because of her looks. Don't get me wrong. I'm not saying that my daughter is an angel, but I know that her problems have come from her looks, and the way she carries herself, because she carries herself well. She's not loud. Don't get me wrong: She can be crazy when she and her friends get together. She has one good girlfriend; the rest of them are all guys and they love her and treat her with the utmost respect. She said she doesn't have to worry about competition or them backstabbing her. Then, the girls walk around and call her a hoe [whore] or a "B." That's why I say her problems started in school. I was sending her to school every day, praying over both of my daughters and all of the kids, that nobody would jump her, which was her worst fear. Since seventh grade, she has had a lot of problems with females. People come up to her and ask her if she's a model. Even before they know her, they've already judged her, saying, "She thinks she's all that," and they don't even know her. I would like for you to come over one day and just see her. You would love her.

One girl actually did come to my house and fought her outside of my house. My daughter makes jokes about it. Normally, I come straight home, but that day, I stopped at the store. The girl gave her two choices: Either she was going to kick her butt here at home, or kick her butt at school. That was her sophomore year. They were friends at one time. That's the sad thing about it. I think she just wanted to fight her.

At first, both Mary and her husband underestimated the magnitude of their oldest daughter's problems at school. Ironically, Mary herself had had similar experiences during high school. She recounted:

I was fearful, but because I had more fear of my dad than of the girls who hated me, I couldn't let it affect my grades. My father was very strict. We didn't have the love and compassion as far as sitting down and telling them how our day was. So, you carried all that inside. I would try to get out of class early to make it home, or in high school I would get a ride from a guy friend. One day, I was in the school bathroom, and it was like a whole herd of elephants came in. You would have thought that every Black girl in the whole school was there. But, then, my sister walked in with her crowd. I don't know what would have happened that day. That was about the scariest thing that happened to me in high school. Another girl wanted to fight me over a boy that asked me to go to the Prom. One girl can get twenty girls against you and they don't even know you. That's how it works. But it wasn't as bad as it is now. Back then, it was a fight; now, it's knives and blades. Maybe it was like that back then, but I don't remember it being as bad as it is now.

Several incidents that Mary personally witnessed involving harassment of her daughter by other girls convinced her that her daughter's safety was in jeopardy. Mary said:

One day, we were in Target and we were going up the aisle. There were three girls going across the aisle. They happened to look at me and my daughter, and if eyes could kill, we both would have been dead. I said, "Baby, do you know them?" She said, "Mom, I've never seen them a day in my life." And, if I wasn't there, I can't tell you what would have happened. That's how bad the looks were. And she said, "Mom, this is what I've been trying to tell you, what I go through."

Because of the different things she has encountered with girls, nowadays she doesn't even go around the corner by herself. She will not walk to school. She has met girls that she had an argument with in third grade that still want to jump her now. This is what she goes through. We went to graduation last year and to a pizza place. My daughter and her best friend went to the rest room about five minutes apart. So her best friend was already in the stall when my daughter walked in. Three girls—somebody that she knew in sixth grade—now, this is six years later, walked in and said, "Shut the door behind you." The other two girls blocked the door, waiting for my daughter to come out of the stall, not knowing that her best friend was in the other stall. Now I'm at the counter outside paying for food, not knowing what's going on behind me. This is what my daughter goes through. I'm fearful for her to go anywhere without me around. That's how bad it was getting. It got to the point where she couldn't get on the school bus after school. Since junior high, I've been picking her up from school, whenever I can get away from work long enough to drop her off at home. Now she has Mace. A sister in the church gave it to her. She doesn't leave home without it. It's just sad. It really is sad. I look at these girls and to me, they're all beautiful.

Once Mary realized how serious her daughter's problems were, she had trouble convincing her husband. She stated, "It got to the point where it was causing problems between me and my husband. At first, he wasn't taking it seriously, thinking that girls are crazy anyway. They roll their eyes at each other, etc. But I was taking it seriously because I know that these girls would have jumped her, cut her face up, or even killed her." However, once her husband realized that the problems were serious, he, too, became extremely concerned and often attended meetings with Mary, their daughter, and school officials.

Unbeknownst to the parents, by ninth grade their daughter's problems began to have a serious effect on her grades. She started ditching school and ended up failing classes. According to Mary, "She said she ditched because of the girls bothering her, she had a boyfriend, and the classes were boring." Because she was lacking course credits, Mary's daughter ended up going to a continuation school. At this school, she was also harassed by certain girls. One teacher, a young African American woman, befriended her and helped her cope with the harassment. When her daughter was unable to graduate on time, Mary said, "She cried because her friends were graduating and she wasn't. She wasn't even going to go to her best friend's graduation, but I had to coax her to do it. It hurt her to see everybody graduating and it hurt me too." After continuation school, Mary's daughter took Adult Education classes. When she started, she was lacking sixty-five credits toward graduation. At the time of Mary's interview, her daughter only needed to make up two credits.

Although her daughter wanted to attend college after earning her last two credits, Mary suspected that fear and safety issues would probably dissuade her from doing so. She stated, "Even at Adult Ed, it's still the same thing. She doesn't even want to go to the local community college because of the girls there. But she wants to go on with her education."

Whereas Mary was unsure whether or not most school administrators and teachers fully understood the magnitude of her daughter's problems and how they affected her schooling, she was certain that preventive measures must be taken in order to protect other students from having similar experiences. She explained:

I don't know if administrators are aware of the situations that kids go through. There should probably be seminars, especially for our young girls, to equip them for the future. Instead of just having Black History Month, I'd rather see them have after-school seminars to teach, equip, motivate, build up self-esteem, and let the girls know that they are special, and that the person sitting next to them has a heart and red blood just like them, hurts like them, and cries like them. We need to let those girls know that they should stop only focusing on the outward appearance. If we think about it, the school has our children or sees our children more than we do. They have our children in their hands eight hours a day. So, we're entrusting our children in their hands, from eight in the morning until school ends. That's a lot of time for you not to know what's going on in order to improve it. Now, that's a scary thought. By the time we parents get them, they're not even up for eight hours before bedtime. So, the school has our children. The things that we're seeing now in the schools, we never heard of.

SUMMARY

This chapter presented specific concerns that three African American mothers had about their children's safety at school. Each mother's concerns were also related to her own schooling experiences. For example, Sandra was concerned about her stepdaughter, who was being bullied in elementary school. Lynette and Mary said that their daughters were subjected to harassment from other girls, starting in middle school/junior high school. In each case, the children's experiences affected both parents and children and in at least one case, another sibling as well.

One way it affected Lynette's and Mary's daughters was that it had a negative impact on their achievement. For example, before the threats started, Mary's daughter had been on the Honor Roll. By ninth grade, her grades had declined. She started ditching school and ended up failing to graduate on time. Lynette's two daughters were suspended during middle school. Although Sandra did not attribute her stepchildren's academic problems to the teasing and bullying that they experienced, it is possible that the two were linked. Maslow's Hierarchy of Needs posits that until deficiency needs are met—including the need for survival, safety, a sense of belonging, and self-esteem—growth needs, such as the need for intellectual achievement, aesthetic appreciation, and self-actualization, cannot be met (Eggen & Kauchak, 2001). Therefore, all of the children who experienced harassment at school may have found it difficult to concentrate on schoolwork when they feared that they would be unsafe at school. A second way it affected Mary's daughter was that it made her fearful both at school and away from school. For example, Mary said that her daughter was not only afraid to walk to school, but "She doesn't even want to go around the corner by herself."

The problems also had an adverse effect on the parents. Sandra felt compelled to walk her "babies to school every day." As a child, she had been unable to protect herself from constant bullying and abuse, but she was determined to protect her stepchildren as well as she could. Mary had been picking her daughter up from school since junior high, "whenever I can get away from work long enough to drop her off at home." Moreover, she was fearful about letting her daughter go anywhere without her.

Another message from the interviews was that the mothers were dissatisfied with how school principals had responded to their concerns. Sandra did not think the principal was taking her concerns seriously. Lynette believed that the principal had disciplined her daughters for fighting, but had not enforced the punishment against the girl that her daughters had fought. According to Lynette, this girl had even threatened to cut her daughter with a knife. Mary wanted schools to take preventive measures that would address sources of conflict that lead to violence. The mothers' frustration with school principals' responses to their daughters' problems was typified by Lynette. She felt angry enough to take matters into her own hands. Regarding the girl who had threatened to cut her daughter, Lynette stated, "Don't let me catch her in the dark. I will put a bag over her head, and knock her out."

Lynette's statement is important in that it is indicative of the dilemma facing many African American parents/guardians. On the one hand, African American parents/guardians, like Canada (1995) want their children to be nonviolent, and they themselves want to practice what they teach. On the other hand, they do not want their children to be victims. Therefore, many African American parents/guardians teach their children to fight back when bullied. Teaching them to "turn the other cheek" is not only unrealistic, but it is totally irrational as well. In urban schools, children who do not defend themselves are merely subjected to more harassment. Canada (1995) wrote, "I have counseled so many children who've said they acted violently because their parents told them to. . . . The parents, inevitably single women raising children in the midst of an urban war zone, come with similar stories of children being victimized again and again" (p. 6). Therefore, when some parents/guardians believe that schools are failing to protect their children, they see no alternative but to teach their children to protect themselves.

This problem facing African American parents/guardians is compounded because many schools have "Zero Tolerance" policies. This means that when students fight, even the child who was merely reacting in self-defense—as advised or even ordered by his/her parents/guardians—will be punished along with the perpetrator. This factor could be one of the causes of the high suspension and expulsion rates of African American students. The feedback from the mothers suggests that the public school system must improve its policies pertaining to fighting at school. These policies are diametrically opposed to the messages that many African American children get at home. Whereas parents/ guardians tell their children not to be victimized, current school policies appear to promote victimization. A more logical policy might be stated as follows: "Perpetrators and instigators of fights will be held accountable." As it stands now, however, the victim is also punished in many school districts.

12

Peer Pressure and the Lure of Street Life

Although the current study did not seek to address issues pertaining to peer pressure, during the interview phase of the study several parents/guardians mentioned that they were concerned about how peer pressure was affecting their children's attitudes about school. It turned out that some of the parents/guardians had been distracted from their own schooling because of peer pressure and the "lure of street life." These issues have also surfaced in numerous autobiographies of African Americans.

For example, in *Makes Me Wanna Holler*, McCall (1994) illustrated why street life is often more alluring than the values that parents attempt to instill in their children. McCall found himself increasingly becoming bored with school and more attracted to life outside of school. However, this decision led him to the underside of street life, which resulted in his eventual arrest and incarceration. At the time when he wrote his autobiography, however, McCall, had used his reading and writing skills to improve the quality of his life. He had become a reporter for the *Washington Post*.

Like McCall, in *From the Mississippi Delta*, Holland (1997) recounted how she chose the vices associated with street life over a more constructive lifestyle. Holland was eventually kicked out of high school. Later, she became involved in the civil rights movement and decided that a formal education was necessary to improve her life. At the time her autobiography was published, she had earned a Ph.D. and was a professor at a prestigious private university.

In *Out of the Madness*, Ladd (1994) described his struggle to survive poverty, the violence that was prevalent in his neighborhood, and the effects of growing up with a heroin-addicted mother. Unlike McCall and Holland, he coped by using reading and his strong desire to overcome the dead-end life of the projects as a means of escape.

Whereas Ladd chose to ignore the lure of the streets in favor of a formal education, and Holland and McCall succumbed to peer pressure and the lure of street life but later redeemed themselves, Shakur (1993) is still suffering from the consequences of choices that he made during elementary school. Shakur, a former Boy Scout, wrote a vivid account of the forces that compelled him to join a faction of the Los Angeles Crips when he was only eleven years old. During his thirteen years as one of the city's most notorious gang members, his ruthless acts of violence earned him the moniker "Monster." Shakur's godfather, Ray Charles, the famous musician, attempted to have a positive impact on him, but it was not enough to keep Shakur from joining the gang and encouraging his younger brother to do so as well. He wrote, "My sixth-grade graduation was my first and last. Actually, it was the last time I ever seriously attended school—for academic purposes. My homeboys became my family—the older ones were father figures" (p. 25).

In addition to the lack of father figures, however, the chronic violence of inner city neighborhoods is another reason why some youths give in to peer pressure to join gangs. Garbarino, Dubrow, Kostelny, and Pardo (1992) found that some victims of chronic violence cope by collaborating with their aggressors. Joining a gang is one way that such victims unite with their aggressors. Shakur (1993) said, "Early on I saw and felt both sides of the game being played where I lived. It was during my time in elementary school that I chose never to be a victim again, if I could help it . . ." (p. 100). Moreover, the high incidence of violence, as well as negative peer pressure, in many communities makes parenting more difficult for even the best-intentioned parents. For example, Shakur's mother tried many times to dissuade her sons from gang life, but it was too late. "Mom was the enemy at home," Shakur explained. "Mom was, to me, what antiwar protesters were to Westmoreland" (p. 168).

Golden (1995) described the difficulty of raising African American boys in America and examined ways in which parents might deter them from joining gangs and becoming involved in socially unacceptable activities. One of her conclusions was that, regardless of socioeconomic status, many African American mothers live in fear that they will lose their sons to violence from street life or police brutality. Of her own experience, Golden wrote, "As the mother of a Black son, I have raised my child with a trembling hand that clutches and leads" (p. 7). She also said, "I want my son to grow up to be smart, productive, and content. But like every Black mother I know, I want my son mostly to live" (p. 16).

Garbarino, Dubrow, Kostelny, and Pardo (1992) said that the fear of losing their children to gangs often leads parents in violent neighborhoods to employ "restrictive measures" that have the opposite effect. They wrote, "The ironic result is greater susceptibility to the negative forces abroad in the community" (p. 65). However, McCall (1997) said that even middle-class African American youths are tempted by the lure of street life. Describing one group of Black middle-class youth who dressed like "gangstas," McCall wrote, "They're wanna-bes who are just acting out, pretending to be the gritty street warriors they see" (p. 118).

The aforementioned autobiographies and research illustrate how peer pressure and the lure of street life can lead to underachievement among African American students or even a total rejection of the education system. The current chapter presents feedback from several African American parents/guardians about the effects of peer pressure and the lure of street life on their own schooling experiences and those of their children. The purpose of this chapter is to broaden educators', researchers', and policymakers' awareness of additional factors that can impact African American students' achievement.

THE PRESSURE: THE PRESSURE WAS GETTING TO ME

Whereas most of the parents/guardians who participated in the interview phase of the study often spoke passionately about their own and their children's schooling experiences, May, a mother of two, like Sandra in Chapter 11, actually cried. Like many other interviewees, thirty-two-year-old May's determination to ensure that her children received a good education was rooted in her own schooling experiences.

While growing up in Virginia, May attended schools that were predominantly African American and Native American. She described her elementary school years as mostly positive. "Back then, we had to stay in school," she explained. "We couldn't miss a day. It was positive because most of the parents were always there: one parent home and one parent working. I didn't have a dad, so my mom had to do everything." In middle school, however, things changed for May. Because she didn't fit in with her peers, she was singled out. She recounted:

There were some people I didn't get along with, and I didn't want to. I told my mom that I didn't want to be there. People pick on you. People would say, "I have more than you have. You don't have this." I didn't mingle with most of the people because I didn't care for them. Because what they were doing—drinking, smoking, and hanging out—I wasn't doing. I didn't do those things.

During high school, May eventually succumbed to the peer pressure. She explained:

I wore bifocals until I was in the tenth grade. In eleventh grade, I lost my bifocals. I wanted to do what my friends were doing. I wanted to hang out. I wanted my own job, and I wanted to get what I could get. My mom tried to stop me. She would say, "Baby, keep on going; keep on going." But I stopped at the beginning of twelfth grade.

The pressure, the pressure was getting to me. My friends were doing this, so I said, "I'm stopping everything. I'm going to do what my friends are doing." I went and got a job, and I kept on working. Then, I got pregnant. It hurts. I don't like talking about it, because I get depressed.

According to May, the most painful aspect of her decision to drop out of school pertained to the effect that decision had on her ability to help her own children—a fourth grade boy and a sixth grade girl—with their studies. Her son was struggling in school with math, science, writing, and discipline. Her daughter was struggling with math, science, and writing. Although May worked assiduously to assist her children by helping with their homework, staying in regular contact with teachers, attending school functions, and involving them in church and community programs, often she was unable to assist them when they needed her help. "When I can't help them, I'll ask somebody else, or take them to the Homework Center," she said. "Mostly, it's the math." Moreover, despite the fact that she talked to them regularly about the importance of doing well in school and attending college, she feared that her children, particularly her daughter, would end up failing to graduate from high school, as she had. Regarding her daughter, May stated, "I don't think she enjoys what she's doing in school. She says, 'Mom, it's too hard. I can't do it.' It seems like she just gave up, but I kept pushing and pushing. I said, 'Baby, you need to keep on pushing. You need to keep on going.'"

Because her daughter continued to have difficulty remaining focused during class, May agreed to have her placed in the Resource Specialist Program (RSP), so that she could receive additional help. "I want them to grow up and get what I stopped getting," May said. "I want them to get more. I want them to succeed. It really hurts me, because I didn't make it. I tell my kids that elementary school is the beginning. You need to keep on going and going, and don't stop. It hurts me really bad."

In addition to supporting her children academically and continuing to encourage them to attend college, one of May's immediate goals was to earn her General Education Diploma (G.E.D). "I'm planning on doing what I have to do," she stated. "I'm planning on continuing to take tests and get my G.E.D and go from there."

IT'S THE STREETS THAT YOU HAVE TO WORRY ABOUT

Twenty-eight-year-old Paul was one of several interviewees who had attended school in the same district in which his child was currently enrolled. There were two similarities between his interview and May's. First, like May, he was committed to preventing his daughter, a kindergartner, from following in his footsteps. Second, like May's story, Paul's experiences illustrate not only how peer pressure and the lure of street life can compete with the school system for the attention of African American students, but also that they can even deter students from completing their K–12 schooling.

In the beginning, his schooling experiences were mostly positive. Although Paul described himself as being "hardheaded, like my daughter," he felt that his elementary teachers tried to "counsel me into getting back on the right track, instead of getting on my case and throwing me off on a worse track than I was on." Despite the fact that he had some conflicts with students and adults on campus, Paul said that he earned good grades during elementary school and middle school.

As with May, in high school things changed for Paul. Three factors contributed to his decision to eventually drop out of school: (1) peer pressure and the lure of street life; (2) a boring curriculum and unqualified teachers; and (3) harassment from adults at school. Concerning the role that peer pressure and the lure of street life played in his decision to drop out of school, Paul explained, "There were more conflicts when I was in high school because I was harder. I wanted to run the streets more then. I wanted to be bad, like everybody else. I wanted the fast money like everybody else and fast cars. I wanted all the girls to look at me."

As a result, Paul dropped out of school during eleventh grade. However, the boring curriculum and unqualified teachers also contributed to his decision. According to Paul:

In tenth grade, I learned a lot of stuff about science and biology. It made me look at stuff in a different light than I had known about. After that, it was starting to repeat itself. We were learning the same things over again. But when I had a question that was higher than that, nobody knew anything.

The only thing I could say about the educational system is we need more qualified teachers. Make sure they know what they're doing and know what they're talking about, and that they're qualified to do their jobs. I could say that in junior high and high school, some of the teachers could have gone back to school with me. They knew about as much as I knew. They could have been sitting in a desk right next to me. They could have been learning something just like me. That's probably one reason why I left, because I felt like I wasn't learning anything.

The third factor that prompted Paul to drop out of school was the way that school counselors and school police treated him. Paul felt that they singled him out for harassment. He said:

There was a lot of drama at school. "Some of the counselors and school police didn't like me. They wanted to put us through a hassle all day. I just didn't want to go through all of that. They'd try to talk to me and I'd just give them a crazy look and keep going. I remember that I had counselors that didn't really care. They just wanted to do their eight hours, to get paid, and go home. I know that there's some that care, but I know there's some that really don't care either.

Bored with school and seeking to make money quickly, Paul resorted to selling illegal drugs. As a result, he ended up spending five years in a state prison. During his incarceration, Paul earned his G.E.D. When he was released, he was determined to change his lifestyle. He enrolled in a nursing program with the intention of eventually working in a convalescent home. However, the passage of a proposition that was designed to provide substance abusers with rehabilitation instead of jail time convinced Paul to seek a counseling certificate instead. His goal was to work with teenage drug addicts but also to keep his daughter headed in the right direction. Regarding his daughter, he said that, in addition to reading to her, playing computer games with her, and teaching her that there are consequences for bad behavior, he often took her to college with him. "She knows that I go to school," he said. "She'll bring my backpack to me. I take her to classes with me and everybody wants to hug her and talk to her. I take her up there a lot."

When asked what, if anything, the public school system can do to prevent other African American students from dropping out of school because of peer pressure and the lure of street life, Paul shared several ideas. Although he felt that many negative aspects of street life are deeply entrenched in schools, he also believed that there are definitive measures that parents/guardians and school officials can take to keep African American youths in school. He said:

It's the streets that you have to worry about that's more or less in schools now. There are drugs and guns and people trying to pressure you. And it's more in the schools now, than it is in the streets. Parents can help by telling kids that they can't run the street and go to school at the same time. They should tell them not to listen to what people on the street have to tell you, 'cause nine times out of ten, they just want to get you in trouble. The peer pressure and wanting money, cars, and women, instead of sitting at home reading books causes a big conflict. Seeing other people with things that you don't have will make you want those things to outdo that person.

The schools should try to mix it up a little bit, by bringing a little street into the school, without the violence and the drug part. They could have arcade games, crafts, ping pong, pool, and video games for the students that are doing what they have to do. They could make it a privilege. Those who don't want to work and do what they need to do wouldn't be able to go into the game room.

SHE'S A LOT LIKE ME. . . . I BARELY MADE IT THROUGH MY SENIOR YEAR

Whereas Paul and May were hopeful that their children would not follow in their earlier footsteps, Ashanté had already come to the painful realization that her daughter would not graduate. Although her eldest son was attending college and her two other children—a seventh grade boy and an eleventh grade girl—were doing well in school, her daughter, a high school senior, was failing every one of her courses. According to Ashanté:

She needs help with everything, but it's too late, because she's supposed to graduate on the 14th. She will probably not try and pursue a G.E.D. She'll probably end up working full time and then going from there. She may take classes here and there, but she's a lot like me. That's how I was. I barely made it through my senior year and then I graduated and ended up working and going to cosmetology school later. I don't think she's going to be getting her diploma; I really don't. But I have to wait until that day comes, for the 14th to come, and see if those teachers are going to take her off the Fail List.

Despite the fact that she had resigned herself to the strong likelihood that her daughter would not graduate, Ashanté still retained a sliver of hope that manifested itself through her actions. During the interview she was actually typing make-up work for her daughter to hand in to her teachers. "Her American Government teacher gave her eighteen chapters to turn in Monday," Ashanté explained. "I'm sitting here typing, because she doesn't know how to type."

Ashanté's disappointment was exacerbated by the fact that her daughter had done well in previous years and had been looking forward to graduating. However, meeting an older boy during her senior year had caused her to change her priorities. Ashanté recounted:

She was a good student, and she was a good girl, and this boy just turned her whole world upside down. What I did was the same thing, got caught up with some boy. My mom and dad were up there [at school], just like we're up there for her. I told them, "My daughter can do it. We know she's smarter than she's pretending to be." So, I don't know what happened. I really honestly believe that they pushed me through the system. I think they gave me "C's" and let me out. I'm glad they did because with that high school diploma, I went back to school. I got my education and what I needed to be where I am today. I feel that we've done everything we can for my daughter and she refuses to do her schoolwork because of this boy.

She only had to carry four classes per semester during her senior year. She was planning to finish early. She said, "Oh mom, I'm going to graduate. After these four classes, I'm going to be done. I could just kick it all year." We were like, "Cool! You can do it." We had all our kids on track until she met this boy, and it all went downhill. She didn't do anything at school. Well, me and her dad chased the boy away, cussed him out on the phone. We went to the school. He was coming up there. My husband went up there and told him to stay away from her. We would go to my sister's house and the boy was over there. She is just all caught up on this boy. He claimed he graduated last year, but we think he's twenty-one years old. He lies about everything—his age, when he graduated. We really don't know anything about him. Everything he says is a lie, but that doesn't phase her. She didn't do any work during her senior year.

Instead of gratitude, Ashanté found her efforts to assist her daughter by typing her work and trying to motivate her to do her work were met with resistance and bitterness on both sides. According to Ashanté:

My husband and I are the bad ones. I'm sitting here doing her work for her all the time and she says, "Oh, mom, finish my work." And then, she's just trippin' out on us, like we're the bad ones. She's the one that sat in the class and didn't do any work because she wanted to be with that boy. If you look in her textbook, she has that boy's name all up in her book. She wants out of this type of environment. I pick her butt up from school every day and she doesn't want to speak to us. She thinks we're bad people.

SUMMARY

The autobiographies that were included at the beginning of this chapter and the three narratives that followed illustrate how peer pressure and the lure of street life can affect the schooling experiences of African American students. These stories indicate that the problem is not new. Children in previous eras faced similar situations. For many, street life with its appeal to excitement and fun, looks a lot more interesting than the "drudgery" and routine that are often associated with school. For lower-socioeconomic-status African American children who cannot afford the material possessions that some of their class-mates might have, the possibility of earning money on the street may compound the problem. For example, Paul stated that he wanted "fast money and fast cars," so that all the girls would notice him.

Although schools cannot become the panacea for all of society's ills, the school system can take measures that might dissuade some African American youths from dropping out of school as a result of peer pressure. First, as noted previously, schools must address factors and practices that are associated with the early negative labeling of African American children, particularly African American boys. Several interviewees stated that their sons or grandsons were singled out and labeled as discipline problems. Paul said that one factor that contributed to his decision to drop out of school was the way that he was treated by school counselors and security personnel. Ferguson (2001) said that the public school system engages in practices that propel African American boys toward prison. These practices, which include early negative labeling and det-rimental discipline polices, must be eradicated.

Another way that the school system can decrease the likelihood that African American youths will reject school for street life is to improve the quality of teachers and the curriculum. These recommendations have also surfaced re-peatedly in previous chapters, particularly in Chapter 9. In fact, another factor that contributed to Paul's decision to drop out of school was that "We were learning the same things over and over again. But when I had a question that was higher than that, nobody knew anything." Paul recommended that schools should try to "mix it up a little bit, by bringing a little street into the school, without the violence and drug part." Teachers can do this in a number of ways that could make the curriculum more interesting and relevant to students (Thompson, 2002). Inviting guest speakers from the local community to share their personal stories of resiliency and how peer pressure affected them is one way. Another way is by using autobiographies and biographies of African Americans as tools that will enable students to read about, write about, and discuss the pros and cons of giving in to peer pressure.

13

College

Although there are many definitions of success, in the United States the attainment of a college degree has traditionally been one measure of success used by mainstream society. More important, the attainment of a college degree is widely believed to increase opportunities for socioeconomic mobility. The procurement of jobs in the most highly respected professions, such as medicine, science, and law, for example, not only requires college degrees, but this procurement tends to be equated with prestige and higher salaries as well. Because disproportionately high percentages of African Americans live in poverty, at the very least, a good K–12 education is imperative. Without a strong academic foundation and the prerequisite knowledge and skills that are necessary to pass the college entrance examinations, acceptance into four-year universities becomes more difficult—if not impossible. As a good example of this, when Affirmative Action was outlawed in California, the number of African American students who were admitted into University of California institutions decreased. In spite of the fact that many of the African American students who applied had high grade point averages, low scores on college entrance exams prevented them from being admitted. Since then, the University of California system has decided to take a more comprehensive look at candidates for admission. Nevertheless, in many regions throughout the United States, particularly in impoverished and urban areas, the students who are most in need of socioeconomic mobility are the least likely to obtain a college degree as a means of improving the quality of their lives. Among the most well-known reasons are that these students are often underprepared to do college-level work as a result of inadequate math preparation (Drew, 1996; Polite, 1999) and they have not had access to college preparatory courses, particularly Advanced Placement courses (Burdman, 2000; Dupuis, 1999).

In *African American Teens Discuss Their Schooling Experiences*, Thompson (2002) described the students' future plans, attitudes about college, and whether or not they believed that the public school system had adequately prepared them for college. The teens were also given an opportunity to explain "how public schools can better prepare students for college." The most frequently cited recommendations were (1) teach better study skills; (2) provide more counseling about college; (3) offer college preparatory classes to all students; (4) provide better math preparation; (5) hire better teachers; (6) improve college preparatory classes; (7) increase parent involvement; and (8) offer more writing practice.

The parents/guardians who participated in the current study were also given an opportunity to address numerous issues pertaining to college. Many of the questions were similar to those that were answered by the high school students who participated in Thompson's earlier study. As noted in the Introduction, the region in which most of these parents/guardians resided has one of the lowest college attendance rates in California. Furthermore, during the 2000–01 academic year, the majority of African American students in this region and statewide did not do well on the new state-mandated California High School Exit Exam. This exam will eventually be used to determine if students can graduate or not. Additionally, in the region in which the majority of parents/guardians resided, African American high school seniors who took the Scholastic Aptitude Test (SAT) and/or the ACT in 2000, had lower average scores than seniors from other racial/ethnic groups (California Department of Education, 2001).

Therefore, there is clearly a need not only to improve the quality of the K–12 schooling that African American students in this region receive, but also to increase the likelihood that they will attend college and be prepared to do college-level work. This chapter presents several issues pertaining to college, including the parents'/guardians' views of college, messages that they conveyed to their children about college, whether or not their children planned to attend college, how the public school system could better prepare African American students for college, the value that they placed on their children's education, and a related narrative.

THE VALUE THAT AFRICAN AMERICAN PARENTS/ GUARDIANS PLACED ON THEIR CHILDREN'S EDUCATION

Ninety-two percent of the parents/guardians who completed the questionnaire said that their children's education was *very important* to them. In explaining why her children's education was extremely important to her, a mother of four stated:

I want them to have the best. I want them to be the best that they can be. My mom wanted me to have more than she had. I want my kids to have more than I have. I want them to do very well and be independent. I don't want my son to depend on a woman. I don't want my girls to depend on a man. I want them to have their own. I want them to make sure that the person that they end up with has what they have on the same level or higher. But if they fall in love with somebody that doesn't have it, they have to live with them, not me! That's what I teach them. I want them to enjoy life.

The value that the parents/guardians placed on their children's education was correlated to sixteen other questionnaire items. Five of the six variables that were inversely related to the value that they placed on their children's education can be perceived as negative aspects of schooling. For example, the parents/guardians of children who had been expelled from school and/or who experienced racism at school from adults or from both adults and children were less likely to say that their children's education was very important to them. The same was true of parents/guardians whose children had problems with history and/or pronunciation, and who disliked school. Additionally, parents/guardians who placed less value on their children's education were unlikely to state that they assisted their children academically in "other" ways than the ones that were listed on the questionnaire.

The questionnaire items that were positively correlated to the value that the African American parents/guardians placed on their children's education included their beliefs about the benefits of their children's elementary school homework and their high school course work. Parents'/guardians' self-rating and how they rated the public school system were also positively correlated to this variable. This suggests that those who believed that they did an *excellent* or *good* job of assisting their children academically and those who believed that the public school system had done an *excellent* or *good* job were more likely to say that their children's education was very important to them. Parents/guardians who assisted their children by buying books for them, who encouraged them to check over their work, who talked to them regularly about school and/or college, and who contacted teachers on an ongoing basis were also likely to state that their children's education was very important to them. These parents/guardians also tended to believe that most teachers care about students (see Table 13.1).

A grandmother who said that her grandchildren's education was very important to her explained:

Well, the world is changing—all this technology that we have. It's not simple and cut and dry like it used to be, when people were doing things manually. If our children are not taught about the modern technology—the computers and the new procedures that they have—where's it going to leave them? They're going to be doing janitorial work or flipping burgers. But if they keep up with modern technology, they're not gonna need them to flip burgers. Education is their key. That's what's gonna give them some power no matter what color they are.

ENCOURAGING AFRICAN AMERICAN CHILDREN TO ATTEND COLLEGE

Seventy-four percent of the questionnaire respondents said that they encouraged their children to attend college or talked to them about college on a

Table 13.1
Variables That Were Correlated to the Value African American Parents/
Guardians Placed on Their Children's Education in the Order of the
Strength of Each Correlation

Variable	Strength of Correlation	Significance
Assisting children in "other" ways	-.70	$p < .001$
History problem	-.43	$p < .001$
Source(s) of racism	-.37	$p < .03$
Pronunciation problem	-.36	$p < .001$
Benefits of high school course work	.32	$p < .03$
Talking with children about school regularly	.28	$p < .002$
Parents'/guardians' self-rating	.25	$p < .01$
Expulsion	-.25	$p < .01$
Contacting teachers regularly	.24	$p < .01$
Disliking school	-.23	$p < .01$
Talking to children about college	.22	$p < .02$
Parents'/guardians' beliefs about whether or not teachers care	.22	$p < .03$
Encouraging children to check their work	.21	$p < .02$
Buying books for children	.20	$p < .03$
Public school system rating	.19	$p < .04$
Benefits of elementary school homework	.19	$p < .04$

$N = 129$

regular basis. This variable was correlated to fourteen other questionnaire items. Some of the same variables that were correlated to the value that African American parents/guardians placed on their children's education were also correlated to this variable.

However, some questionnaire items that were associated with this variable differed from those that were correlated to the previous one. For example, the number of school-age children per family was positively correlated to encouraging children to attend college. Therefore, parents/guardians with multiple school-age children were more likely than those with one school-age child to encourage their children to attend college on a regular basis. Gender was also positively correlated to this variable: Female parents/guardians were more likely than males to encourage children to attend college on a regular basis. In addition to encouraging their children to attend college, these parents/guardians also were more likely than others to assist their children academically by limiting television viewing, helping them study for tests, helping with homework, encouraging them to read, and encouraging them to use the school libraries regularly. Moreover, parents/guardians who encouraged their children to attend college on a regular basis were unlikely to have children who struggled with spelling or reading comprehension (see Table 13.2).

The parents/guardians who participated in the interview phase of the study were asked the following question: "In your opinion, how important is a college education?" The majority of interviewees replied that it was *very important*. The most frequently cited reason was that a college education would improve their children's economic status and give them more access to higher-paying jobs. In explaining why she believed that a college education was very important, a woman who was the legal guardian of three of her school-age relatives stated, "Back in the day, I didn't know that it was that important, but now, I know. I know that people who have a college education have the best jobs and they make good money. Some of the people I work with have a college education, and I see how well they're doing. They drive nice cars and own their own home. That's why I think it's very important." Some parents/guardians said they regretted that they had not gone to college or had not gone as long

Table 13.2
Variables That Were Correlated to Encouraging Children to Attend College in the Order of the Strength of Each Correlation

Variable	Strength of Correlation	Significance
Encouraging children to check their work	.55	p < .001
Talking with children about school regularly	.47	p < .001
Limiting television viewing	.46	p < .001
Helping children study for tests	.41	p < .001
Helping with homework	.38	p < .001
Encouraging children to read	.36	p < .001
Contacting teachers regularly	.34	p < .001
Buying books for children	.33	p < .001
Encouraging children to use school libraries	.27	p < .002
Spelling problem	-.24	p < .01
Value placed on children's education	.22	p < .02
Parents'/guardians' gender	.21	p < .02
The number of school-age children	.20	p < .03
Reading comprehension problem	-.19	p < .04

$N = 96$

as they'd planned to. Others said that they still valued a college education even though they were not using the degrees that they'd earned to the extent that they could. However, a more common explanation was that parents/guardians wanted their children to use a college education to avoid some of the choices that they had regretted making.

For example, a mother of six said:

I see too many people working now and it's not because they know how to do the job, or it's not even really because they have the smarts. But it's because they have the paperwork behind them. They got an A.A., B.A., or M.A. It doesn't mean that they're smarter than you or I. They just have a degree and a nice resumé. I wanted to go for my master's. I messed up, instead of finishing my college education. I should have followed through, instead of getting married. The only good thing I got out of it was my kids.

A mother of two daughters said, "I don't want them to go through what I've gone through as far as waiting that long to go back to school. And then, of course, ending up getting married, having children, then getting involved in church, and trying to take care of things at the house." A mother of four stated, "I don't have a college education, but I have certificates. A college education will take you much further. One of my sons is already in college. He will be able to make his dreams come true."

BELIEVING THAT ONE'S CHILDREN PLANNED TO ATTEND COLLEGE

Ninety-one percent of the questionnaire respondents said that their children planned to attend college. This belief was correlated to ten other questionnaire items. Most of these variables have already been cited in Tables 13.1 and 13.2. However, several additional variables surfaced.

The parents/guardians whose children owned books were more likely than others to believe that their children planned to attend college. Conversely, parents/guardians of children who experienced racism from adults or from both adults and students, and who attended schools in certain districts, were unlikely to believe that they planned to attend college (see Table 13.3).

During the interview phase of the study, parents/guardians were able to discuss in more detail the reasons that they believed their children did or did not plan to attend college. The most frequently cited reason was that children had already expressed a desire to pursue a profession that would require a college degree. For example, a mother of three explained:

I try to let them know how important it is to go to college. My daughter wants to be a lawyer. I try to let them know if they further their education, they can be what they want to be. My daughter knows she has to go to law school in order to be a lawyer, and I think she might end up being a lawyer. She's really looking forward to going to

Table 13.3
Variables That Were Correlated to Believing That One's Children Planned
to Attend College in the Order of the Strength of Each Correlation

Variable	Strength of Correlation	Significance
Racism source(s)	-.37	p < .04
Talking to children about school regularly	.36	p < .001
Buying books for children	.26	p < .004
Children owning books	.24	p < .01
Contacting teachers regularly	.23	p < .01
Parents'/guardians' beliefs about administrators' treatment	.23	p < .02
Helping with homework	.22	p < .02
Encouraging children to check their work	.21	p < .02
Encouraging children to read	.21	p < .02
School district location	-.20	p < .03

N = 117

law school. She reads a lot and is looking into books about law. One of her teachers is a real good teacher. He's good and I really like him.

A mother of two said that, although her older daughter did not want to attend college, the younger one, a middle school student, did. "She wants to be everything!" her mother exclaimed. "She wants to be a doctor, a teacher, and a dancer. I want her to know that she can do all things through Christ, but she is going to have to focus on one profession, because that is a little too much." A mother of four stated that although her son was labeled a discipline problem at school and had been diagnosed with ADD, he still wanted to go to college to become a doctor.

The second most frequently cited reason why parents/guardians believed that their children planned to attend college was that the parents/guardians had indicated that they wanted this for their children or that the children had no choice: A college education was mandatory. For example, the mother of a seventh grader stated, "I've been telling her since she was born that she's going to college." A mother of two said, "I told them they have to get through school to get to college. I want them to go straight through and go on to get that college degree. I told them that they would have more choices and better life-styles." A mother who attended community college for less than a year said, "All of them better be going to college, because that is something I want them to do to educate themselves in order to get better-paying jobs."

Conversely, some interviewees said that their children did not plan to go to college. Several expressed ambivalence about the importance of a college education. For example, a father said that he did not know if his daughter planned to go to college because she was too young to understand much about college. As far as whether or not she should eventually go, he stated, "It depends on what you're going for. There's certain things that won't help you get a job and others that will." A cosmetologist who owned her own business said that, although her children had expressed a desire to go to college, "I've seen people who had a college education who couldn't even get a good job. I didn't go to college, but my children don't have to follow in my footsteps. If they want to go, I want them to go."

Several interviewees also stated that their children wanted to join the military instead of going to college. For example, one mother said that she was hoping that her two youngest children would eventually go to college, but her oldest son, who had been offered several scholarships, had decided not to go. She explained, "He said he wasn't ready for school anymore. He had enough of it and he wanted something different. Well, he got it. He decided to go into the Marines. They wanted to pay for his education. I'm hoping that the youngest two will go to college because this is my goal. So I'm praying and putting aside money right now for their college education."

MESSAGES THAT AFRICAN AMERICAN PARENTS/ GUARDIANS CONVEYED TO THEIR CHILDREN ABOUT COLLEGE

There were two main messages that most parents/guardians who participated in the interview phase of the study sought to convey to their children about college: (1) A college education is important and (2) a college education will provide you with more options. For example, an interviewee who worked as a clerk said:

I keep telling my oldest child, "If you go to school, you won't have to worry about getting paid on Thursday and being broke on Friday." That's why I want her to go to school. So, when she gets around twenty-four or twenty-five, she will already be set in a nice profession, making double digits, instead of starting out with one figure and trying to get up there. I try to really impress the fact that in order to have a better life and decent job, you need to go to college. I even asked her to go to school with me at night.

A mother of three said she tells her children:

That piece of paper—that B.A. or M.A.—is going to make you have a better life and better living. You can get what you want and be able to take care of a family, if that is what you want. Take care of yourself first and get what you need out of life. I tell the girls, "Don't start having all those babies. You can't have all those babies and go to school. You're going to need child care; that baby needs to be fed. You can't go to college and do that. It's going to be very hard and mom and dad are not babysitters. We both work." I told my son, "Don't go having babies all over the place." College is very important. My son is always talking about that Lamborghini. I said, "If you go to college, you're going to get a Lamborghini" and he's so excited. He works now, but he's hard up for money.

A mother of four said that she uses practical examples to instill positive messages about college in her children, particularly her fifth grade son. She explained, "When I see people on the street—street people with nowhere to go—I show him what life could be like. I tell him that he has choices in life. I try to make him understand that he needs to make good choices and think before he does things." A mother of a middle school daughter said that she constantly told her daughter that college was merely an extension of her K–12 schooling. "I would include examples like 'College is part of school, like grammar is a part of school,'" she stated. "'High school is a part of school; college is a part of school. That's how long you have to go to school. It's not like it's exclusive in your education. It's part of your education.' I think my daughter really doesn't know that she has an option not to go to college."

Another mother said, "I tell them that college is very important and they should take advantage of it, because it can make them really be somebody. That's why I tell them to read about what they want to be now, so when they get to college they'll already know. Not just skip around and change their mind about what they want to do, because they'll never get finished." However, a grandparent wanted her three grandchildren to know that whereas a college degree is important, the college education must be used wisely. She stated, "I'm trying to teach them that it takes more than a college degree. 'You don't want to be foolish with the education that you have.' It's what's going to get them ahead, so they can have more choices and not just be stuck. I try to teach them, 'You don't want to get out there and just have a job.' "

WHAT AFRICAN AMERICAN PARENTS/GUARDIANS CAN DO TO ENCOURAGE MORE AFRICAN AMERICAN STUDENTS TO ATTEND COLLEGE

The interviewees were also asked, "In your opinion, what can African American parents do to encourage more African American students to go to college?" Most of the interviewees believed that talking about college and encouraging children to attend college when the children are very young are the best ways to do this. A stepparent said that parents should "participate, be at every award ceremony, make their children feel proud of everything that they accomplish, and make them want to go to college."

One mother said:

Parents can insist that it is part of your schooling. You don't quit in high school. High school is just one of the items you need to get where you need to go. You can't quit elementary school; you can't quit at junior high. You can't quit high school. You've got to keep going. A lot of parents who haven't gone to college don't know what you need to do or what courses you need to take to prepare for college.

A mother of four believed that reading to children, teaching them kindergarten readiness skills, and talking to them about college at an early age are extremely useful strategies. She explained:

You need to start training them and prepping them from elementary school. The main thing is reading to kids. You have to read to those kids. You have to teach them their ABCs and their numbers. You have to teach those babies. Teaching should take place at home also, not just in the schools.

When my girls were little, we'd be riding in the car. "ABCDEFG" and they would be singing and doing their numbers. I had flashcards. I still have them in my closet now. I went to a book fair last year, and I bought a whole bunch of children's books, because when my friends bring their kids over I like to read to them. I like to flash my cards at them. Kids have to be taught when they're young. From two or three years old, you start teaching kids how to read. I don't know if they make them read in class now. If they don't want to read, because they can't, pull them to the side and say, "Why didn't you read the story to me?" Those kids are scared when they get into high school, even middle school. Those kids are scared to read out loud because those kids don't know how to read. Those kids are being pushed out of school not knowing how to read or count or speak proper English. They don't know how to use their grammar properly. My kids used to until they got into high school, hanging around those silly kids up there. Now, they're talking like, "Dope. Got a lot of flo." You know that's not the proper way to say it or spell it. They know the proper ways. You have to go in and get those kids while they're young and prepare them for this.

Some interviewees said that sharing personal experiences and examples with children are additional ways that parents/guardians can motivate African American students to attend college. For example, a mother of two daughters urged parents/guardians to "just talk to them; share your experiences. I don't want my girls to go through what I have financially. I don't want that. I want them to be able to stand on their own." A mother of three said, "I think they should show their children differences, comparisons or something. They could say, 'These people right here had to go to college to become this. And this person over there had to go to college to become that.' I do that a lot." A mother of two urged parents/guardians to "Keep on talking to them and letting them know that a mind is a terrible thing to waste. I wasted mine. Now, here I am, thirty-two years old, trying to get what I can get. That's a waste. Just do what you got to do and then it'll come. Save up for college. As African American parents, that is what we should put in our kids' heads."

Another recommendation to parents/guardians was to stay extremely involved in their children's lives as a strategy to motivate them to attend college. For example, a mother of three advised African American parents/guardians to "be more involved with every aspect of school. Be there when they get awards. Volunteer at school. Encourage more, instead of discouraging children.

I love my people. Basically, if you can get parents to lift children up, instead of putting them down, it will bring us such a great generation of children." Another parent recommended that parents/guardians "Be involved in your children's life. I would ask my three sons, 'So who do you think is cool?' Well, they told me that the drug dealer was and I told them, 'No, that's not cool.' I showed them another guy who worked. He works, has a car, owns his own house. He's working to get this stuff without taking the chance of getting put in jail for what he does to make his money. That kind of surprised my kids."

WHAT THE PUBLIC SCHOOL SYSTEM CAN DO

When asked, "In your opinion, what can the public school system do to encourage more African American students to go to college?" the interviewees gave several recommendations. These recommendations included the following: (1) Give African American students a stronger academic foundation; (2) provide parents/guardians with more assistance to help their children academically; (3) improve the curriculum; and (4) provide African American students with more positive messages about college through lectures, guest speakers, and visits to college campuses.

Concerning academic preparation, a mother urged schools to "Prepare them for college. Tell them what they have to do, and what they need to learn in order to be able to go." A parent who was concerned about the number of African American students who leave high school unprepared to do college-level work said:

They need to get with each one of those children to see if they can read and write. They need to say, "Hey, what do you want to be? Everybody write down your five-year plan. What do you want to be? If you want to be an astronaut, this is what you need to do." Take them to some job fairs to get information packets on each one of those jobs that those elementary students want to do, and let them look. Tell the students, "This is what you need to do to become an astronaut. This is the requirement to be a nurse, doctor, or lawyer. This is how long you will need to go to college."

Let them know what is required of them to do those things. That is what the teachers can do. Then, the kids can say, "That's too much" or "Hey, I have a lot of work ahead of me. I better start working toward this." Let kids do more research in the library. Read to those kids, and have them read out loud. I don't know what happened to Spelling Bees. I used to love Spelling Bees when I was in school. Do Spelling Bees and have an incentive for them to do this. That's going to help them more with the reading. The math scares me when I look at it. I told my husband, "If I had to do the math those kids are doing, I would have dropped out of school. I couldn't have done that." That algebra stuff: I look at that, and there is no way I could have done that. I look at that stuff and it looks like a foreign language. I would have been a dropout.

Regarding providing parents/guardians with more assistance to help their children prepare for college, a grandmother stated that parents/guardians and the school system were both in need of improvement. She explained:

First, parents need to start taking more interest in their children at home, as far as their education is concerned, and I know it's difficult for some parents. I know one third grader whose parents can't help him. He's in third grade, but should be going to fifth grade. His mother can't help him with his homework because she can't half read, and she's thirty-seven years old. But that's where the school should be of support. If I don't know how to do something, I tell my grandson, "All right. You find out from your teacher tomorrow how you're supposed to do this." If he comes back, and he can't explain it to me, then it's my job to go up there and talk to his teacher. At least that's the way I feel about it.

A mother of two said that educators needed to improve their communication with parents. She said, "They need to get together and talk, saying, 'I can help you do this. I can help you do that. You need help with your child. I need help to do this with your child. Let's sit down, and let's do this if you want your child to go to college.'"

Many interviewees said that school curricula should automatically include information about college, but curricula should also be culturally relevant. For example, another mother stated:

I feel they should do more things that pertain to our culture. You find a lot of things that have to do with Whites or about some of our kids in the lower class, but not about a part of the world that they don't even know exists. Teaching about George Washington and Abraham Lincoln is great. But teach me about some Black people. Not only in February, the shortest month of the year, but teach me that all year long, because I want to know. I might be like them one day. Just like you do George and Lincoln, teach me about them all year long. African American children need to know more about their people. They need to know more about what their people have accomplished. I sit in the class. Half of the kids are looking up at the ceiling, even though they should learn that, because it's a part of history. But come on! Mix it. Make it favorable. Give me some of my people. I'm not being prejudiced, because I'm not. I just want to hear about my people.

Many interviewees also encouraged schools to provide African American children with more positive messages about college through lectures, guest speakers, and field trips. One parent was pleased that one of her son's teachers actively encouraged him to go to college. She stated, "My older son has a teacher that talks to them, and gives them different brochures on colleges and whatever they want to do. My oldest son wants to be a lawyer." A father urged schools to "Have more lectures. Have somebody come down from the college with a little pamphlet or some pictures, something that'll catch the eye. Some of the boys might want to play football. Have the football coach come down there with his little cards or something. Girls might want to play basketball, so the basketball coach should come down." A mother of two urged educators not only to discuss the benefits of a college education with African American students, but to convey the message that their hard work will pay off. She said:

Keep enforcing and reinforcing. Have seminars and let them know that McDonald's is not a put down but it's not what you want to do for the rest of your life, unless you own it. Nowadays, kids want to have nice things. They want name brands. In order for them to have name brands, they need money. We just have to keep letting them know it is there, and they can obtain it, but they have to work for it. They have to be told that society is not going to give it to you. We have to reinforce the message that education is the best way. Have seminars, starting in elementary school. Don't wait until they get to high school and plant it. That is what schools can do.

The narrative that follows is based on an interview with a college-educated mother of two girls.

IT'S JUST SOMETHING WE'VE TALKED ABOUT EVER SINCE THEY WERE YOUNG

Among the parents/guardians who participated in the interview phase of the study, thirty-seven-year-old Yvonna was unique in three ways. First, both she and her husband had earned bachelor's degrees at the same university; second, neither of her children was struggling academically; and third, most of her comments about her own and her children's schooling experiences were overwhelmingly positive, despite the fact that her children attended school in the same district in which the children of the majority of questionnaire respondents were enrolled.

Yvonna, an accounts manager for a well-known nonprofit organization, grew up in Los Angeles. She attended public schools, and stated that her elementary, middle, and high school experiences were positive. "I enjoyed all of school," she said. "I just remember having good teachers. I remember liking my teachers and teachers liking me. I just remember liking school. I guess the teachers had a lot to do with it."

Yvonna's love for education, which stemmed from her own positive schooling experiences, permeated her entire interview. Moreover, she had successfully passed this attitude on to her own daughters, a seventh grader and a ninth grader, as evidenced by their own schooling experiences. Before they started school, she read to them and purchased books for them. After they started school, she attempted to assist them academically in other ways. Yvonna explained:

I just ask them questions about what's going on at school. Even though my oldest daughter is kind of independent, I still ask her about what's going on, and if she needs help with anything. I'm involved in her school. I'm on the School Site Council. I've always been involved in PTA and helping out in the classrooms. For a lot of years, I didn't work, so I could be there. When I started working, I did less of it. My husband and I support education. We try to show how important we think it is by our attitudes.

The strong academic foundation that Yvonna and her husband gave to their daughters paid off at school. During elementary school both girls were placed in the Gifted and Talented Education Program (G.A.T.E.). During middle school, they were accepted into a prestigious college preparatory public school. This school has historically had the school district's highest standardized test scores and it is considered to offer a more rigorous curriculum than other middle schools in the district. Yvonna rated her children's elementary and middle school teachers as *good* and the public school system as *excellent*. In explaining how her daughters were faring academically, she stated:

The oldest has never really needed help. She always just came in and did what she had to do and caught on easily. She's really disciplined, more so than a lot of young people. Since she was little, I never really had to help her at all. She just kind of does it on her own.

Now, the younger one, she's a good student and she makes good grades, too. But, sometimes, she just needs to be pushed a little bit. She's more of a procrastinator. So, I have to stay on her more, you know, ask her about her assignments. She complains about science. She gets "B's" in science. So, as far as I'm concerned, she's fine. If she has a most difficult subject, that would be it. She says she tries to get "A's," but she hasn't been able to.

In addition to doing well academically, one of the benefits of being targeted for success when they were very young was that Yvonna's children constantly heard positive messages about college. At school, they not only received a college preparatory curriculum, and had teachers with higher expectations, but they were also invited to participate in programs that gave them more exposure to college. These programs included field trips to colleges for both students and their parents/guardians, invitations to attend seminars about college, and opportunities to hear guest speakers discuss their college experiences.

At home, just as Yvonna and her husband started preparing their children for academic success long before they entered kindergarten, they also started instilling positive messages in them about college when they were very young. According to Yvonna:

It's just something we've talked about ever since they were young. We told them that in order to do this or be happy in certain careers, you have to go to college. They've gone to college programs during the summer. My oldest one recently participated in a workshop at a college. They've been on college campuses. We've taken them over to the college that my husband and I graduated from. It's something we've always talked about.

However, although Yvonna said that she believed that a college education was very important, she realized that it was not for everyone, and it was not the sole determinant of success in life. She explained:

I think it's very important, but I don't think it's absolutely necessary. It depends. I just know there are people out there who did not go to college. Maybe, they went to vocational school, but they succeeded in careers where college wasn't necessary to get a good job, get a decent salary, take care of their family. They're still members of society.

That's the route that they chose. I mean there are some things that people will decide to do in life that won't require a college degree. Maybe, they have to take another avenue.

Nevertheless, Yvonna was convinced that her own daughters would indeed go to college. "My kids plan to go," she said. "They'll have to go to college to have the careers that they want and the things that they talk about wanting. I have not heard them say that they are not interested or that they don't want to go, or that college is going to be hard, or that they're going to do something else. I have not heard any of that conversation."

Yvonna also shared her thoughts about how African American parents/guardians and the public school system can encourage more African American students to go to college. She said, "Parents should talk to kids, especially parents who have been to college themselves. Just talk to them about college, and tell them how college prepared them for their careers. Let them know that, generally speaking, people who go to college can earn more money than those who don't and have more options and better jobs." She believed that the public school system could encourage more African American students to attend college by providing them with access to programs, such as those to which her own children had access. These programs would result in constant exposure to college and lots of positive messages about college.

SUMMARY

Throughout this study, there have been numerous indicators that most of the parents/guardians who participated were extremely concerned about their children's education. When asked directly, the majority of the questionnaire respondents said that their children's education was very important to them. However, five factors had a negative impact on the value that parents/guardians placed on their children's education. The parents/guardians of children who were expelled from school, experienced racism at school from adults or from both adults and children, who disliked school, or who had a problem with history and/or pronunciation were less likely than others to say that their children's education was very important to them. The most obvious difference between the two groups was that parents/guardians who placed less value on their children's education were also less likely to assist them academically in "other" ways, such as by serving on school committees, attending school functions, and participating in school events.

The majority of the African American parents/guardians who completed the questionnaire also said that they encouraged their children to attend college on a regular basis. Results from the interview phase of the study indicated that such parents/guardians were likely to tell their children that a college education was important and/or that a college education would give them more job options. Women and the parents/guardians of multiple school-age children were more likely than others to do this. Conversely, parents/guardians of children who struggled with reading comprehension or spelling were less likely to do so.

The majority of the parents/guardians who completed the questionnaire also said that they believed that their children eventually planned to go to college. Parents/guardians of children who experienced racism from students and from adults at school were less likely to believe that their children planned to go to college.

All of the interviewees believed that both parents/guardians and the school system could use specific strategies to encourage more African American children to go to college. Parents/guardians could do so by being actively involved in their children's education, talking to their children about college, and encouraging them to plan to attend college, starting when they are very young. They also stated that it was beneficial for parents/guardians to share their own personal experiences, and the experiences of others, with their children. The school system could encourage more African American children to attend college by ensuring that they receive a stronger academic foundation; improving the curriculum; and giving African American children more information about college through visits to college campuses, guest speakers, and positive messages about college (Thompson, 2002). Finally, the school system could do so by providing more assistance to parents/guardians in areas in which they are unable to help their children academically.

14

Conclusion

In this study, African American parents/guardians described numerous aspects of their own schooling experiences and those of their children. Four key points surfaced: (1) The majority of African American parents/guardians who participated in the study placed a high value on their children's education; (2) most African American parents/guardians in the study used numerous strategies to assist their children academically; (3) African American parents'/guardians' beliefs about teachers, administrators, course work, homework, and the public school system are interrelated; and (4) many African American parents/guardians are pleased with the public school system as a whole; however, they have numerous concerns that must be addressed. Although some of the results were based on small subsets of the larger group of participants and many of the correlations were low, taken together, the feedback from the parents/guardians can be utilized to improve the schooling experiences of African American children throughout the nation. Moreover, it can be utilized to improve relations between African American parents/guardians and educators. Improving relations between parents/guardians and educators is necessary in order to increase parent/guardian participation in schools and in their children's formal education.

The first key point was that African American parents/guardians in the study placed a high value on their children's education. This is important because it negates the widely held assumption among educators that African American parents/guardians are apathetic about their children's education. Both interview and questionnaire data contained information that refuted this common misperception. Most African American parents/guardians in the study not only wanted their children to eventually attend college, but they talked to their children about college on a regular basis and tried to convey positive messages about college to them. Furthermore, they wanted parents/guardians and schools to make a stronger effort to encourage more African American children to attend college. Some of their recommendations were similar to those of the students who participated in the study *African American Teens Discuss Their Schooling Experiences* (Thompson, 2002).

The second finding was that most African American parents/guardians in the study used multiple strategies to assist their children academically. Contrary to popular opinion among educators, who believe that African American parents/guardians are not involved in their children's formal education, 80 percent of the parents/guardians rated their level of involvement as *excellent* or *good*. This finding is similar to that of Thompson (2002), in which the majority of the African American teens reported that their parents/guardians had been extremely involved in their formal education. In the current study, there were eleven specific strategies that most of the parents/guardians utilized. The majority (1) listened to their children read; (2) talked to their children about school; (3) contacted their children's teachers; (4) encouraged their children to attend college; (5) helped with homework; (6) encouraged their children to check over their schoolwork and homework; (7) bought books for their children; (8) read to their children; (9) encouraged their children to read during their spare time; (10) limited children's television viewing; and (11) helped their children study for tests. This finding is extremely noteworthy in that it reveals that educators must cease to view parent involvement through the traditional limited paradigm of attendance at Back to School Night and Open House. Conversely, educators must realize that many African American parents/guardians are not only highly involved in their children's education, but that the strategies that they utilize may be invisible to educators. Broadening educators' perspectives of parent involvement is a pivotal first step in improving their relations with African American parents/guardians.

The third finding was that African American parents'/guardians' beliefs about teachers, administrators, course work, homework, and the overall quality of their children's schooling experiences are interrelated. The majority of the parents/guardians believed that most public school teachers cared about students and that most teachers had treated their children fairly. Furthermore, the majority rated their children's elementary and middle school teachers as *excellent* or *good*, but slightly less than half the participants who had children in high school gave a high rating to their children's high school teachers. The majority of parents/guardians also believed that most public school principals and counselors cared about students and that they had treated their children fairly. Most parents/guardians also believed that most of their children's elementary, middle, and high school course work and homework were beneficial. Moreover, the majority gave a high rating to the public school system as a whole. When parents/guardians were satisfied with one aspect of their children's schooling, they tended to be pleased with others. Conversely, negative schooling experiences pertaining to racism, suspension, expulsion, certain academic problems, and children's attitudes about reading and school tended to be linked to parents'/guardians' dissatisfaction with some aspects of their children's schooling. Moreover, in some school districts parents'/guardians' dissatisfaction tended to be higher than in others. Because they are sources of concern for African American parents/guardians and can affect their children's schooling experiences, these problems warrant more attention.

The fourth finding was that although most of the African American parents/guardians were pleased with the public school system as a whole, they had numerous concerns and recommendations that must be addressed. These concerns surfaced repeatedly throughout the study. One concern was that, whereas many African American parents/guardians truly wanted to assist their children academically, often, they were ill-equipped to assist them with particular academic problems. For example, while some parents/guardians were unable to help their children with reading comprehension, a more common complaint was that parents/guardians were unable to help their children with math. Several interviewees attributed this to their own weak math skills; others said that children are being required to do higher-level math at a younger age. The parents'/guardians' inability to assist their children with these academic problems resulted in frustration. Some complained that teachers were unwilling to assist them and their children in ways that could resolve these problems. The need for outstanding math teachers, starting in elementary school (Drew, 1996), was underscored by this concern.

Another problem that concerned many parents/guardians related to disciplinary practices at school. Numerous parents/guardians said that their children, particularly boys, were labeled as behavior problems early in their schooling. These labels resulted in negative expectations and unfair treatment by adults at school. One grandmother compared her grandson's treatment to that of an ex-con who had paid his debt to society but was still suffering the negative consequences. A father said that being singled out at school had contributed to his decision to drop out of high school, which was similar to White-Johnson's (2001) research. Additionally, some parents/guardians said that even when their sons or grandsons were telling the truth, school personnel assumed that they were lying. Ferguson's (2001) study addressed many of these issues, and it should be required reading in teacher training institutions, as well as for the professional development of in-service teachers and administrators.

A frequently cited problem of great concern to many parents/guardians was that their children had been identified by teachers or counselors as suffering from ADD or ADHD. A few parents/guardians believed that the diagnosis was correct; others were skeptical. Some were told by doctors that the diagnosis was incorrect. Some found the drug that was prescribed for their children to be ineffective. Several were fearful of the long-term effects of the drug. This issue warrants further investigation and it raises several questions, including the following: Are teachers qualified to identify ADD/ADHD? Should teachers be telling parents/guardians that they suspect that their children have ADD/ADHD? A more important question is this: Is ADD/ADHD the real problem or is it merely being used as an excuse to medicate children who are perceived to be problematic? Still another important question is: What messages are children who are being medicated for ADD/ADHD inferring about problem-solving? In other words, are they learning that a pill will solve their problems as opposed to finding more appropriate ways of handling difficult circumstances?

Another concern that surfaced was that African American children often get mixed messages from home and school. For example, communication styles that are acceptable at home often become problematic at school. Some parents/guardians said that, at home, their children were encouraged to explain themselves and to ask questions. Moreover, in some African American homes, "talking loud" is perceived as normal behavior. However, these practices—which are normal to many African American children—can result in punishment at school. Kochman's (1981) research into contrasting styles of discourse among African Americans and Whites addressed some of these issues. For example, he described the African American style of discourse as passionate or "argumentative" and urged educators to learn to differentiate between passionate speech that is driven by anger and passionate speech that is infused with the desire to stress a point. Kochman's book can be used in teacher training institutions and for professional development workshops to inform teachers and administrators about cultural misunderstandings that originate from ignorance about differences between African American and "White" styles of discourse.

Another conflict between home practices and school practices involves fighting. In many African American homes, children are taught to defend themselves and to prevent themselves from becoming victims (Canada, 1995). However, in some schools, both victim and victimizer receive the same punishment. Several parents/guardians described problems that their children had at school after being targeted by other students. These problems affected both parents/guardians and their children in numerous ways. Furthermore, some parents/guardians were dissatisfied with school administrators' responses to their concerns about their children's safety. Inviting African American parents/guardians to discuss more realistic policies with school officials might alleviate these problems.

Another issue that concerned some parents/guardians was that they felt unwelcome at school. On the one hand, teachers and administrators have complained about the lack of parent participation in schools. On the other hand, some African American parents/guardians have inferred that there is a lack of sincerity on the part of school personnel regarding parent participation. For example, some parents/guardians believed that only certain parents, particularly Spanish-speaking parents, were welcome at school. In addition, at least two interviewees said that school personnel actually appeared to be intimidated by their presence at their children's schools. Furthermore, even African American parents/guardians who offered to serve as classroom volunteers were sometimes told that their help was not needed. One mother who offered to help in her children's classroom stated that teachers told her "We don't need help." "But at the end of the school year, they have a problem with my kids," she pointed out. If teachers and administrators are sincere in their efforts to increase parent/guardian participation, they need to create an environment that welcomes all parents/guardians (Lynn, 1997b; Mapp, 1997; Vail, 2001b), instead of pitting parents/guardians from different racial/ethnic groups against each other.

Another problem that concerned many African American parents/guardians was the quality of their children's teachers, the instructional practices in the classroom, and the curriculum. Even some parents/guardians who gave high ratings to most of their children's teachers expressed concern about the number of underprepared teachers in public schools. Some complained about teachers who only appeared to be focused on collecting a paycheck. Others complained about teachers who were unable to assist their children with certain academic problems. Several complained about poor classroom management skills and a nonchallenging, boring curriculum. These issues have been well documented and addressing them is critical to effective school reform.

Another issue that concerned many of the interviewees was that their own schooling experiences had been more positive than those of their children. Several of the parents/guardians had attended racially segregated schools and believed that having had caring and effective African American teachers who lived in their communities was invaluable. However, even some of the interviewees who had attended racially mixed public schools believed that they'd had better teachers and better schooling experiences than their own children. The high number of underprepared teachers in public schools, teachers who are working with Emergency Credentials and Waivers, and teachers who are underprepared to work effectively with children from diverse backgrounds are problems that also have been well documented and addressing them is crucial for effective school reform.

In conclusion, the African American parents/guardians who participated in this study were unique in some ways and similar in others, which illustrates the diversity that exists among African Americans. The participants included biological parents in two-parent homes, single parents, grandparents, foster parents, and stepparents who were rearing school-age children. Some had been deterred from completing their own formal education as a result of peer pressure, temptation outside of school, or stressful circumstances. Others had positive schooling experiences and stable childhoods. Regardless of the differences in their background experiences, however, the majority of the parents/ guardians were single-minded about wanting a better life for their children. They were unwavering in their belief that a good K–12 education and a college education were crucial to their children's socioeconomic advancement. Most also believed that there was much hope for the public school system. Moreover, they did not expect the schools to do it all. African American parents/guardians are willing to work with teachers and administrators to ensure that their children receive a quality education. However, if the persistent achievement gap is to ever be eradicated, teachers, administrators, researchers, and policymakers must become more willing to view African American parents/guardians as assets. They must become more willing to invite African American parents/guardians to verbalize their concerns. Then, they must take those concerns seriously and work with African American parents/guardians to effect meaningful and lasting change in the public school system. Finally, as noted repeatedly throughout this book, the fact that some of the results were based on small subsets of the total sample of participants underscores the need for other researchers to conduct studies involving larger groups of African American parents/guardians.

Bibliography

Anderson, J. D. (1988). *The education of Blacks in the South: 1860–1935.* Chapel Hill: University of North Carolina Press.

Armstrong, T. (1995). *The myth of the A.D.D. child: 50 ways to improve your child's behavior and attention span without drugs, labels, or coercion.* New York: Penguin Books.

Bempechat, J. (1998). *Against the odds: How "at-risk" students exceed expectations.* San Francisco: Jossey-Bass, Inc.

Burdman, P. (2000). Extra credit, extra criticism. *Black Issues in Higher Education, 17* (18), 28–33.

California Department of Education (2001). Enrollments, Staffing, Testing. http://www.cde.ca.gov/dataquest.

Canada, G. (1995). *Fist stick knife gun: A personal history of violence in America.* Boston: Beacon Press.

Chall, J. S. (1967). *Learning to read: The great debate.* New York: McGraw-Hill Book Company.

Clark, R. (1983). *Family life and school achievement: Why poor Black children succeed or fail.* Chicago: University of Chicago Press.

Coles, G. (1999). *Reading lessons: The debate over literacy.* New York: Hill & Wang Publishers.

Comer, J. P., & Poussaint, A. F. (1992). *Raising Black children: Two leading psychiatrists confront the educational, social, and emotional problems facing Black children.* New York: Penguin Books.

Cook, P. J., & Ludwig, J. (1998). The burden of "acting White": Do Black adolescents disparage academic achievement? In C. Jencks & M. Phillips (Eds.), *The Black-White test score gap,* 375–400. Washington, DC: The Brookings Institution.

Cruickshank, D. R., & Haefele, D. (2001). Good teachers, plural. *Educational Leadership, 58* (5), February, 26–30.

Davis, J. E., & Jordan, W. J. (1995). The effects of school context, structure, and experiences in African American males in middle and high school. *Journal of Negro Education, 63* (4), 570–587.

Delpit, L. (1995). *Other people's children: Cultural conflict in the classroom.* New York: The New Press.

Drew, D. (1996). *Aptitude revisited*. Baltimore: Johns Hopkins University Press.

Dupuis, J. (1999). California lawsuit notes unequal access to AP courses. *Rethinking Schools Online, 14* (1).

Eggen, P., & Kauchak, D. (2001). *Educational psychology: Windows on classrooms* (5th ed.). Upper Saddle River, NJ: Merrill Prentice Hall.

Ferguson, A. A. (2001). *Bad boys: Public schools in the making of Black masculinity*. Ann Arbor: University of Michigan Press.

Ferguson, R. F. (1998a). Can schools narrow the Black-White test score gap? In C. Jencks & M. Phillips (Eds.), *The Black-White test score gap*, 318–374. Washington, DC: The Brookings Institution.

————. (1998b). Teachers' perceptions and expectations and the Black-White test score gap. In C. Jencks & M. Phillips (Eds.), *The Black-White test score gap*, 273–317. Washington, DC: The Brookings Institution.

Ferrandino, V. L. (2001). Challenges for 21st-century elementary school principals. *Phi Delta Kappan*, February, 440–442.

Fink, E., & Resnick, L. B. (2001). Developing principals as instructional leaders. *Phi Delta Kappan*, April, 598–606.

Fleming, J. E. (1976). *The lengthening shadow of slavery*. Washington, DC: Howard University Press.

Flesh, R. (1986). *Why Johnny can't read and what you can do about it*. New York: HarperCollins.

Flores, B., Tefft-Cousin, P., & Diaz, E. (1991). Transforming deficit myths about learning, language, and culture. *Language Arts, 68*, 369–378.

Floyd, C. (1995). African American high school seniors. Unpublished doctoral dissertation. Claremont, CA: Claremont Graduate University.

Ford, D. (1995). Desegregating gifted education: A need unmet. *Journal of Negro Education, 64* (1), 53–62.

Fordham, S., & Ogbu, J. (1986). Black students' school success: Coping with the burden of "acting White." *Urban Review, 18* (3), 176–206.

Foster, M., & Peele, T. B. (1999). Teaching Black males: Lessons from the experts. In V. C. Polite & J. E. Davis (Eds.), *African American males in school and society: Practices and policies for effective education*, 8–19. New York: Teachers College Press.

Garbarino, J., Dubrow, N., Kostelny, K., & Pardo, C. (1992). *Children in danger: Coping with the consequences of community violence*. San Francisco: Jossey-Bass Publishers.

Gardner, H. (1991). *The unschooled mind: How children think & how schools should teach*. New York: Basic Books, HarperCollins Publishers.

Goldberg, M. F. (2001). Leadership in education: Five commonalities. *Phi Delta Kappan*, June, 757–761.

Golden, M. (1995). *Saving our sons: Raising Black children in a turbulent world*. New York: Anchor Books, Doubleday.

Goodman, K. (1996). *On reading: A commonsense look at the nature of language and the science of reading*. Portsmouth, NH: Heinemann.

Gordon, D. T. (1999a). Rising to the discipline challenge. *The Harvard Education Letter, 15* (5), 1–4.

————. (1999b). Turning frustration to fulfillment: New teachers need more help with discipline. *The Harvard Education Letter, 15* (5), 2–3.

Graue, E. M., & DiPerna, J. (2000). Redshirting and early retention: Who gets the "Gift of Time" and what are its outcomes? *American Educational Research Journal, 37* (2), 509–534.

Grissmer, D., Flanagan, A., & Williamson, S. (1998). Why did the Black-White score gap narrow in the 1970s and 1980s? In C. Jencks & M. Phillips (Eds.), *The Black-White test score gap,* 182–226. Washington, DC: The Brookings Institution.

Haberman, M. (1995). *Star teachers of children in poverty.* West Lafayette, IN: Kappa Delta Pi.

Hacker, A. (1992). *Two nations: Black and White, separate, hostile, unequal.* New York: Ballantine Books.

Harris, A. J., & Sipay, E. R. (1990). *How to increase reading ability: A guide to developmental and remedial methods* (9th ed.). New York: Longman.

Harris, V. J. (1992). African-American conceptions of literacy: A historical perspective. *Theory Into Practice, 31* (4), 276–285.

Haycock, K. (1998). Good teaching matters: How well-qualified teachers can close the gap. *Thinking K-16, 3* (2), 1–2.

Hedges, L. V., & Nowell, A. (1998). Black-White test score convergence since 1965. In C. Jencks & M. Phillips (Eds.), *The Black-White test score gap,* 149–181. Washington, DC: The Brookings Institution.

Holland, E. I. M. (1997). *From the Mississippi delta.* New York: Simon & Schuster.

Honig, B. (2000). *Teaching our children to read: The components of an effective comprehensive reading program* (2nd ed.). Thousand Oaks, CA: Corwin Press.

Jencks, C. (1998). Racial bias in testing. In C. Jencks & M. Phillips (Eds.), *The Black-White test score gap,* 55–85. Washington, DC: The Brookings Institution.

Kochman, T. (1981). *Black and white styles in conflict.* Chicago: University of Chicago Press.

Ladd, J. (1994). *Out of the madness: From the projects to a life of hope.* New York: Warner Books, Inc.

Ladson-Billings, G. (1994). *The dreamkeepers: Successful teachers of African-American children.* San Francisco: Jossey-Bass Inc.

———. (2001). *Crossing over to Canaan: The journey of new teachers in diverse classrooms.* San Francisco: Jossey-Bass Inc.

Langdon, C. A., & Vesper, N. (2000). The sixth Phi Delta Kappa poll of teachers' attitudes toward the public schools. *Phi Delta Kappan,* April, 607–611.

LeMoine, N. (2001). Language variation & literacy acquisition in African American students. In J. L. Harris, A. G. Kamhi, & K. E. Pollock (Eds.), *Literacy in African American communities.* Mahwah, NJ: Lawrence Erlbaum Associates, Publishers.

Lynn, L. (1997a). Family involvement in schools: It makes a big difference, but remains rare. *The Harvard Education Letter, 13* (5), 3–5.

———. (1997b). Teaching teachers to work with families. *The Harvard Education Letter, 13* (5), 7–8.

Mapp, K. (1997). Making the connection between families and schools. *The Harvard Education Letter, 13* (5), 1–3.

McCall, N. (1994). *Makes me wanna holler.* New York: Random House.

———. (1997). *What's going on?* New York: Random House.

McQuillan, J. (1998). *The literacy crisis: False claims, real solutions.* Portsmouth, NH: Heinemann.

Moses, R. P., & Cobb, C. E., Jr. (2001). *Radical equations: Math, literacy, and civil rights.* Boston: Beacon Press.

Murrell, P., Jr. (1999). Responsive teaching for African American male adolescents. In V. C. Polite & J. E. Davis (Eds.), *African American males in school and society: Practices & policies for effective education,* 82–96. New York: Teachers College Press.

National Center for Education Statistics. (1996). *NAEP Mathematics Report Card for the nation and the states,* Table 2.3, p. 30.

———. (2000). *Fourth grade reading highlights.* Jessup, MD: U.S. Department of Education.

———. (2001). *The nation's report card mathematics 2000.* Jessup, MD: U.S. Department of Education.

Newsom, J. (2001). Leadership 101: A shortage of qualified administrators has sparked a boom in principal preparation programs. *American School Board Journal,* November, 30–33.

Nieto, S. (2000). *Affirming diversity: The sociopolitical context of multicultural education* (3rd ed.). New York: Longman.

Oakes, J. (1999). Limiting students' school success and life chances: The impact of tracking. In A. C. Ornstein & L. S. Behar-Horenstein (Eds.), *Contemporary issues in curriculum* (2nd ed.), 224–237. Needham Heights, MA: Allyn and Bacon.

Paige, R. (2001, December 19). Keynote address at the U.S. Department of Education's Improving America's Schools conference. San Antonio, Texas.

Phillips, M., Brooks-Gunn, J., Duncan, G. J., Klebanov, P., & Crane, J. (1998). Family background, parenting practices, and the Black-White test score gap. In C. Jencks & M. Phillips (Eds.), *The Black-White test score gap,* 103–145. Washington, DC: The Brookings Institution.

Phillips, M., Crouse, J., & Ralph, J. (1998). Does the Black-White test score gap widen after children enter school? In C. Jencks & M. Phillips (Eds.), *The Black-White test score gap,* 229–272. Washington, DC: The Brookings Institution.

Polite, V. C. (1999). Combating educational neglect in suburbia: African American males and mathematics. In V. C. Polite & J. E. Davis (Eds.), *African American males in school and society: Practices & policies for effective education,* 97–107. New York: Teachers College Press.

Poplin, M., & Weeres, J. (1992). *Voices from the inside: A report on schooling from inside the classroom.* Claremont, CA: The Institute for Education in Transformation at the Claremont Graduate School.

Quality Counts. (2000). *Education Week, XIX* (18).

———. (2001). *Education Week, XX* (17).

Reitzug, U. C., & Patterson, J. (1998). I'm not going to lose you! Empowerment through caring in an urban principal's practice with students. *Urban Education, 33* (2), 150–181.

Roderick, M., & Camburn, E. (1999). Risk and recovery from course failure in the early years of high school. *American Educational Research Journal, 36* (2), 303–343.

Rodney, L. W., Crafter, B., Rodney, H. E., & Mupier, R. M. (1999). Variables contributing to grade retention among African American adolescent males. *The Journal of Educational Research, 92* (3), 185–190.

Rose, L. C., & Gallup, A. M. (2000). The 32nd annual Phi Delta Kappa/Gallup poll of the public's attitudes toward the public schools. *Phi Delta Kappan,* www.pdkintl.org/kappan/kpol0009.htm.

———. (2001). The 33rd annual Phi Delta Kappa/Gallup poll of the public's attitudes toward the public schools. *Phi Delta Kappan,* September, 41–58.

Routman, R. (1996). *Literacy at the crossroads: Crucial talk about reading, writing, and other teaching dilemmas.* Portsmouth, NH: Heinemann.

Sbarra, D. A., & Pianta, R. C. (2001). Teachers' ratings of behavior among African American and Caucasian children during the first two years of school. *Psychology in the Schools, 38* (3), 229–238.

Scott, J. C., & Marcus, C. D. (2001). Emergent literacy: Home-school connections. In J. L. Harris, A. G. Kamhi, & K. E. Pollock (Eds.), *Literacy in African American communities.* Mahwah, NJ: Lawrence Erlbaum Associates, Publishers.

Shakur, S. (1993). *Monster: The autobiography of an L.A. gang member.* New York: Penguin Books.

Thompson, G. (1999). What the numbers really mean: African-American underrepresentation at the doctoral level. *Journal of College Student Retention Research, Theory & Practice, 1* (1), 23–40.

———. (2000). California educators discuss the reading crisis. *Educational Forum,* Spring.

———. (2002). *African American teens discuss their schooling experiences.* Westport, CT: Bergin & Garvey.

Tirozzi, G. N. (2001). The artistry of leadership: The evolving role of the secondary school principal. *Phi Delta Kappan,* February, 434–439.

U.S. Department of Education. (1998). *Tools for schools: School reform models supported by the national institute on the education of at-risk students.* Washington, DC: Office of Educational Research and Improvement.

———. (1999). *Digest of education statistics.* Washington, DC: National Center for Education Statistics.

———. (2000a). *Eliminating barriers to improving teaching.* Washington, DC: U.S. Department of Education.

———. (2000b). *National assessment of educational progress, NAEP trends in academic progress* (various years). Washington, DC: National Center for Education Statistics.

———. (2001a). *Family involvement in children's education: An idea book* (Abridged Version). Jessup, MD: Office of Educational Research and Improvement.

———. (2001b). *No child left behind.* Washington, DC: Office of the Secretary.

Vail, K. (2001a). How much is too much? Homework problems. *American School Board Journal,* April, 24–29.

———. (2001b). Teaching the parents: Sometimes the best way to help students is to first help their parents. *American School Board Journal,* September, 23–25.

White-Johnson, A. F. (2001). "Peas 'N Rice or Rice 'N Peas"—Which are we really ordering? The plight of African American male students engaged in educational exchange processes. *Urban Education, 36* (3), 343–373.

Wilson, W. J. (1996). *When work disappears: The world of the new urban poor.* New York: Alfred Knopf, Inc.

———. (1998). The role of the environment in the Black-White test score gap. In C. Jencks & M. Phillips (Eds.), *The Black-White test score gap,* 501–510. Washington, DC: The Brookings Institution.

Wright, R. (1998). *Black boy* (Rev. ed.). Upper Saddle River, NJ: Prentice Hall.

Index

About the Author

GAIL L. THOMPSON is Associate Professor, School of Educational Studies, Claremont Graduate University.

Made in the USA
San Bernardino, CA
06 May 2019